Approaches to Teaching the Works of Margaret Atwood

Approaches to Teaching the Works of Margaret Atwood

Approaches to Teaching the Works of Margaret Atwood

Edited by

Lauren Rule Maxwell

The Modern Language Association of America
New York 2025

85 Broad Street, New York, New York 10004
www.mla.org

To order MLA publications, visit www.mla.org/books. For wholesale and international orders, see www.mla.org/bookstore-orders. The EU-based Responsible Person for MLA products is the Mare Nostrum Group, which can be reached at gpsr@mare-nostrum.co.uk or the Mare Nostrum Group BV, Mauritskade 21D, 1091 GC Amsterdam, Netherlands. For a copy of the MLA's risk assessment document, write to scholcomm@mla.org.

Approaches to Teaching World Literature 183
ISSN 1059-1133

Library of Congress Cataloging-in-Publication Data

Names: Maxwell, Lauren Rule editor
Title: Approaches to teaching the works of Margaret Atwood / edited by Lauren Rule Maxwell.
Description: New York : Modern Language Association of America, 2025. | Series: Approaches to teaching world literature, 1059-1133 ; 183 | Includes bibliographical references.
Identifiers: LCCN 2025017358 (print) | LCCN 2025017359 (ebook) | ISBN 9781603297219 hardcover | ISBN 9781603297226 paperback | ISBN 9781603297233 EPUB
Subjects: LCSH: Atwood, Margaret, 1939—Study and teaching | Atwood, Margaret, 1939—Criticism and interpretation | Canadian literature—Study and teaching
Classification: LCC PR9199.3.A8 Z535 2026 (print) | LCC PR9199.3.A8 (ebook)
LC record available at https://lccn.loc.gov/2025017358
LC ebook record available at https://lccn.loc.gov/2025017359

CONTENTS

ACKNOWLEDGMENTS

When the MLA acquisitions editor Jaime Cleland approached me about editing this volume, I knew it would be a project worth making time for. I'd like to thank all the contributors for feeling the same way and for their patience throughout the editorial process. We are teachers because we care about our students and think that teaching them literature matters, and we know that sharing new approaches invigorates the learning experience for everyone. I am grateful for all the students who have enriched our classrooms and helped us develop these approaches. The Margaret Atwood Society has been incredibly supportive; I view Atwood's works and how to go about teaching them differently because of that community. The team at the Daniel Library was invaluable in securing sources, the staff at the Thomas Fisher Rare Book Library was welcoming and helpful, and the librarians Danielle Moore and Chelsea Humphries provided insight into what works I should include as materials. To my faithful readers, Anna Judy de Torres, Lee Frew, Martine Watson Brownley, and Marguerite Trossevin, thank you for making my words better. I am so grateful to Jason, my husband, for his support in this and all endeavors, and to my daughters, Carson June and Caroline, who inspire me every day. Thank you for understanding when I sat for so many hours surrounded by papers at my computer. Finally, I would like to acknowledge the keen eye and generous manner of our copyeditor, Zahra Brown, and the contributions of the editorial staff members who prepared the manuscript for publication. Thank you for helping us bring this book to life.

Introduction: Margaret Atwood, More Relevant Than Ever

Lauren Rule Maxwell

Amid challenges from climate change, the COVID-19 pandemic, and attacks on truth and democracy, millions of people around the world are turning to the works of Margaret Atwood to make sense of their realities. Perhaps more than any other author of our time, Atwood compels us to confront the crucial issues we face and start conversations about our relationships to the world around us and with each other—about what matters most.

Atwood is best known for *The Handmaid's Tale* and other speculative dystopian novels that seem especially relevant today, but her works have been shaping intellectual and cultural thought for six decades. Now the author of more than sixty books in a wide range of genres, Atwood began her literary career as a poet: her first major published work, a collection of poetry called *The Circle Game*, won the Governor General's Award for Poetry from the Canada Council for the Arts. The volume's titular poem explores the power of language to create boundaries, "to hold" individual bodies, groups, and communities "in their proper places" (144, 146). Like the poem's speaker, who "want[s] to break . . . all the glass cases," Atwood consolidated the power of her words to make invisible barriers visible, particularly those restricting women (286, 290). Atwood has explained that "at the time I became a poet, . . . I had no idea . . . that I was about to step into a whole set of preconceptions and social roles which had to do with what poets were like, how they should behave, and what they ought to wear; moreover, I did not know that the rules about these things were different if you were female" (Waterstone's Poetry Lecture). She published many poetry collections in the following decades, including *Power Politics*, *You Are Happy*, *Two-Headed Poems*, and *True Stories*, which explored, among other themes, gender dynamics and violence against women. With the underlying assertion that "[a] word after a word / after a word is power" (*True Stories* 64), Atwood's early poetry presaged the long-lasting influence of her writing in movements for women's liberation and empowerment.

This influence derives from her work in many genres, including fiction, children's books, graphic novels, essays, letters, and reviews. Forty years after its publication, *The Handmaid's Tale* continues to inspire one of the most visible representations of women's empowerment, employed particularly in protests against state control of women's bodies. As a student in my spring 2021 graduate fiction seminar explained at the beginning of his final paper on *The Handmaid's Tale*, "Margaret Atwood's handmaids have been busy":

> In Washington, D.C., a group of about thirty women donning the iconic handmaid's uniform—long red dresses and oversized white coifs—gathered

> to protest a proposed health care bill that planned to defund Planned Parenthood. Then, a similarly dressed group in Columbus, Ohio, publicly opposed a bill set to ban the dilation and evacuation procedure, the state's most common abortion method. NARAL Pro-Choice also organized protests at the Texas state capitol, where more women clad in the red uniforms rallied against restrictive abortion laws. Even more handmaid attire appeared in Concord, New Hampshire, as women called for the expulsion of State Representative Robert Fisher after reports appeared detailing his contributions to a Reddit forum known for its misogynistic content. More of the same followed: protests at the Missouri state capitol concerning women's reproductive rights, a "March for Truth" rally in Washington, D.C., about Russia's possible involvement in the 2016 presidential election, a public push in Albany, New York, for improvements in reproductive health and contraceptive care acts. All of these protests occurred in 2017 alone, and all saw a number of women adorning the highly visible handmaid's uniform. And many more have followed in the years since.

With the continued popular success of the Hulu TV series inspired by *The Handmaid's Tale* and the publication of Atwood's Booker Prize–winning sequel to it, *The Testaments*, the handmaid's uniform has become even more ubiquitous.

One reason Atwood's fiction has become central to current debates about public policy is that the things that she writes about have actually happened or are in the process of happening. As Atwood, a thorough researcher, explains about *The Handmaid's Tale*, "One of my rules was that I would not put any events into the book that had not already happened" (*Handmaid's Tale* xiv).[1] Writing what she describes as "speculative fiction" with "[n]o imaginary gizmos, no imaginary laws, no imaginary atrocities" (xiv), Atwood bears witness to the past—including "group executions, sumptuary laws, book burnings, the Lebensborn program of the SS and the child-stealing of the Argentine generals, the history of slavery, the history of American polygamy"—while reminding us that these acts could happen again (xviii). Reframing these realities within the dystopian world of the novel prompts readers to draw contrasts and comparisons between the society of the novel, Gilead, and that of our lives today, a thought exercise especially compelling for readers in the United States, given that in the novel, the Gileadean regime has overthrown the United States government.

In recent decades, Atwood's speculative fiction has focused more centrally on environmental threats that result from human causes. We see this concern to some degree in *The Handmaid's Tale* as well; as Atwood has pointed out, "In the novel, the population is shrinking due to a toxic environment, and the ability to have viable babies is at a premium" (*Handmaid's Tale* xiv). Atwood goes on to note that in "today's real world," studies "showing a sharp fertility decline" have already demonstrated that environmental pollutants are starting to affect reproductive health (xiv). Examinations of human effects on the environment become much more prominent, however, in Atwood's MaddAddam trilogy, which includes *Oryx and Crake*, *The Year of the Flood*, and *MaddAddam*. This trilogy explores a world all too similar to our own in which humans are nearly extinct following a bioengineered plague. Depictions of the world before the plague, in which gene-splicing biocapitalist corporations dominate the economy amid accelerated ecological decline, and the world after, in which the remaining humans coexist with the genetically engineered Crakers and reconsider connections with each other, nonhuman animals, and the surrounding environment, have shaped how readers imagine their relation to the natural world. Like *The Handmaid's Tale*, the MaddAddam trilogy presents what has already happened or is now happening. Atwood's papers at the Thomas Fisher Rare Book Library reveal the extensive research she conducted when writing the trilogy: there are hundreds, if not thousands, of clippings, scientific studies, magazine articles, and other materials that inspired the novels. From climate change to infertility to declining bird populations to genetically modified food products to Dolly, the cloned sheep, to forever chemicals to bioterrorist threats, Atwood's work reflects the world around us. As Atwood has insisted when interviewed about the worlds she creates, in her writings she is reflecting our own realities.

Atwood in recent years has enjoyed a visibility that reflects her growing prominence as an author, activist, and public intellectual. On *X*, formerly known as *Twitter*, Atwood shares her timely musings with a diverse international audience that has widened to more than two million followers with the success of the Hulu television series *The Handmaid's Tale* and the Netflix miniseries *Alias Grace*. The Hulu series has achieved both popular and critical acclaim, winning the 2017 Emmy Award for Outstanding Drama Series and reinforcing Atwood's status as a cultural icon. In addition to Booker Prizes for *The Blind Assassin* in 2000 and *The Testaments* in 2019, Atwood has received numerous other honors, including the PEN USA Lifetime Achievement Award, Governor General's Awards for both fiction and poetry, the Peace Prize of the German Book Trade, the *Los Angeles Times* Innovator Award, the *Stylist* 2020 Icon of the Year ("Remarkable Women"), a 2021 Artists against Racism Humanitarian Award, and the Sun Valley Writers' Conference 2024 Writer in the World Prize. Elisabeth Moss, who won the 2017 Emmy for Outstanding Actress in a Drama Series for her portrayal of Offred on the Hulu series, sums up Atwood's broad appeal in a statement paying homage to Atwood as "a champion, a heroine, a rebel, and a fighter for freedom and equality" who "has given a voice to so many who could not use their own, . . . given us her heart and soul as readers, [and] asked us to wake up and not only look around but to act and resist."

With recent aired interviews on PBS and NPR and features in publications such as *The Guardian*, *Time* magazine, and *Glamour*, where she was honored as a 2019 Woman of the Year and Lifetime Achievement Award winner, Atwood has used her authorial platform to motivate readers to think and act (Atwood,

Interview [*Dialogue*] and Interview [*Wild Card*]; Allardice; Freeman; Feldman; "Best Moments"). Samira Wiley, another Emmy Award–winning actress in Hulu's *Handmaid's Tale* series, has said, "She makes you look. She makes you terrified—particularly about reproductive rights. And then she makes you brave. Along with millions of fans around the globe, she has expanded my idea of the impact I can make in this world. And I am certain that we all dream bigger because of Margaret Atwood" ("Best Moments").

Atwood serves, in the words of the 16 September 2019 *Time* cover, as a "reluctant prophet." With her frank, commonsense approach to confronting the world's problems, she has become a spokesperson for things worth fighting for and believing in—the arts, the environment, human rights, justice, and free speech among them. In doing so, she has also reminded the public at large of the power of words, that they move us to act. Tapping into that power, teachers around the world have developed new strategies for using Atwood's works to demonstrate why words and literature matter. How instructors are approaching the teaching of Atwood's writings in this critical moment has been a consistent focus of panels that the Margaret Atwood Society, an allied organization of the MLA, has hosted at recent conventions. The society has adopted the unofficial slogan "now more relevant than ever" to promote scholarly engagement with Atwood's work, and that relevance transfers to our classrooms, where students and teachers alike have adopted innovative ways of engaging with Atwood's texts.

Since the MLA's *Approaches to Teaching Atwood's* The Handmaid's Tale *and Other Works* was published in 1996, Atwood has become a truly international presence and one of the most famous living authors of our time. Atwood has continued to publish extensively in a variety of genres, writings that for their artistry are as timeless as they are timely. Her novels since the 1996 volume include *Alias Grace*, *The Blind Assassin*, *Oryx and Crake*, *The Penelopiad*, *The Year of the Flood*, *MaddAddam*, *The Heart Goes Last*, *Hag-Seed*, and *The Testaments*. She has also published four collections of short stories, *The Tent*, *Moral Disorder*, *Stone Mattress*, and *Old Babes in the Wood*; three books of poetry, *The Door*, *Dearly*, and *Paper Boat: New and Selected Poems, 1961–2023*; children's books; graphic novels, most notably the *Angel Catbird* series; and collections of essays and nonfiction. Atwood's prolific and wide-ranging literary production has provided teachers with an even greater range of literary styles and topics with which to engage their students.

Because Atwood's works are being taught and written about by teacher-scholars around the world, this volume seeks to share approaches that can be used in many different educational settings. When asked what they would like to see included, teachers of Atwood's works discussed presenting Atwood in context, exploring both adaptations of her writings and the challenges and opportunities of teaching her works in a digital age. Offred reiterates in *The Handmaid's Tale* that "[c]ontext is all" (144, 192); one respondent to the MLA survey asked that we not forget that Atwood's writing provides social critique about this context, that we "[d]ispel the notion . . . that the craft is 'apolitical.'" The imperative to examine how Atwood's work informs and responds to our politics is echoed by those specializing in the study of her writings: Artpolitical, the first ever all-Atwood global conference, whose pre-conference symposium was held in March of 2021 and whose meetings were held over *Zoom* in October of that year, focused on precisely this topic. Noting that for Atwood "politics and art inherently belong together," the organizers, Dunja M. Mohr of Erfurt University and Kirsten Sandrock of Göttingen and Leipzig Universities, hosted conversations about "the interaction between politics and aesthetics in Atwood's oeuvre as well as its various transmedial adaptations" ("Artpolitical"). Teachers who shared their priorities for this volume also wanted to learn about using new adaptations of *The Handmaid's Tale* and other works by Atwood, such as *Hag-Seed* and *Alias Grace*. They asked for interdisciplinary, "cross-sectional," and "cross-genre" approaches and explorations of contemporary feminisms, science fiction, and Atwood's place in the context of twenty-first-century literature worldwide.

One of the most exciting opportunities we have in this volume is investigating new modes of teaching Atwood's writing in the digital age. Since teachers used *Zoom* and other web-based technologies to provide instruction during the COVID-19 pandemic, these applications have become permanent fixtures in many classrooms. To reflect the increasing reliance on videoconferencing as a medium for academic discourse, I incorporated an Atwood-focused *Zoom* conference for one class session of my spring 2021 graduate fiction course, even though the class usually met in person. For this assignment, I asked students to prepare a ten-to-twelve-minute presentation on the contemporary relevance of Margaret Atwood's work. The presentations had to reference *The Handmaid's Tale*, which we were reading for the class, but they could focus on Atwood's other works, social media, and popular culture. I pitched the assignment to the students as a low-stakes conversation-building exercise that would give them an opportunity to hone their presentation skills on *Zoom*. The students presented on a range of topics, including *The Handmaid Tale's* descendants in recent young adult fiction, the Me Too movement, the cinematography of the Hulu series, surveillance and threats to freedom, Atwood's poetry, and the use of historical precedents in *The Handmaid's Tale*.

The students all said that they enjoyed the conference because it fostered rich discussion and learning; in one student's words, "the end result was fantastic." They also recommended integrating the assignment into future classes. Surprising feedback came from students teaching full-time in high school settings who said that they would like to adapt the assignment for their own classrooms. One student shared that she was inspired by the conference "to look at [her] own teaching and explore ideas [she] had never considered before."

Looking more closely at the teaching of Atwood's works and exploring new, innovative ideas and approaches are the aims of the present volume.

One commenter on the MLA survey raised some concerns about this project, explaining, "I am incredibly uneasy about teaching her work given her very public political defence of [Steven] Galloway at UBC from sexual assault charges. Indeed, I would urge anyone who is working on Atwood and not familiar with this situation to think carefully about the complexities of teaching Atwood without fully narrativizing the contradictions that abound in her writings." The writer was referring to the controversy over Atwood's signing of an open letter that criticized the University of British Columbia for suspending Steven Galloway without due process after he was accused of sexual assault (Freeman). One of the goals of this volume is to consider the impact of Atwood as a public figure on our understanding and reading of her works; exploring her writings in this way helps initiate and contextualize conversations about controversial issues that extend beyond Atwood and that often stymie class discussion. In the Atwood *Zoom* conference discussed above, for example, one student directly tackled the controversy arising from Atwood's political stances in her presentation, "*The Handmaid's Tale* as Protest." Detailing the letter, the backlash, and Atwood's response to it, the presenter highlighted the controversy itself as "a very important moment" in examining the intersection of universal human rights and feminist discourse. While some in the class disagreed with the presenter's assertion that Atwood's stance in fact furthers women's best interests, all agreed that examining the controversy sheds light on Atwood's relevance while causing readers to consider in more depth the treatment of justice and equality in her works.

The present collection aims to share a wide range of new approaches to demonstrate how teachers are using Atwood's works to create meaningful learning opportunities for today's students in a variety of classroom types. The essays all focus on the ways the authors are teaching Atwood's works in their classrooms, providing readers with compelling strategies that they can put into practice. The approaches in this volume focus on Atwood's works that are most frequently taught today; instructors can find strategies to teach earlier works that now are not taught as widely, such as *Surfacing*, *Survival*, *Bodily Harm*, and *Wilderness Tips*, in the first Approaches volume. In addition to covering the texts students are most likely to encounter in the classroom, this volume aims to provide methods for a wide variety of classroom types, from high school to graduate settings, and ideas about how to adapt approaches according to students' needs.

First, a "Materials" section details the works Atwood has written to date, notable adaptations of her works, and other resources that can be helpful for teachers. From the Margaret Atwood Papers Manuscript Collection at Toronto's Thomas Fisher Rare Book Library to the Margaret Atwood Society's annotated bibliographies, and from online interviews featuring Atwood to recent works of literary criticism, the "Materials" section highlights comprehensive and current resources that can aid in engaging more deeply with cultural and critical conversations about Atwood's works.

Six groups of essays in this collection, while not mutually exclusive in regard to content, place approaches to teaching Atwood's works into specific contexts. Justin Omar Johnston's essay "Teaching *Oryx and Crake* in a Science and Literature Course during a Pandemic" begins the first group of approaches, "Atwood in the Digital Age." Johnston discusses pairing *Oryx and Crake* with scientific texts and describes how creating "apocalypse survival groups" helped students process the early months of the COVID-19 pandemic. He explains that Atwood's vision of the posthuman informs our understanding of a world in which we anticipate another pandemic. Olivia Guillet's "Teaching *The Handmaid's Tale* to Generation Z" details using online and multimedia assignments to introduce high school students to considerations of genre and representation while also asking them to think about what concepts like freedom and anarchy mean in the society where they live. Incorporating the Hulu series and students' own creative works inspired by the novel, Guillet shows how Atwood's work illuminates the relationship between technology and social and legal identities as well as the necessity of forming meaningful connections with others. The last essay in this group, Amanda Licastro's "'Under His Eye': Atwood and Surveillance," investigates portrayals of surveillance in *The Handmaid's Tale* and the MaddAddam trilogy and reveals what students can learn when they write about these depictions using platforms like *Twitter* (now *X*), which employ the very technologies about which they are writing.

Danette DiMarco's "Considering Nonhuman Animals in World Literature: *The Complete Angel Catbird*," the first essay in the "Fostering Ecological Understanding" section, explores how Atwood's use of the graphic novel defamiliarizes human story and allows readers to better understand the relational aspects that emerge from seeing species' entanglements. She also shows how students have extended this project with their own environmental research, ultimately designing their own creative works. In "Lessons in Teaching and Living *The Year of the Flood*," Shoshannah Ganz discusses her teaching of the MaddAddam trilogy in an applied arts curriculum that bears renewed importance since the onset of the COVID-19 pandemic. By applying lessons from *The Year of the Flood* and adopting a care-based approach to collaboration, her master's-level students worked to develop their own sustainable community. My essay, "Song That 'Goes On Calling': Teaching Atwood's Poetry," explains how students in my graduate poetry seminar traced poets' imaginations of space and place over time to chart the evolution of what we now know as ecopoetics. In readings of Atwood's poems ranging from her early work to her 2020 collection, *Dearly*, students noted the capacity of poems to mimic songs of the natural world and, in so doing, to call us to protect the home we all share.

The third group of approaches explores a range of cross-disciplinary applications for studying Atwood's works. Its first essay, "Testimony, Truth, and Judgment in *Alias Grace*," by Melissa Ganz, uses Atwood's novel to investigate the causes and consequences of criminality while weighing the difficulties of legal and moral judgment in the light of the gendered nature of criminal justice. The next essay, Rebecca Dixon's "Race and Reproductive Rights in *The Handmaid's Tale*," argues that what in art and society appears to be "raceless" really is not. Dixon asserts that *The Handmaid's Tale* generates fruitful conversations about reproductive rights, health care, and lifestyle choices and that to fully understand the novel's engagement with these issues, those discussing the novel should consider its resonances not only with the exploitation of Black women's reproductive capacity under American slavery but also with racial inequities in the current US health care system. Theodore Sheckels's essay on *The Blind Assassin* considers a pedagogical dilemma: If a teacher could include only one Atwood novel in a course, what would be the best choice? In answering, Sheckels weighs considerations of genre, structure, narrative perspective, symbolism, and messaging, ultimately settling on Atwood's first Booker Prize–winning novel, *The Blind Assassin*; his discussion of Atwood's other works may also be helpful to teachers who would like to learn more about overarching characteristics of her fiction. The final essay in this group, Patrick Thomas Henry's "Messages and Message-Bearers: Teaching Atwood's Fiction in the Creative Writing Workshop," discusses applying Atwood's messenger model of sharing words across time and space in a creative writing workshop to develop a process-based pedagogy in which students both develop their own writing strategies and treat research as a creative activity that stimulates the imagination.

"Intertextual Analysis and Adaptation Theory," the fourth grouping, begins with Melissa Caldwell's essay, "The Value of Atwood's Adaptations for Twenty-First-Century Students," which makes a case for studying adaptation as both process and product. Caldwell argues that her teaching of *The Penelopiad* and *Hag-Seed* in this framework allows for not only a richer interpretation of the works themselves and literary history, but also students' developing their own voices as writers. In "Teaching *The Handmaid's Tale* in Adaptation," Katherine Snyder notes that the political relevance and continual adaptation of *The Handmaid's Tale* provide a pedagogical opportunity to apply adaptation studies theory and inspire students to create their own compelling adaptations of the novel. In addition to discussing how *The Testaments* acts as an adaptation of the original story, Snyder explains how the development of the Hulu series after the first season "expands and deepens the Gileadverse" with new characters, locations, and storylines. Ultimately, Snyder says, these adaptations have something to teach instructors not only about the worlds of these works but also about teaching itself. Heidi Tiedemann Darroch's "Atwood's Canadian Shakespeare: Allusions and Intertextuality in *Cat's Eye* and *Hag-Seed*" uses Atwood's novels to explore the influence of both Shakespeare and Atwood on Canadian literature. Noting the prominence of Shakespeare in Canadian education, Darroch explains that Atwood's works serve as colonial allegories and that their Shakespearean intertexts represent the extent of Britain's colonial influence. The last essay in this group, Gina Hausknecht's "Sea Changes: *Hag-Seed*, Shakespearean Adaptation, and Prison Representation," claims that *Hag-Seed* explores what is at stake in retelling Shakespeare's *The Tempest* and what this modern-day retelling suggests about the representation of prisons and prison programs. Examining intersections of incarceration and education, Hausknecht explains that at the heart of this adaptation, as in so many of Atwood's works, is an examination of power.

The fifth grouping of approaches focuses primarily on Atwood's *The Penelopiad.* A case study of *The Penelopiad* is warranted (as was a case study of *The Handmaid's Tale* in the 1996 Approaches volume) because of the novel's wide adoption across classroom types; I believe it is now the most frequently taught Atwood work after *The Handmaid's Tale. The Penelopiad* appeals to instructors as a counterpoint to canonical texts, as a point for discussion about gender and history, and as a medium for exploring perspective and narration. It also serves as a gateway to other Atwood works.

The first essay in the case study, Marguerite Raymond's "Rethinking Archetypes in the High School Classroom with *The Penelopiad,*" discusses why *The Penelopiad* is particularly well-suited for high school students and how using the novel alongside *The Odyssey* forces students to reassess what it means to be a hero. *The Penelopiad,* Raymond explains, foregrounds the theme of survival—of a narrator or hero and even of myth itself—in different contexts than *The Odyssey* while encouraging higher-level practices of close reading, research, and argument formation. Lisa Tyler's essay describes teaching *The Penelopiad* at a two-year community college. Tyler explains that this selection works so well in her classrooms in part because Penelope's perspective resonates with her predominantly female students, whose life and work experience inform their understanding of the story's marital dynamics and of the prospect of justice for the wronged maids. *The Penelopiad* also accommodates readers at various levels of ability, Tyler says, allowing a greater range of students to find meaning in the text. The last essay in the group, Katja Pilhuj's "Cadets Weaving Connections: Teaching Conflict and Leadership through *The Penelopiad,*" centers on teaching to yet another group of students, a mainly male corps of cadets at a US military college, many of whom will either serve in the US military or pursue a defense-oriented career. Pilhuj demonstrates how she teaches principled leadership through contrasting Atwood's and Homer's texts to explore the challenges leaders must overcome when prioritizing the best interests of the people they will lead and completing the mission they have accepted.

The last section of this volume focuses on new approaches to *The Handmaid's Tale.* The first essay in this group, Tarshia Stanley's "Reproductive Ransom and Self Recovery: Mothering in *The Handmaid's Tale* and *Wild Seed,*" demonstrates that the power of mothers in both these novels is not limited to birthing babies. While examining the role of the procreating body and its limits, the novels present bodies as producers of story and record and affirm the multiple ways to read motherhood. Helen Thompson's "*The Handmaid's Tale* as Campus Book Pick: Dystopia, Dominance Feminism, and Satire" describes her experience in organizing her university's campus-wide reading program around a study of *The Handmaid's Tale.* Thompson discusses how the program's speakers and activities prompted her to more closely examine the novel's depiction of the protectionist premise of dominance feminism and its mobilization against pornography. The novel's satire highlights the hypocrisy of the righteous pretensions of both Gilead and our world today, Thompson explains. The final approach in this collection is Debrah Raschke's "Teaching *The Handmaid's Tale* and *The Testaments* through the Theoretical Zeitgeist," which discusses how Atwood's works incorporate theoretical concepts drawn from the cultural context in which they are written. Contrasting the poststructuralist fragmentation of *The Handmaid's Tale* with the possibility for reconnection in *The Testaments*, Raschke locates *Oryx and Crake* as the turning point between these theoretical movements. Today, she notes, students find solace in recognizing that language itself provides a medium through which "resistance can actually occur."

This collection aims to inspire both teachers and students to enter into a deeper engagement with Atwood's works, to show them how they might find greater meaning in the texts themselves and their relation to the real world. As Katherine Snyder explains in the conclusion to her essay, "the creative and interpretive interventions that we make as teachers, like adaptations themselves, are part of what makes texts continue to matter. The explorations that we undertake in the classroom . . . provide windows onto the texts we study, and even doors that we walk through in order to enter these texts more fully." Bringing together instructors from various teaching contexts, this volume provides many new gateways through which readers can explore Atwood's rich body of work. Collectively, these intellectual journeys demonstrate the force of Atwood's writing, which is now more relevant than ever.

NOTE

1. This essay cites the 2017 Anchor edition of *The Handmaid's Tale*.

Part One

MATERIALS

Atwood's Writings

With a literary career spanning six decades and counting, Margaret Atwood is the most prolific major author of our time. While a comprehensive list of her major works and small press editions to date appears at the end of this section, it is helpful for teachers of Atwood's works to understand the breadth and depth of her literary production. Atwood was first published as a poet, but she has written extensively in many other genres, including novels, short fiction, children's books, graphic novels, literary criticism, essays, occasional pieces, book reviews, and collected lectures. Constantly producing new work, Atwood has published more than sixty books to date and continues to develop new literary projects.

Atwood is best known for her novels. Her first, *The Edible Woman*, which uses satire in its depiction of consumerism, social expectations for women, and the politics of food, distinguished her as a writer of prose as well as poetry. Other early Atwood novels include *Surfacing*, whose narrative deals with alienation, abortion, and mental health, and *Bodily Harm*, which presents the experiences of a writer recovering from cancer who becomes embroiled in political upheaval and a problematic romance abroad. *Cat's Eye* looks at how prior relationships, including those with mean girls of her childhood, affect a painter's adult life and work. These early novels depict the inner lives of women and feminist themes that are even more fully developed in Atwood's later works.

I have discussed at length in the introduction the importance of Atwood's speculative dystopian novels, but it is worth noting that Atwood has also received critical acclaim for her historical fiction. Like her speculative fiction, Atwood's historical fiction encourages a closer examination of gendered power dynamics of the past as well as a consideration of the power of words themselves to make history. Based on an 1843 double murder that took place not far from Toronto, where Atwood now lives, *Alias Grace* presents a character study of Grace Marks, the woman convicted of being an accomplice in the murders. The novel explores how gender inflects the exchanges between Grace and Dr. Simon Jordan, a fictional mental health expert researching the case, and how bias clouds the interpretation of her accounts by supposedly objective medical and legal professionals. *The Blind Assassin*, Atwood's first Booker Prize–winning novel, reveals bit by bit the story of Iris Chase Griffen, who tries to redefine her legacy in her retrospective account of the formative events of the 1930s of her youth. Both Grace and Iris are psychologically complex characters, and they realize that the words they use in their accounts have the power to shape their legacies. Collectively, these novels highlight how women, despite societal constraints, have used the platforms available to them to tell their own stories.

Atwood has claimed that "[w]e . . . judge good stories . . . by the way they strike us" (*Writing with Intent* 68). As an editor of *The Best American Short Stories* and two Oxford collections of Canadian short stories in English (Atwood and Weaver, *New Oxford Book*, *Oxford Book*), Atwood has thought critically about "our notions of what a story is" and the impact that "the voice of the story" has on the reader (*Writing with Intent* 70). Atwood explains that the voice in a good story is "a speaking voice like the singing voice in music, that moves not across space, across the page, but across time" and that "every written story is a score for voice" (71). Atwood has shown her versatility as a storyteller by developing compelling voices brought to life not only in her seventeen novels but also her nine collections of short stories. From the 1977 collection *Dancing Girls* to her most recent book of short stories, *Old Babes in the Wood*, Atwood has continued to publish short fiction, demonstrating her command of voice with scores of various lengths.

Atwood's remarkable versatility as a writer extends beyond her fictional offerings to works in other genres. In Atwood's nineteen collections of poetry, spanning from *The Circle Game* to *Paper Boat: New and Selected Poems, 1961–2023*, readers will find wide-ranging formal diversity, subjects, and figurations. Her seven children's books use art and sound to playfully appeal to younger readers, and her more recent graphic novels encourage young adult and adult readers to expand their frames of reference, as with the reimagining of hybridity and interspecies entanglements in the *Angel Catbird* volumes (2016, 2017). Atwood's eleven nonfiction collections to date chart her contributions to literary and intellectual thought over time. Particularly noteworthy are *Survival: A Thematic Guide to Canadian Literature*; *Second Words: Selected Critical Prose*; *Negotiating with the Dead: A Writer on Writing*; *Writing with Intent: Essays, Reviews, Personal Prose, 1983–2005*; *Payback: Debt and the Shadow Side of Wealth*; *In Other Worlds: SF and the Human Imagination*; and *Burning Questions: Essays and Occasional Pieces, 2004–2021*. Atwood also shapes cultural conversations through her online writings and social media posts, described below under "Other Resources."

Translations and Adaptations

According to Atwood's website, her works have been published in more than forty-five countries and have been translated into many languages, including Catalan, Danish, Dutch, Estonian, Finnish, French, German, Greek, Hebrew, Icelandic, Italian, Japanese, Norwegian, Polish, Portuguese, Romanian, Russian, Serbo-Croatian, Spanish, Swedish, Turkish, and Urdu. In addition to the recent television productions of *The Handmaid's Tale* and *Alias Grace*, Atwood's works have been adapted for radio, film, opera, and ballet, among other media, providing teachers with many new modalities to offer their students when considering the implications of Atwood's writing. Atwood has also created noteworthy adaptations that challenge canonical writings and the notion of the canon itself. One such work that is taught widely in both high school and collegiate settings is *The Penelopiad*, which retells the Odysseus myth from the point of view of Penelope. Another, the *New York Times* best-selling *Hag-Seed: William Shakespeare's* The Tempest *Retold*, uses the novel form to reimagine Shakespeare's play. Adaptations by Atwood and of her works have engendered rich reimaginations of storytelling as well as reconsiderations of the import of art in society.

Literary Criticism

Because Atwood is so prolific, publishing so many different works and generating wide-ranging critical interest, there are too many works of literary criticism to include a comprehensive listing here. To compile these recommended sources, I consulted with Danielle Moore, the deputy director of The Citadel's Daniel Library, and Chelsea Humphries, a public services librarian at the Grenfell Campus of the Memorial University of Newfoundland, to select prominent texts within Atwood criticism as well as the most frequently held books on Atwood's work according to *WorldCat*, a global database of library holdings. This list represents only a starting place for those interested in exploring books and articles that focus on Margaret Atwood's writings. Consult the essays in the "Approaches" section for additional sources as well as explanations about how instructors might incorporate them in their teaching.

Books

Building on key collections like Sherrill Grace and Lorraine Weir's *Margaret Atwood: Language, Text, and System*, Kathryn VanSpanckeren and Jan Garden Castro's *Margaret Atwood: Vision and Forms*, Arnold Davidson and Cathy N. Davidson's *The Art of Margaret Atwood: Essays in Criticism*, J. Brooks Bouson's *Brutal Choreographies: Oppositional Strategies and Narrative Design in the Novels of Margaret Atwood*, Judith McCombs's *Critical Essays on Margaret Atwood*, and Hilde Staels's *Margaret Atwood's Novels: A Study of Narrative Discourse*, many books on Atwood and her works have been published since the 1996 MLA volume *Approaches to Teaching Atwood's* The Handmaid's Tale *and Other Works*. Notable volumes include Coral Ann Howells's *The Cambridge Companion to Margaret Atwood* and *Margaret Atwood*, Sharon R. Wilson's *Margaret Atwood's Textual Assassinations: Recent Poetry and Fiction* and *Myths and Fairy Tales in Contemporary Women's Fiction: From Atwood to Morrison*, Bouson's *Critical Insights: Margaret Atwood*, Reingard M. Nischik's *Engendering Genre: The Works of Margaret Atwood* and *Margaret Atwood: Works and Impact*, Fiona Tolan's *The Fiction of Margaret Atwood*, Harold Bloom's *Margaret Atwood*, Margaret Reynolds's *Margaret Atwood: The Essential Guide to Contemporary Literature*, Shannon Hengen and Ashley

Thomson's *Margaret Atwood: A Reference Guide, 1988–2005*, Nathalie Cooke's *Margaret Atwood: A Critical Companion*, and Donna Bickford's *Understanding Margaret Atwood.*

The major biographies of Margaret Atwood are Rosemary Sullivan's *The Red Shoes: Margaret Atwood Starting Out*, Cooke's *Margaret Atwood: A Biography*, and Lorraine York's *Margaret Atwood and the Labour of Literary Celebrity*. Books focusing exclusively on *The Handmaid's Tale* include Bouson's *Critical Insights:* The Handmaid's Tale and Bloom's *Margaret Atwood's* The Handmaid's Tale. To explore Atwood's works and feminism, see Tolan's *Margaret Atwood: Feminism and Fiction*, Martine Watson Brownley's *Deferrals of Domain: Contemporary Women Novelists and the State*, Theodore F. Sheckels's *The Political in Margaret Atwood's Fiction*, and Atwood's foreword in Nahid Shahalimi's *We Are Still Here: Afghan Women on Courage, Freedom, and the Fight to Be Heard*. If seeking books on Atwood's postapocalyptic vision, see Karma Waltonen's *Margaret Atwood's Apocalypses*, Susan Watkins's *Contemporary Women's Post-apocalyptic Fiction*, and Sławomir Kuźnicki's *Margaret Atwood's Dystopian Fiction: Fire Is Being Eaten*. A source for looking at adaptations of Atwood's work is Shannon Wells-Lassagne and Fiona McMahon's *Adapting Margaret Atwood: The Handmaid's Tale and Beyond*.

Articles

Online databases can help users locate the most current Atwood criticism in peer-reviewed journals and books. With thousands of articles published on Atwood's works, I have opted to prioritize recent work here while also considering a diversity of approaches.

Three articles that could help situate Atwood's writings and her public persona in recent conversations about her relationship to feminism are Hadley Freeman's "Playing with Fire: Margaret Atwood on Feminism, Culture Wars and Speaking Her Mind," Julie Rak's "Margaret Atwood and Sexual Assault," and Susanne Bach's "May I Laugh about Women's Lib? or, The Difficult Relationship of Humour and Feminism, Caryl Churchill, and Helen Fielding." These essays explore Atwood's reluctance to assume the mantle of being a "feminist" writer. As Freeman explains in her article, Atwood's "clear-eyed focus on what's fair and true over any kind of ideology, with little concern about public criticism, is part of what has made her personally so inspiring and her work so enduring." For more on the politics of Margaret Atwood's literature, see the introduction to the special section of essays on this topic in *Margaret Atwood Studies* by Dunja Mohr and Kirsten Sandrock. Those wanting to read scholarly assessments of recent protests that invoke *The Handmaid's Tale* might consult Lauren Wright's "Mayday: Rethinking Reproductive Justice Protests Utilizing Margaret Atwood's *The Handmaid's Tale*" and Kam Meakin's "Restorative Nostalgia and Historical Amnesia in *The Handmaid's Tale* Protests." For a broad examination of gender and surveillance, see Claire Wrobel's "Gender and Surveillance in Margaret Atwood's Novels, from *Bodily Harm* (1981) to *The Testaments* (2019)."

Teachers interested in learning more about Atwood's recent poetry collections, such as *Morning in the Burned House*, *The Door*, and *Dearly*, could consult Carla Scarano D'Antonio's "Transformation through Storytelling in Margaret Atwood's Latest Poetry." Three articles that readers of *Alias Grace* might be interested in are Maysaa Jaber's "'I Am a Celebrated Murderess': Female Criminality and Multiple Personalities in Margaret Atwood's *Alias Grace*," Maria J. Lopez's "'You Are One of Us': Communities of Marginality, Vulnerability, and Secrecy in Margaret Atwood's *Alias Grace*," and Chloe Harrison's "Ninety-Nine Ways to Retell a Story: The Styles and Functions of Narrator Reconstrual." Alaina Kaus's "Liberalities of Feeling: Free Market Subjectivities in Margaret Atwood's *The Blind Assassin*" provides an interesting reading of that novel, and two works worth reviewing on *Hag-Seed* are Melissa Caldwell's "'The Isle Is Full of Noises': The Many Tempests of Margaret Atwood's *Hag-Seed*" and Wolfgang Klooβ's "Margaret Atwood's *Hag-Seed*: The Aesthetics of Retelling Shakespeare's *The Tempest*."

There is, of course, a preponderance of critical material on *The Handmaid's Tale*, but some pieces that might be of particular interest are Jonathan Alexander and Sherryl Vint's "Feminism, Violence, and the Anthropocene in *The Handmaid's Tale*," Riley Thomas's "Women's Rebel Spaces in Margaret Atwood's *The Handmaid's Tale*," and Barbara Eckstein's "Beloved in the Attic: Harriet Jacobs's Confinement." Two essays that focus on the continuation of the storyline of *The Handmaid's Tale* in *The Testaments* are Alistair Rolls's "Telling Tales: The True Story of *The Handmaid's Tale*" and Fiona Tolan's "Twenty-First-Century Gileads: Feminist Dystopian Fiction after Atwood."

As the scrutiny of climate change has increased, so has the amount of literary criticism on the MaddAddam trilogy. Among noteworthy approaches instructors might consider are Robert Marzec's "Margaret Atwood's *Oryx and Crake* and *The Year of the Flood* as Cli-Fi," Dunja Mohr's "Critical Hope: Relationalities in Twenty-First-Century Speculative Fiction and Art," Sayan Aich Bhowmik's "Pandemic and the End of the World in Margaret Atwood's *Oryx and Crake*," Liza B. Bauer's "Reading to Stretch the Imagination: Exploring Representations of 'Livestock' in Literary Thought Experiments," and J. Brooks Bouson's "A 'Joke-Filled Romp' through End Times: Radical Environmentalism, Deep Ecology, and Human Extinction in Margaret Atwood's Eco-Apocalyptic MaddAddam Trilogy." Two works exploring the trilogy's relation to religion are Emrah Atasoy and Thomas Horan's "Prayer Had Broken Out: Pandemics, Capitalism, and Religious Extremism in Recent Apocalyptic Fiction" and David Morris's *Public Religions in the Future World: Postsecularism and Utopia*, which also discusses the work of Octavia E. Butler.

Those interested in learning about how Atwood's works are taught around the world can start with pieces like Vera Benczik's "The (Post)Apocalypse in Hungary: American Science Fiction and Social Analysis," P. Seethalaxmi's "Teaching Philosophy of Life through the Select Ghost Novels of Toni Morrison and Margaret Atwood," Pilar Somacarrera's "A Prince of Asturias Award for the Queen of Canadian Letters: Reading Margaret Atwood's Texts in Spain," and my essay "'To See Clearly and without Flinching': Teaching the Works of Margaret Atwood."

Other Resources

Archival Materials

The Thomas Fisher Rare Book Library's Margaret Atwood Papers Manuscript Collection is the best resource for those wanting to deeply explore Atwood's writing process and research interests firsthand. As the library boasts on its collection highlights page, "The archive is a near-complete representation" of Atwood's "literary output since the early 1960s up to the present day" ("Margaret Atwood Papers"). In addition, the library houses a collection of Margaret Atwood juvenilia that reveals Atwood's growth as a writer from the illustrated stories of her youth.

Housed in the University of Toronto, the Margaret Atwood Papers Manuscript Collection at the time of this writing contains 717 boxes (nearly 350 linear feet), which are very well organized and catalogued. These materials, which continue to grow as Atwood continues to publish, include holograph drafts, typescripts, galleys, and page proofs in addition to a trove of unpublished material, including correspondences that reflect Atwood's active role as an author and public figure, doodles and other marginalia, and files upon files of research Atwood has compiled—magazine clippings, scientific studies, newspaper articles, brochures—as inspiration for her writings.

The collection provides researchers and students a special opportunity to incorporate these various archival materials in their own work. Teachers able to travel to the library can similarly enrich their classes' experiences by introducing their students to fascinating artifacts that can inspire critical thinking and creative work.

Margaret Atwood Society Annotated Bibliographies

Demonstrating the depth and breadth of recent literary criticism on Atwood's works, the Margaret Atwood Society's Annual Atwood Bibliography of publications by or about Atwood provides the most comprehensive compilations of current Atwood criticism (atwoodsociety.org/bibliography/).

Atwood's Website

Margaret Atwood's website (margaretatwood.ca) contains many standard features, such as the author's biography and bibliography, but it also offers teachers compelling resources like a *Flipboard* collection of "Margaret Atwood's MaddAddam World" linking to articles and blogs that focus on issues central to the MaddAddam trilogy (flipboard.com/@MargaretAtwood). For those teaching *Oryx and Crake*, *The Year of the Flood*, and *MaddAddam* who cannot travel to the Fisher Library, this website brings some of the real-world inspiration for the trilogy to life. Another resource for teaching the MaddAddam trilogy is the "*MaddAddam* Media" page, which provides hyperlinks to Atwood's interviews on the project (margaretatwood.ca/maddaddam-media).

Atwood's site also has some fun features. The A/V dropdown menu offers comics Atwood has created over the years, videos, and photos of her life, starting with a 1942 image of her watching her father make a campfire. Notable options in the FAQ menu are the "Resources for Writers" page, which addresses common questions about writing and publishing with humor and practical advice, and the "Your Online Presence" page, which gives helpful words of warning and discussions of possibilities and drawbacks of authors' use of online platforms, including *Twitter* (known as *X* as of July 2023), blogs, *Goodreads*, and *Facebook*, among other options. Here Atwood gives this sage advice: "there's no rule that says you can't try one of these tools out and then decide it's not for you. On the Internet, one size does not fit all."

Atwood's Social Media Sites

Margaret Atwood has embraced social media as an opportunity to connect with others and share ideas. She has more than two million followers on *X*, and she uses *Substack*, a platform that allows her to publish directly to her audience.

Interviews

Many of today's students have grown up learning on devices and through video clips. Teachers can search selectively through hundreds of videos and broadcasts featuring Atwood on the Internet to find one that matches their lesson plans. The Canadian Broadcasting Corporation has produced many interviews with Atwood that could enrich classroom discussions. Another interview teachers may want to share with their students is a five-minute clip in which Atwood shares how she got started as a writer and insights into writing her memoir ("Margaret Atwood Reveals"). On 25 July 2022, Atwood gave an hour-long interview, "Telling Tales from the Future," discussing global warming, plastics in the ocean, and how her works reflect the urgency of action regarding the environment ("Margaret Atwood: Telling Tales"). Focused on *Burning Questions*, Russia's invasion of Ukraine, and why her works resonate with so many readers, Atwood's 9 March 2022 interview with ABC News runs about six minutes and relates her writings to world events ("World 'Moving'"). For those teaching from the Hulu series, students will want to see *Nightline*'s behind-the-scenes glimpse into the making of the second season of *The Handmaid's Tale* ("Behind the Scenes").

Atwood's Works to Date

Novels

The Edible Woman (1969)
Surfacing (1972)
Lady Oracle (1976)
Life before Man (1979)
Bodily Harm (1981)
The Handmaid's Tale (1985)
Cat's Eye (1988)
The Robber Bride (1993)
Alias Grace (1996)
The Blind Assassin (2000)
Oryx and Crake (2003)
The Penelopiad (2005)
The Year of the Flood (2009)
MaddAddam (2013)
The Heart Goes Last (2015)
Hag-Seed (2016)
The Testaments (2019)

Short Fiction Collections

Dancing Girls (1977)
Murder in the Dark (1983)
Bluebeard's Egg (1983)
Wilderness Tips (1991)
Good Bones (1992)
The Tent (2006)

Moral Disorder (2006)
Stone Mattress (2014)
Old Babes in the Wood (2023)

Children's Books

Up in the Tree (1978)
Anna's Pet (with Joyce Barkhouse, 1980)
For the Birds (1990)
Princess Prunella and the Purple Peanut (1995)
Rude Ramsay and the Roaring Radishes (2003)
Bashful Bob and Doleful Dorinda (2004)
Wandering Wenda and Widow Wallop's Wunderground Washery (2011)

Graphic Novels

Angel Catbird, vol. 1 (illustrated by Johnnie Christmas, 2016)
Angel Catbird, vols. 2 and 3 (illustrated by Johnnie Christmas and Tamra Bonvillain, 2017)
War Bears (illustrated by Ken Steacy, 2018)

Poetry

The Circle Game (1966)
The Animals in That Country (1968)
The Journals of Susanna Moodie (1970)
Procedures for Underground (1970)
Power Politics (1971)
You Are Happy (1974)
Selected Poems (1976)
Selected Poems, 1965–1975 (1976)
Two-Headed Poems (1978)
True Stories (1981)
Interlunar (1984)
Selected Poems 2: Poems Selected and New, 1976–1986 (1986)
Selected Poems, 1966–1984 (1990)
Margaret Atwood Poems, 1976–1986 (1991)

Morning in the Burned House (1995)
Eating Fire: Selected Poetry, 1965–1995 (1998)
The Door (2007)
Dearly (2020)
Paper Boat: New and Selected Poems, 1961–2023 (2024)

Nonfiction

Survival: A Thematic Guide to Canadian Literature (1972)
Days of the Rebels, 1815–1840 (1977)
Second Words: Selected Critical Prose (1982)
Strange Things: The Malevolent North in Canadian Literature (1995)
Negotiating with the Dead: A Writer on Writing (2002)
Moving Targets: Writing with Intent, 1982–2004 (2004)
Curious Pursuits: Occasional Writing (2005)
Writing with Intent: Essays, Reviews, Personal Prose 1983–2005 (2005)
Payback: Debt and the Shadow Side of Wealth (2008)
In Other Worlds: SF and the Human Imagination (2011)
Burning Questions: Essays and Occasional Pieces, 2004–2021 (2022)
Book of Lives: A Memoir of Sorts (forthcoming)

Edited Collections

The New Oxford Book of Canadian Verse in English (1982)
The Oxford Book of Canadian Short Stories in English (with Robert Weaver, 1986)
The Canlit Foodbook (1987)
The Best American Short Stories (with Shannon Ravenel, 1989)
The New Oxford Book of Canadian Short Stories in English (with Robert Weaver, 1995)

Interview Collections

Earl G. Ingersoll has edited two volumes of interviews, *Margaret Atwood: Conversations* and *Waltzing Again: New and Selected Conversations with Margaret Atwood*. A collection of interviews with Victor-Lévy Beaulieu is published in both English and French (*Two Solicitudes*; *Deux Sollicitudes*).

Theater

The Penelopiad: *The Play* (2007)

Small Press Editions

Poetry

Double Persephone (1961)
Kaleidoscopes Baroque: A Poem (1965)
Talismans for Children (1965)
Speeches for Doctor Frankenstein (1966)
Marsh, Hawk (1977)
Notes towards a Poem That Can Never Be Written (1981)
Snake Poems (1983)

Fiction

Encounters with the Element Man (1982)
Unearthing Suite (1983)
Bottle (2004)
I Dream of Zenia with the Bright Red Teeth (2012)

Part Two

APPROACHES

Teaching *Oryx and Crake* in a Science and Literature Course during a Pandemic

Justin Omar Johnston

Scientific experimentation seeks to isolate specific phenomena by controlling for other variables, whereas literary works are much more interested in following the expansive interaction between many variables. Inherently interdisciplinary, novels, at their best, trace the historical forces that condition their composition and allow these multiple discourses to develop according to their own interactive logic. It's this fact that makes science and literature courses especially well-suited for confronting social realities emerging from technoscientific and environmental change. This essay will discuss my approach to teaching Margaret Atwood's novel *Oryx and Crake* and how that approach was complicated, for better and worse, in spring 2020 by the COVID-19 pandemic. After describing how and why I typically pair Atwood's novel with a selection of scientific and theoretical texts by Sarah Franklin, Melinda Cooper, and Elizabeth Grosz, I turn toward the move to online instruction during the first wave of the pandemic and how the novel helped students process in real time what was happening as part of a larger set of economic, social, and technological factors. Finally, I address how Atwood's vision of the posthuman might inform our understanding of the so-called postpandemic world.

Overview of the Course

My intermediate science and literature course, Novel Laboratories, is designed to engage mostly English majors around the question of human belonging in twenty-first-century literary and technoscientific cultures. I divide Novel Laboratories into three interrelated, sequential thematic clusters, each of which reimagines "the human" from a different scientific or philosophical perspective: the biotech revolution, the human-animal divide, and the Anthropocene. Along the way we explore theories of posthumanism, transhumanism, human capital theory, and liberal humanism as they emerge in both literary texts and nonfiction works by well-known scientists, such as the climatologist Paul Crutzen and the biologist E. O. Wilson. The novels I teach in the course are meant to address an urgent dilemma in the humanities: What are the status and standing of the human in a world marked by both growing inequality and increasing ecological and technological interdependence? Among other things, these works feature human clones, animal-human hybrids, artificial intelligence, and whole societies radically transformed by the chemical composition of their environments. As I explain to students, I see it as our job to help one another parse the social, political, and ethical meanings of species, nature, kinship, evolution, and energy as they are represented in these contemporary works.

Given the structure of the course, I almost always begin the semester with a careful and slow three-week reading of *Oryx and Crake*. The novel opens on a beach soon after the near-extinction of humans from Earth, but many large sections of the novel flash back to a dystopian, pre-apocalyptic world dominated economically, socially, and politically by biotech firms. The novel thus oscillates between a "last man" survivalist story—full of lyrical contemplations about hunger, pain, and nature—and a biting political satire of biocapitalism amid ecological degradation. Likewise, its protagonist's identity is divided between the pre-apocalyptic "Jimmy," a white middle-class boy from the suburbs, and "Snowman," the name Jimmy gives himself after the "Great Rearrangement" (103). This "Great Rearrangement" is not only Snowman's euphemism for the death of his species but is also a great melodramatic tear in history whereby Atwood rearranges the novel's setting and choreographs a rhythmic pattern of flashbacks, juxtapositions, and tonal shifts.

Oryx and Crake is packed with imagery and discourse about cellular life, biocapitalism, and lateral gene transfers; the novel not only serves as a critical introduction to the biotech section of the course but also functions as a critical survey for the course as whole. Indeed, later in the semester, when students read other contemporary novels, including Kazuo Ishiguro's *Never Let Me Go*, J. M. Coetzee's *The Lives of Animals*, Han Kang's *The Vegetarian*, Jeanette Winterson's *The Stone Gods*, and Ben Lerner's *10:04*, they invariably return to Atwood's novel by way of comparison in both their essays and our class discussions. *Oryx and Crake* is as much about animality and ecological destruction as it is about biotechnological breakthroughs. In this way, like a "ChickieNob" with its tentacles reaching in every direction (202), *Oryx and Crake* is the literary and pedagogical creature at the center of Novel Laboratories. That it could be assigned at any point during the semester is the reason I teach it first.

Moreover, in many ways, *Oryx and Crake* is a novel about pedagogy (even as it clearly satirizes the education system in the corporate-owned suburban compounds). To better understand the purpose of Atwood's satire, I begin our first class by asking students to interpret one of the epigraphs to *Oryx and Crake*, which is taken from Jonathan Swift's *Gulliver's Travels*: "I could perhaps like others have astonished you with strange improbable tales; but I rather chose to relate plain matter of fact in the simplest manner and style; because my principal design was to inform you, and not to amuse you." Here students grasp that Atwood's comic mode is satirically instructive only insofar as they move beyond mere amusement at ridicule and confront the "plain matter" before them. Atwood's satire of contemporary biotechnology is a send-up not only of genetic experimentation but also of those who might dismiss such projects outright. I show them excerpts from an interview in which Atwood adjures readers, "Please don't make the mistake of thinking that *Oryx and Crake* is anti-science." On the contrary, Atwood, whose father was a biologist, believes that "science and fiction both begin with similar questions" but that "the experiments of science should be replicable, and those of literature should not be (why write the same book twice?)" (Atwood, "Interview"). Atwood's rejection of "strange improbable tales" in favor of stories that are "design[ed] . . . to inform" points to her pedagogical project: to use fiction to explore the unfolding technical, social, and political implications of what is already scientifically possible in the present.

To emphasize the importance of Atwood's goal here, I use the novel's epilogue to segue into a brief discussion of Atwood's well-known public debate with Ursula K. Le Guin about the definitions of *science fiction*, *speculative fiction*, and *fantasy*. Using slides, I show students excerpts from Le Guin's review of Atwood's *The Year of the Flood* that object to Atwood's "arbitrarily restrictive definition" of "science fiction" as "fiction in which things happen that are not possible today." For Atwood, the world-building in "speculative fiction" differs from "science fiction" precisely because it is constrained by what can be extrapolated from already-available technologies. For Le Guin, Atwood's distinction is "designed to protect her novels from being relegated" to the "literary ghetto" of science fiction. Atwood's response to Le Guin, which I also project on slides, comes from the introduction to her nonfiction book *In Other Worlds*. There Atwood rebuts the implication that she is a "genre-traitor" and reformulates the matter by asking, "Is *Nineteen Eighty-Four* as much 'science fiction' as *The Martian Chronicles*?" (*In Other Worlds* [Anchor] 2). Perhaps so, but whether such works are called "science fiction" or "speculative fiction" is not the point. The real purpose of staging this debate for students is to highlight Atwood's pedagogical commitment to embedding her novels within the epistemological horizon of what is scientifically possible at present. This is worthwhile because I structure our reading of *Oryx and Crake* around three nonfiction texts that influence the novel's depiction of biological experimentation, species patenting, and evolution.

Three Lessons: Cellular Biotech, Species Patents, and Evolution

The first of three relatively accessible nonfiction texts I teach alongside *Oryx and Crake* is the first chapter of Sarah Franklin's book *Dolly Mixtures: The Remaking of Genealogy* (19–45). To help facilitate and focus our discussion of nonfiction texts, I always prepare slides for a few key passages. Franklin's chapter, "Sex," is useful not only because it illustrates the technique (somatic cell nuclear transfer) used by Ian Wilmut at the Roslin Institute to clone Dolly the sheep in 1997 but also because it situates animal cloning within a larger epistemological shift in the biological sciences: "Reversing the usual determinism attributed to DNA as the blueprint or master plan for cellular development, the Dolly technique contributed to a new emphasis on *situated biological communication*, in which the powerful egg cytoplasm replaces DNA as the origin of developmental 'instructions'" (42). Franklin's focus on the cellular turn in biology echoes Atwood's depiction of porous cellular membranes, which in the novel opens the nucleus to various forms of cross-species genetic experimentation. To illustrate Atwood's interest in permeable cells, I ask students to consider Jimmy's mother's explanation of how a disease works: "A disease, she continued in that calm, stretched voice, a disease got into you and changed things inside you. It rearranged you, cell by cell, and that made the cells sick. And since you were all made up of tiny cells, working together to make sure you stayed alive, . . . if enough of the cells got sick, then you [got sick]" (Atwood, *Oryx* 21).

Because living bodies are "made up of tiny cells" that are semiporous, they are always already available to "invisible" and "small" microbes that can "fly through the air or hide in the water" (20). This vision of cellular vulnerability not only foreshadows the Great Rearrangement but also helps students conceptualize the biological processes that scientists in the novel use to produce hybrid species like wolvogs and ChickieNobs. Indeed, as Franklin puts it, "microbes and bacteria, which have a famously loose ability to exchange genes, are equally recombinant to the higher organisms" (19–20).

Importantly, Atwood contrasts this image of biological promiscuity with her depiction of corporate-owned biotech compounds that seek to wall off and segregate their gated communities from outsiders. These wealthy suburban communities have their own private infrastructure, education system, water supply, food production, and police forces, but they are primarily defined by their paranoid exclusion of the poor "pleeblanders" who live in the decaying urban centers beyond the compound walls (164). Ultimately, this apartheid produces a key contradiction that drives the novel's preoccupation with biocapitalism: on the one hand, contemporary biotechnology relies on the porousness of cellular life and the interoperability of the genetic code to produce novel forms of hybrid life which surpass species boundaries. On the other hand, to profit from their creations, these new hybrids must be patented and secured as both species and intellectual property. In other words, they must be prevented from undergoing any further promiscuous mixing.

To ground this point in historical context, the second nonfiction text I assign alongside *Oryx and Crake* is the first chapter of Melinda Cooper's book *Life as Surplus: Biotechnology and Capitalism in the Neoliberal Era* (15–50). Cooper offers students a mini-history of the rise of the biotech industry, which she persuasively links to a shift in the mode of capitalist production:

> The difference lies merely in their temporalities: while industrial production depletes the earth's reserves of past organic life (carbon-based

> fossil fuels), postindustrial bioproduction needs to depotentialize the future possibilities of life, even while it puts them to work. This counterlogic is perhaps most visible in the use of patented sterilization technologies, where a plant's capacity to reproduce itself is both mobilized as a source of labor and deliberately curtailed, thus ensuring that it no longer reproduces "for free." (25)

One such self-sterilizing plant is Monsanto's Roundup Ready soybean. Indeed, drawing on audio excerpts from the oral arguments in the 2013 Supreme Court case *Bowman v. Monsanto*, I show how Monsanto uses soybeans' reproductive capacity as a source of living labor while at the same time it seeks to genetically control where and how this reproductive capacity can be legally expressed ("Bowman v. Monsanto").

For Atwood, this image of bioproduction is crystalized by the figure of the ChickieNob, one of the biotech compounds' most perplexing and profitable inventions. Described as an "animal protein tuber," the ChickieNob has a "bulblike . . . head in the middle," consisting solely of a large "mouth opening at the top" with "no eyes or beak or anything" (*Oryx* 202). Out of this bulbous head grow "twenty thick fleshy tubes," which sprout into chicken breasts at each end. According to the corporate scientists, the ChickieNob "feels no pain" because all "brain functions that had nothing to do with digestion, assimilation, and growth" have been removed (203). The ChickieNob is meant to function as a living machine whose vital processes are designed to provide automatic labor. At this point, I ask students to share their feelings about the creature. I ask them, "Would you eat a ChickieNob?" and "How are ChickieNobs different from already available forms of chicken nuggets?" Reliably, this leads to a provocative discussion that lays the groundwork for the middle section of the course devoted to animality. Drawing on Cooper, I also suggest that the real horror of the ChickieNob derives not from intermixing the genes of different species but instead from the economic subsumption of every aspect of its life into calculable reproductive labor: "you get chicken breasts in two weeks"—that's a three-week improvement "on the most efficient low-light, high-density chicken farming operation so far devised" (203). No matter how biologically hybrid, the ChickieNob is a trademarked species whose genetic purity is policed by biotech corporations deeply invested in individualized patented species. While the biotech corporations apparently celebrate the dynamic potential of interspecies reproduction, they also disavow the profound and uncontrollable promiscuity of interspecies evolution.

Having framed the tension between the novel's representation of porous cellular membranes and securitized corporate compounds, during the third and final week with *Oryx and Crake*, I assign chapter 2 of Elizabeth Grosz's book *Time Travels: Feminism, Nature, Power* (35–42). Grosz's philosophical interpretation of Darwinian thought prepares students to engage in a discussion about the end of the novel and the catastrophe it imagines. While Atwood's

Great Rearrangement depicts the near-extinction of the human species, it also offers us an image of punctuated evolution, as Earth is suddenly and primarily populated by biotechnologically engineered species, including the humanoid Crakers. Along these lines, I ask students to consider Grosz's radical view: "The movement of evolution is in principle unpredictable, in principle historical, in the sense that the nature of species in the past prefigures and provides the raw material for present and future species but in no way contains, limits, or directs them to any particular goal or destination" (38).

Grosz's insight that Charles Darwin opened up a radical futurity where *nature changes* is both inspiring and terrifying. It allows students to interpret the Crakers as evolving from humans rather than merely displacing them, thus allowing them to reconsider the historicity of their own species. It also helps students move beyond moralizing indictments of Crake as a character to consider how Atwood is both evoking and setting aside the "mad scientist" trope.

That said, the ending of *Oryx and Crake* is strategically overdetermined, and it offers readers at least three different frames for interpreting the Great Rearrangement. Therefore, I structure the final discussion of the novel around how to read Crake's decision to wipe out nearly all humans from Earth: Is it an act of genocide? Is it a metaphor for political revolution? Or is it a depiction of evolutionary change? Because all three interpretations are defensible, these questions invariably lead to a rich final discussion about the ethical stakes of becoming posthuman as an act of violence, as an act of political transformation, or as an act of adaptation. However, in the spring of 2020 this discussion took on an uncanny dimension.

The Pandemic

On 18 February 2020, a little less than a month before Stony Brook University transitioned all its classes online in response to the COVID-19 pandemic, my Novel Laboratories class finished reading *Oryx and Crake*. As I recall, the class made a few semiserious references to COVID-19 near the end of our reading of the novel, in our discussions of potential future communicable diseases. But our attitudes toward COVID quickly changed. By 21 February, there were thirty-four reported cases in the United States and seventeen in Italy (Wang). By the end of the following week, there were sixty-five reported cases in the United States, several of which could not be linked to international travel (Baker). Increasingly, my students wanted to talk about the disease, and Atwood's novel provided an imaginary lens for processing its spread. On February 24, for example, a quarter of the students' writing responses to a different assigned novel, Kazuo Ishiguro's *Never Let Me Go*, referred to *Oryx and Crake* and its ending.

In March 2020, COVID dominated everyone's attention. News came fast and students were scared. For example, on 11 March alone, the World Health Organization declared COVID-19 a pandemic, the National Guard established a "containment area" in New Rochelle, New York, and the president of Stony Brook University announced that we would be moving to remote instruction after spring break (Nir). On 12 March I held my last in-person session of Novel Laboratories for that semester, having made attendance optional. Only about two-thirds of the students attended, several having e-mailed me that they had relatives with compromised immune systems or that they were too frightened to attend.

In many ways, *Oryx and Crake* could have distorted students' perceptions of the COVID pandemic. The pandemic in the novel, engineered to eliminate humans from Earth, is even more deadly and sinister than the one we faced and continue to face. And while no students expressed any paranoid or conspiratorial views about COVID-19, I shared with them my concern that they might conflate the novel's fictional circumstances with our actual ones. Meanwhile, I also fretted about Atwood's semicomical style and her somewhat cynical depiction of the Great Rearrangement, which certainly didn't do justice to the students' feelings of embodied fear. The spread of COVID-19 was not a metaphor for evolution or political change: it was moment of tremendous uncertainty that, for the most part, resisted critical reflection.

Nevertheless, *Oryx and Crake* proved an especially helpful tool for transitioning students to online classes. It gave us a pandemic text to draw upon collectively. On the last day of in-person class I asked students to create "apocalypse survival groups." Each group of five to six students exchanged e-mail addresses and came up with a group name. Many of the groups picked names that directly or indirectly referenced Atwood's novel, such as "Carers and Crakers," "Craker Oats," "ChickieNobs," "Atwood's Angels," the "Plague Gang," and the "Clones." I collected the groups' information and added the names of students who couldn't attend that day. As members of these newly formed groups, students left campus feeling understandably fearful but also fortified by their attachments with others. Even as we sometimes needed to isolate ourselves physically, these "survival groups" came to affectively contrast the "containment area" established by the National Guard and the securitized compounds of Atwood's novel. Heeding Grosz's lesson that nature changes, our class was now experiencing the promise and anxiety this contingency brings. As the semester progressed, some students cared for sick relatives and some lost beloved family members. Some students' part-time jobs suddenly became riskier and more stressful as they were deemed "essential workers," and some students suffered from depression after losing work and losing opportunities to socialize. We were undeniably porous and vulnerable, yet the groups we had formed gave us a means of collectively supporting and safeguarding one another.

For many students, the apocalypse survival groups became much more important than I could have predicted. Friendships were born as most groups moved well beyond "peer review" to offer members compassionate understanding, patience, humor, and a sense of social belonging during a time of terrible insecurity. As a professor, it has long been my hope that students take the literature and analysis from class into their lives to better understand and shape their worlds. In spring 2020, I saw students rely on their readings of *Oryx and Crake* to process in real time the volatility of bodies, both political and biological. I saw students in turn bring their personal experiences to bear on their readings of the novels, creating new modes of thought and deeper attachments to the texts. Students that semester turned in some of the best, worst, longest, and shortest essays I've ever received. But I also knew, given the shifting circumstances, what it took for some students to turn in anything at all—it took their tremendous effort as well as sustained support from their peers.

The Posthuman, Postpandemic

Now back in the classroom, I teach *Oryx and Crake* in a so-called postpandemic context, even as the disease continues to spread, mutate, and interact in complex ways with our vaccines and our relative levels of immunity. The pandemic isn't over, but we're learning to live and teach with it in new ways. Going forward, I will certainly create new apocalypse survival groups and will share their history with students. One way to frame this exercise for them alongside Atwood's novel is through posthumanism. Posthumanism marks an understanding of the human body's entanglement with other species and environments. It therefore recognizes assemblages that affirm the power and ethical standing of nonhumans and those who have been deemed less than human. It offers a non-Eurocentric, non-ableist, non-patriarchal, non-anthropocentric image of belonging that is at least partially figured by Atwood's humanoid Crakers. But this concept might also be related to the apocalypse survival groups. What began as a somewhat cheeky term for supportive peer groups might now be expanded to probe and recognize larger assemblages without whom "survival" would be difficult. For example, can we recognize our symbiotic relationship to certain forms of bacteria that allow us to digest and produce critical vitamins? And how should cobalt miners in Congo inform our group's reliance on lithium batteries? Asking students to consider the hidden and nonspeaking members of their survival groups magnifies what made the groups so valuable as the pandemic unfolded. At that time, in the face of real historical unpredictability, students formed collectives that recognized and supported those who faced the greatest precarity. And while this might be read as an example of the students' humanity, I also saw it as a gesture toward forms of belonging that surpass liberal humanism's emphasis on individual sovereignty. The pandemic, like the novel, revealed our cellular vulnerabilities, our relationship to exploited forms of labor, and our undetermined kinship with nature. The apocalypse survival groups were a small example of solidarity and mutual aid that extended well beyond the disciplinary demands of the class and even beyond the promise of a return to normality.

Teaching *The Handmaid's Tale* to Generation Z

Olivia A. Guillet

The teenagers and young adults in today's literature classrooms are the first to approach print literature as a secondary medium; they belong to a technology-dependent generation with constant access to visual and auditory media. In my experience, students of Generation Z raised on apps and the immediacy and entertainment of visual media tend to be more interested and engaged though a visual media approach. For a generation of students whom many teachers have experienced as lacking the desire to read for pleasure and viewing reading as a requirement, not a privilege, Margaret Atwood's *The Handmaid's Tale*—a novel wherein women's right to read are revoked and literature is dangerous—is a particularly effective text to explore. I will address how to teach *The Handmaid's Tale* to high school English students through a range of media, particularly through lessons that focus on scenes from the Hulu television series and that utilize technology students use daily.

When I first taught *The Handmaid's Tale* to high school seniors in England in 2003, they were disappointed in the 1990 film; it simply did not do the novel justice. In August 2018, just after the second season of *The Handmaid's Tale* had aired on Hulu, one of those students, then in his thirties, contacted me through *Facebook*: "I thought you would appreciate knowing that your encouragement of debate lives on. Mssrs. L., B., and I are currently debating the merits of season 2 of *The Handmaid's Tale.*" In my classrooms, both in the United States and in the United Kingdom, the novel has always inspired enthusiastic discussion; however, the new Hulu series has renewed former students' interest and provided an exciting new approach for current students to explore the ideas presented within it. Using the series can inspire Socratic-style debates and encourage students' personal and ongoing engagement with the novel.[1]

I have taught the whole of *The Handmaid's Tale* in an English literature unit, as an examination text, as a coursework text, and simply as an example of genre or theme, depending on the curriculum. Teaching *The Handmaid's Tale* as a dystopian novel inspires the following pedagogical questions: Do we take the two-pronged approach of teaching about genre and the theories of the scholar and educator Amy Devitt before teaching students to write through the remediation of genre? Or do we teach students about genre simply by practicing the writing of texts in different genres and following the traditional route of identifying the "textual features that mark a genre: the meter, the layout, the organization, the level of diction, and so on" (Devitt 575)? *The Handmaid's Tale* allows teachers to utilize what Devitt acknowledges as the new approach to teaching genre: "embracing new notions of genre as dynamic patterning of human experience, as one of the concepts that enable us to construct our writing world" (573).

Modern theories of genre allow the reader to understand genre as being derived from the rhetorical situation, and *The Handmaid's Tale* is a perfect opportunity to teach the dystopian genre from this perspective of the "human experience." I begin my teaching of the novel with a close analysis of the opening pages detailing Offred's human experience at the beginning of Gilead's regime; students respond to Atwood's depiction of the replacement of a familiar world with a new reality. I introduce these pages as an extract, providing no context and no introduction of the author, the rhetorical situation, or the genre. I present my students with the opening pages of "Night," the first chapter, which introduces the Red Center and begins, "We slept in what once had been the gymnasium" (Atwood, *Handmaid's Tale* 3).[2] We discuss their response to the excerpt before introducing the premise of the novel and Atwood as its author, instead of approaching the novel from a definition of the dystopian genre. A close initial reading of the first chapter intrigues students and encourages their questions: Why are the basketball nets gone? What is the effect of Atwood's description of the "palimpsest of unheard sounds," and why are the protagonist and other women sleeping on "the army cots that had been set up in rows, with spaces between so we could not talk" (3)? What is the danger in women communicating with one another? And what is the effect of the juxtaposition between the maternal connotations of the word *aunts* and the description of the "electric cattle prods slung on thongs from their leather belts" (4)? Early teachings in the English classroom about narrative exposition come into play here. What is the effect of the description of the scene in the gymnasium? And what is Atwood doing when she ends the chapter with the following lines: "In the semi-darkness we could stretch out our arms, when the aunts weren't looking, and touch each other's hands across space. We learned to lip-read. . . . In this way we exchanged names, from bed to bed: Alma. Janine. Dolores. Moira. June" (4)? The one-word sentences at the end of the chapter that identify the women in the novel then allow for further discussion about identity and women's rights. These lines lead to our further explorations of identity.

Identity

In the past, I have taught this novel as one in a series of texts exploring the theme of conflict; often, it follows on from the teaching of novels such as George Orwell's *1984* or Ray Bradbury's *Fahrenheit 451*. It has worked particularly well, however, following Arthur Miller's *The Crucible*, where we consider the concept of identity. We explore the replacement of women's names with possessive male identifiers such as *Of*fred and *Of*glen. We make the connection between the significance of the loss of the women's names in *The Handmaid's Tale* and Miller's commentary on identity through John Proctor's lines in *The Crucible*: "Because it is my name! Because I cannot have another in my life!" (Miller 133). This connection allows a series of group discussions and activities that explore the significance of our names in relation to our identity, our place within the world, our integrity, and our honor, and how something as simple as a given name empowers us, or, in the case of *The Handmaid's Tale*, how the removal of names can remove an entire generation of women from their place in society and in the world.

One way of approaching this idea about identity relates to the creation of online identities. Many cautionary tales about young people whose ill-advised tweets or posts have capsized their college or professional careers are used in teaching Internet safety and social media literacy; we teach our students that the images they present on social media make up the way the world sees them and that our online identities are irrevocably connected to our character and our sense of integrity. "Cancel culture" also comes into this concept, and Generation Z students can relate to a discussion about reputation and perception because most high school students utilize at least one social media platform, and many of them have experienced some negative form of public perception through these online communities. This discussion allows for an insight into Atwood's presentation of a world where women's identities are completely removed. They have no authority over their appearance, their diet, their speech, or their bodies. Scenes from early episodes of the Hulu series not only convey how swiftly and effectively this identity is removed but also present how the hierarchy within society is established.

These scenes were not available as visual stimuli and prompts for discussion when I first taught the novel in 2003. At that time, the novel was a shocking, thought-provoking imagining of a future world based on Atwood's interest in "science fiction, speculative fiction, utopias and dystopias"; in creating "an imaginary garden, [she] wanted the toads in it to be real" (Atwood, Introduction [*Handmaid's Tale*] xiv; see also Moore). Atwood has alluded to real-world landmarks, traditions, and histories that inspired elements of the novel, including the Berlin Wall, the red gowns worn by doctoral students at Harvard, and the practices of slavery and polygamy in the United States. However, my current students are making connections between the world of Gilead in the Hulu show and their own world—for example, the role of social media in fighting for social and civil rights and the Me Too movement. Modern technologies and social media allow students of Generation Z to further explore these connections while providing insight into the dystopian concepts of the novel. Simon Firth notes, "While reading and writing both remain essential proficiencies, the technologies with which we can now undertake them are shifting what it means to be literate. So how, in a world of texting, blogs, and social media, do we prepare young people to be excellent readers and writers, and how do we help their teachers impart those skills?" The suggested solution to these concepts is for teachers to use technology more frequently in their lessons so that students can share their discourses and ideas online. For a young generation raised in a society dependent on web-based technologies, many students are more confident in voicing their ideas online than in class; for this reason, teachers must bring these technologies into their teaching to ensure that the opportunity to develop literacy and discourse is available to those who thrive in that medium.

In addition, this approach allows students to respond to their reading in a personal way; for Generation Z students, whose social life is likely bound up with online communication through *Instagram*, X, or *YouTube*, significant elements of their identity and their engagement with the world are based simply on superficial, but carefully edited and curated, snapshots of their lives. Using a posed and filtered photograph, a pithy quotation, or a dramatic statement to sum up how they see themselves and how they wish others to see them, allows for an element of control. We can take this real-world example of how students identify themselves and how they are identified by others through social media, images, and words and use these modes to engage with the text as well as concepts of freedom of speech and freedom of expression. An effective approach to teaching the rhetorical situation is a weekly discussion board, which appeals to Generation Z in that it allows them to work in response to their chosen media. Students are encouraged to write every week a response to a video, a news article, a social media blog, or a post. The topic must be relevant to both a contemporary issue and the reading material assigned for that week. This allows for expressivism—a concept emphasizing the writer's personal experience and the creation of a credible, honest, personal voice—which, according to Richard Fulkerson, is a composition teaching approach that is "quietly expanding its region of command" (655). This engagement with the text and expression of ideas allows for an ironic exploration of the loss of freedom of speech and expression for those living in Gilead. Students are encouraged to find something they can engage with online that relates to their reading of Atwood's novel and to respond to it by writing about this stimulus, online, in a weekly forum. Their peers are then encouraged to write follow-up responses to engage with the topic—either agreeing with and furthering the discussion or countering it with a different idea or argument. This is an exercise in free speech that allows for an engagement in social and contemporary issues and fosters discussion of how Atwood was responding to social, contemporary, and historical issues of her own time by writing *The Handmaid's Tale* as well as anticipating potential future threats to our freedoms.

Freedom

Analysis of a key scene from episode 3 of season 1 of the Hulu series effectively conveys how a society could potentially take away the rights of a specific group, allowing the class to identify moments in the novel where we see this occurring, too, and encouraging analysis of narrative structures and devices. In this scene, Offred's flashbacks show how effectively the removal of women's rights is implemented. Beginning at 3:06, the scene depicts Offred and Moira jogging together in a pre-Gilead America, listening to their music, before stopping at a coffee shop and ordering coffee. The first sign that all is not normal is when Offred asks about the absence of Claire, their usual barista; the second is when her card is declined because, the male barista tells her, the account has "insufficient funds." The conversation then becomes more disturbing when the male barista becomes antagonistic toward the women, calling them "fucking sluts" ("Late" 00:04:27). The narrative continues in Offred's place of work, where she and all other women are told to go home, to pack up their things since "it's the law now" (00:06:11). The viewer sees how swiftly and effectively an entire social group—women, in this case—can have their rights, their financial independence, and their identities taken from them. Discussion of this scene's visuals (the women walk out of their office carrying their possessions in boxes as armed guards are lined up behind them) allows for an interesting exploration of the things we as individuals often take for granted (our names, careers, possessions, financial independence, etc.). In another flashback scene in this episode, female protestors, including June and Moira, are fired upon by armed police to the soundtrack of Philip Glass's Crabtree remix of Blondie's "Heart of Glass" (00:41:30–44:45). The music and the slow-motion visuals are effectively juxtaposed with the sound of gunfire. Both scenes allow students to engage personally with the ideas in the novel and relate them to their own lives and freedoms.

Further discussion of the concept of freedom and women's rights comes through a contemporary exploration of recent social events. In chapter 5, Offred quotes Aunt Lydia when she says, "There is more than one kind of freedom. . . . Freedom to and freedom from. In the days of anarchy, it was freedom to. Now you are given freedom from. Don't underrate it" (24). This raises questions for readers about how we define freedom, an essential question that furthers students' awareness of their own place in society and the freedoms they are privy to. It also allows for the exploration of the social movements that are defining current conversations. The Me Too and Reclaim the Streets movements are both recent real-world contexts that provide some effective and stimulating material for discussion and allow students to consider their own definitions of "freedom" and "anarchy" and their relation to the world created in *The Handmaid's Tale*. Visual materials such as newspaper articles, images of Reclaim the Streets protests in London, and videos, tweets, and news reports detailing women's testimonies in the sexual assault cases against the film producer Harvey Weinstein and the former US women's gymnastics team doctor, Larry Nassar, provide opportunities for Generation Z students to reconsider the conception of freedom that Aunt Lydia poses in the novel. Is Gilead's version of "freedom"—namely, "freedom from" anarchy—simply packaged in such a way as to manipulate the women of Atwood's narrative, or could one argue that their well-being and safety are of paramount importance to the survival of Gilead or of humanity itself? I direct my students to the moment in the text when Offred remembers the time before Gilead, when women "were not protected," and she thinks about "having . . . control" to explore these questions more fully (24).

To explore what freedom means in terms of control and protection, I ask my students to type the words "freedom and women" into a search engine on any social media website. A quick search will provide a plethora of visual stimuli for discussion. The use of social media as evidence of social feeling and influence, particularly with reference to social movements such as Me Too and Reclaim the Streets, is a powerful teaching tool not only to foster students' engagement with Atwood's novel but also to introduce essential questions about human rights, feminism, freedom of speech, the media, and the power of the written and spoken word.

Psychology

My students have always engaged more with a written text when a visual stimulus is provided. When this visual stimulus interests them because it is contemporary, relatable, or even has a great cast, an effective soundtrack, or interesting visual effects, this teaching tool is even more impactful. The first season of *The Handmaid's Tale* checks all the above criteria. Over a ten-episode narrative arc, the producers of the Hulu drama effectively present several of the key themes and concepts of the novel in a richly visual way that students respond to, using the color imagery, food imagery, religious symbolism, and camera work that conveys the oppressive, claustrophobic feel of Gilead. The series also provides more developed depictions of minor characters in the novel, illustrating how existing narratives can beget new narratives. Highlighting the embellished stories of secondary characters in the series, Emily Nussbaum notes that "Some of the smartest moments in the show—like Ofglen's story, and one featuring a Handmaid named Janine—are radical edits from the book, making a passive plot active." These in-depth explorations, offering some of the adaptation's most harrowing details, encourage students to develop their interpretations and understanding of Atwood's characters. In a creative writing exercise, a student might rewrite a scene in the novel from the perspective of one of these minor characters.

One prime example of this character development, or a "radical edit," as Nussbaum describes it, is in the story of Janine. Offred's perspective on Janine in the novel is that of an observer; she notes Janine's deteriorating mental state and the abuse she suffers but displays little sympathy for her. In one scene at the Red Center, the Aunts use Janine's horrific story of being gang-raped at fourteen and subsequently having an abortion to shame her, insisting that the other women join in. Offred notes, "For a moment, even though we knew what was being done to her we despised her" (72). In the birthing scene, later in the narrative, Atwood evokes sympathy for Janine through Offred's voice when she poignantly states, "We ache. Each of us holds in her lap a phantom, a ghost baby" (127). Although the reader empathizes with Janine in this scene, along with Offred, it is the Hulu series that allows for a deeper characterization of her, particularly in the episode "The Bridge," where Aunt Lydia and Offred talk Janine down from jumping to her death with her baby. In this scene, readers are able to experience Janine's painful perspective of having her child taken from her, whereas in the novel, it is only really Offred's haunting flashbacks of the loss of her daughter that the reader experiences. This exploration of how a character can be interpreted and developed further encourages students to explore the intention and purpose in Atwood's narrative.

The rewriting of a scene from Janine's perspective would encourage students to consider Atwood's writing style and structure in addition to her purpose in creating female narratives and voices to question the concepts and contexts of this novel. Effective assignments could include writing from Janine's perspective during "Testifying" in chapter 12 or the birth scene in chapter 21, from Serena Joy's perspective on meeting Offred for the first time in chapter 3, or from Moira's perspective when she sees Offred at Jezebel's in chapters 37 and 38. Students might also be interested in exploring characters such as Nick, Luke, or even one of the nameless Angels, the guards who are working under Gilead's regime. These creative writing exercises encourage students to seek evidence of perspective and tone from within the author's work and to identify the author's craft as a basis for their own continuation of the author's ideas.

A teaching approach that allows for personal connection and interpretation is helpful to all students. Fulkerson expands on the theory behind this teaching approach: "The central activity . . . is interpretation. The interpretation may be of readings, either about cultural theory or the experiences of a group or individual" (660). This approach to the teaching of *The Handmaid's Tale* allows for an understanding of women's rights and the psychological impact of societal control over groups of people in a hierarchical, theocratic community. For students of Generation Z, teaching materials that span various media offer a more contemporary involvement with and deeper critical examination of a text in addition to an appreciation of the experiences of a group or an individual. Online responses to the Hulu show serve as an example of how instructors can engage students in discussions about characters and ideas and encourage them to participate in critical conversations.

In an article about the show for *Vanity Fair*, Laura Bradley suggests that "Janine has emerged as one of the Hulu drama's most important players—a tragic foil to Offred that reminds viewers just how extraordinary Offred's constitution is. Not everyone is that strong; not everyone *can* keep themselves together under these conditions." Madeline Brewer, who plays Janine, talks with Bradley about Janine's and Ofglen's suicide attempts in the show, saying:

> I think a distinction that can be made between those two suicides is Ofglen is letting the world know that they won't break her. . . . And Janine is kind of succumbing to the fact that this world has broken her. I think that the big difference between the two of them is that [Ofglen], all the shit that happens to her, she only gets more and more fire. And Janine, all the shit that happens . . . she's just tired of it. This world hasn't completely broken her. She just doesn't know what else to do.

This distinction between the two women's responses to their experiences is an interesting commentary on the different ways in which people respond to trauma. For the contemporary reader, the effects of COVID-19 on society—particularly on students—can enable some interesting discussions in class on mental health, trauma, and the effects of isolation, quarantine, illness, and grief. A recent psychological study of COVID-19's impact on young people with pre-existing mental health issues adds "to the growing body of literature that suggests adolescents with pre-existing symptoms have been uniquely, and negatively, impacted by the COVID-19 pandemic" (Stewart). Using US health-care data, recent studies identify increases from 2019 to 2020 in the proportion of teenage patients making mental-health-related emergency department visits, the number of teenagers seen by emergency departments for suspected suicide attempts, and the number of teen and adolescent deaths by suicide. They posit that "[o]ne possible explanation for reduced life satisfaction is the increase in the amount of time teens spent alone due to physical-distancing practices during the pandemic" (Kalenkoski and Pabilonia 1).

Encouraging students to reflect on the relevance and contemporary connections that could be made between Atwood's exploration of the psychological effects of the Gileadean regime and what young people are experiencing today allows for a more invested response to the characters in her novel. The exploration of the psychological states of Janine and other secondary characters provides an effective opportunity for an extended writing assignment. An example would be a research paper that allows the students to explore one or more of the characters in the novel in terms of their psychological responses to trauma. The paper would allow for literary analysis, would require secondary research, and could compare Atwood's presentation with the Hulu adaptation.

Further exploration of characterization in both the novel and the Hulu series through Elisabeth Moss's portrayal of Offred allows students insight and encourages rich discussion of interpretation. Similarly, a debate about the casting of Yvonne Strahovski as Serena Joy (making Offred and Serena Joy age peers rather than different generations) allows students to consider how this interpretation of a character can further their exploration of Atwood's ideas about feminism and to what extent they view Serena Joy's character as either a traitor to women's rights or a victim herself. Strahovski's portrayal of Serena Joy in the Hulu adaptation certainly allows for some rich discussion and analysis. Several scenes in the first season physically place Serena Joy above Offred—on the stairs, on the elevated step between the kitchen and the hallway of the house—and her height adds to her haughty demeanor. Bruce Miller, showrunner for *The Handmaid's Tale*, explains in an interview why he cast Strahovski for the part of Serena Joy: "She was so wonderful and terrifying. And she's quite tall, so that works really well with Lizzie who is more small. . . . To have this towering Viking standing over her . . . she's physically intimidating" (Renfro). There are scenes in which Strahovski uses her youth and size in a physically intimidating manner, which provide excellent opportunities for analysis for students. In an improvised moment in episode 3, shot on the first take, Serena Joy pushes Offred to the floor and kneels next to her, shouting at her. The camera, low on the floor, placed next to Offred's head and angled up toward Serena's face, conveys the subordinate and helpless position of Offred, both as a Handmaid and as the subject of Serena Joy's anger, hatred, and jealousy ("Late" 00:48:15–52). This scene is a fascinating one to study and analyze with students and begs comparison of the women in the novel and their hierarchical positions within Gilead.

The Hulu series provides a wealth of moving images to support students' reading of *The Handmaid's Tale*. This and other available technologies and teaching resources do not, of course, replace Atwood's *The Handmaid's Tale*, but for contemporary students reading the novel, they provide an enhanced experience and promote insights into Atwood's characters and ideas. Students who are accustomed to more visual and auditory stimuli can thus engage with a living, breathing narrative that inspires and educates in a way that excites me as a teacher. For students who struggle with literature, or for those who dislike reading, or simply for those who enjoy the novel but want more, teachers can use social media, digital technologies, and the Hulu television series to aid in their exploration and understanding of what is at stake for those in Atwood's Gilead.

NOTES

1. This essay focuses on the first season of the series, since subsequent seasons developed the plot beyond the events of the novel.
2. This essay cites the 2017 Anchor edition of *The Handmaid's Tale*.

“Under His Eye”: Atwood and Surveillance

Amanda Licastro

Margaret Atwood is prolific on social media. As of August 2023, Atwood has more than two million followers on *Twitter* (now known as *X*) and has produced over 50,500 tweets, and her author profile has 230,000 followers on *Instagram* and 518,000 friends on *Facebook*. Each facet of Atwood's social media presence reveals a different approach to cultivating a professional yet personal persona, including everything from public relations campaigns to tips on gardening, and even pictures of family gatherings. While it may be shocking to see an author who expresses unbridled concern about surveillance technologies in her writing share so much of herself on social media, it is also an incredibly useful paradox to explore when teaching Atwood's works. When I teach Atwood's novels, such as *Oryx and Crake* and *The Handmaid's Tale*, students use social media as a conduit through which they explore surveillance theory, both in literary texts and in our culture. For example, students live-tweet their readings of Atwood novels using a custom hashtag in order to track their progress, and they create multimodal compositions in order to perform an intertextual analysis of surveillance across media platforms. These low-stakes assignments lead to a higher-stakes research project, a process that guides students from being passive consumers to being critical makers of emerging media.

Students' sharing their work in the media we are critiquing supports peer-to-peer learning and subverts the expert-novice dichotomy. As an instructor, this approach also gives me insight into my students' reading processes, helping me identify areas that need attention and explanation, thereby enabling me to better utilize our limited class time. More importantly, using social media as a tool to teach Atwood's near-future dystopian fiction provides a context through which we can investigate literary theory and practice digital literacy, demonstrating the relevance of humanistic inquiry in our everyday lives. In this essay, I offer flexible approaches to implementing social media as a tool for literary criticism, including sample assignments and examples of the resulting student work. I will focus on assignments featuring the MaddAddam trilogy and *The Handmaid's Tale* as examples of how I utilize emerging media as a pedagogical tool for connecting the themes in Atwood's works to the lived experiences of students. The goal is to provide reusable and remixable templates that utilize open access tools that can be implemented when teaching Atwood across a variety of contexts.

I have used Atwood's novels as a lens to understand surveillance studies and intersectional feminist theory across many grade levels and institution types, including a first-year writing course at a prestigious liberal arts university, an upper-level literature course at a regional comprehensive college, and a digital humanities class at an Ivy League institution. The assignments presented in this chapter come from a senior seminar focused entirely on Atwood for humanities majors and from a general education course on science fiction literature aimed at engaging students outside the humanities. When I ask my students in these courses about living in a culture of surveillance, they are often already comfortable with the idea that they are constantly monitored. Many can articulate the awareness that everything they do online is discoverable, and in our conversations, students express an understanding that they have never had the freedom of privacy. In other words, they do not lament the loss of privacy because they never had privacy to begin with. For instance, when I ask students if a government or corporation should have access to all the data on their phones, many students claim, "If you aren't doing anything illegal, you have nothing to worry about." Ironically, this is the same claim Jimmy's father makes in *Oryx and Crake* when attempting to calm his wife's fears about living in the HelthWyzer Compound (Atwood, *Oryx* 52). In Atwood's texts, complacency with surveillance culture consistently leads to devastating and oppressive control by a government or corporate entity, a trope students can identify as alarming in relation to their own lives. In reflection essays, students express how reading these texts changed their worldview and led them to be more critical consumers of media across contexts.

Oryx and Crake

Oryx and Crake, the first novel in the MaddAddam trilogy, takes place in a world governed by corporate surveillance culture. The main characters live in corporate compounds that control every aspect of their lives, including their education, health care, banking, transportation, and, most importantly, security. While the compounds, described as "castles" (27), conjure bastions of safety, the pleeblands, urban areas outside the suburban compounds, are marked by lawlessness and promiscuity, creating a caste system in the hierarchy of the novel. The CorpSeCorps, or corporate secret security detail, functions to maintain this separation under the guise of intellectual property and talent management. The CorpSeCorps restricts movement between these realms but also dictates all other aspects of mobility, both geographical and social.

The theme of border crossing, also critical in *The Handmaid's Tale*, features prominently in *Oryx and Crake*, although through corporate, rather than government, regulation. Randolph Lewis, in *Under Surveillance: Being Watched in Modern America*, quotes the former NSA contractor Edward Snowden as saying, "[E]very border you cross, every purchase you make, every call you dial, every cell phone tower you pass, friend you keep, site you visit and subject line you type is in the hands of a system whose reach is unlimited but whose safeguards are not" (Lewis 2). In *Oryx and Crake*, this level of corporate surveillance elicits tension between the characters, as expressed through the unreliable narration of Jimmy, the protagonist. Both of Jimmy's parents work as genetic engineers under the CorpSeCorps security; however, while Jimmy's father trusts in the company to keep them safe, his mother has a mental break that leads her to publicly criticize the "spies" (54) and privately destroy their computers before fleeing the compound. These contradictory depictions of corporate surveillance culture mirror the conflicting opinions of my students and their experiences of increasingly oppressive dataveillance across the digital technologies that mediate their lives.[1]

I first started teaching *Oryx and Crake* at a well-known school in New York City. Although most of the students were not English majors, they had very strong reading comprehension skills, and more than a few garnered a significant social media audience. Since then, I have also taught this novel at a small regional institution in Maryland, where students were more likely to be first-generation college students, underprepared for college-level reading and writing and lacking extensive social media literacy. In both cases, I wanted to devise strategies to help students navigate this intensely detailed text, because, despite the appealing content of the novel, the sheer volume of information is onerous. While discussion board posts, journal entries, and social annotation tools all serve as effective approaches for shorter texts, I sought out a strategy to amplify the cultural relevance of *Oryx and Crake*, which led me to guide students through the process of live-tweeting their readings of the novel.

Because Atwood has a lively fan base and a large following on social media, all her novels garner a great deal of attention in online spaces. Asking students to discuss her work in these spaces not only capitalizes on this active community of readers but also creates a meta-awareness about the platforms themselves. Essentially, students are asked to write about surveillance technologies through the use of a surveillance technology. I choose *Twitter*, now known as *X*, as a platform for this assignment because of the vibrant academic community and my own robust presence on the platform, which allows me to offer guidance and recommendations on how best to craft and disseminate effective posts.[2] Before we begin this exercise, we analyze what attributes lead to impact on the platform: multimodality, humor, tagging, adding handles, and so on. And I encourage students to use the rhetorical currency of the platform, which at times has included abbreviations and emoji to maximize the 280-character limit. We also investigate Atwood's account, noting her rhetorical strategies and engagement with her audience.

However, inviting students to use social media platforms, particularly *Twitter*, warrants careful guidance and thoughtful execution. In *Oryx and Crake*, women, especially women of color, suffer the most under the regime of corporate surveillance. Take, for example, the tale of Oryx, discovered by Jimmy as a prepubescent child trafficked by a predatory porn industry on "HottTotts, a global sex-trotting site" (Atwood, *Oryx* 89), where he assumed "she didn't have a name. She was just another little girl on a porno site. . . . None of those little girls had ever seemed real to Jimmy—they'd always struck him as digital clones—but for some reason Oryx was three-dimensional from the start" (90). Just as Jimmy views the girls on the screen as "digital clones," digital interfaces dehumanize participants; trolling, bullying, and harassment run rampant on social media, and women of color are the most vulnerable to these attacks. That is one of the many reasons this live-tweeting assignment puts safeguards in place to protect students. As Rachel Dubrofsky argues in *Feminist Surveillance Studies*, "In a culture that consistently puts women's bodies on visual display, and where this display can have implications particular to their gendering, any analysis of a technology that has the possibility of achieving these ends needs to contend with the complicated intersection of gender and the politics of the visual" (10). Heeding this advice, I frame the live-tweeting assignment with the work of Lisa Nakamura on race and identity in online spaces as well the scholarship of Safiya Noble on the bias of algorithms. Together, we read and annotate excerpts from these scholars using the open access, open-source tool *Hypothes.is* to create a robust discussion about these issues before embarking on the social media assignment. The readings prepare students to enter the online space thoughtfully and equip them with the language they need to critique the platform.

After carefully considering the space we are engaging in, I give students a variety of options when preparing to live-tweet. First, I allow students to create accounts that they will use only for this course and that are devoid of any other identifying details, asking that they confirm the handle with me so that I know it is authentic. Then, I create a unique, custom hashtag and promise to look only, as far as these accounts are concerned, at posts marked with this tag. This helps mitigate the "creepy treehouse effect," which may occur when an authority figure invades private space by asking students to connect in an environment typically reserved for peers and private contacts (J. Jones). Students know I will not look at their personal profiles or read any content on their custom class account or existing personal account that is not tagged. If a student wishes to use their personal account, I guide them through the process of telling their followers how to mute the class hashtag and tell them to warn their followers about the frequency of posts this hashtag will likely produce.

I am transparent about my intention to use this tool to monitor students' reading progress, and the assignment provides clear guidelines on what qualifies as minimum engagement (for example, five tweets and two replies per chapter). I stress that the goal is for students to share information and learn from one another—to express what delights, disgusts, or intrigues them about a text—but, more importantly, to ask questions and engage in meaningful conversation with their peers and other Atwood readers. Students are aware that they will be graded on the quality of their participation, not on the speed or character count of their responses. If any student is uncomfortable using the platform entirely, they can serve as a "court reporter" who summarizes the weekly engagement in a few paragraphs, including screenshots and analysis of the conversation.

Reviewing the online threads together as a class is an enlightening, hilarious, and endlessly informative experience. Moving the conversation from the classroom to social media manifests casual, ad-lib commentary that provides insights not only into students' reading comprehension but also into immediate reactions that might never make it into a formal writing assignment. Students ask questions on social media to which their peers and the general public often offer expertise in response, going far beyond what I could offer alone. In fact, Margaret Atwood's social media account has responded directly to my students more than once when they have tagged her in questions. In one particularly exciting instance, a student asked if the self-cleaning clothing depicted in the novel was real, and Atwood replied with an explanation and a link to the resource she used as inspiration; the university retweeted the conversation and published about this exchange in their monthly newsletter. My student said they felt famous.

Accolades aside, my intentions with this assignment also include underscoring the unseen surveillance practiced by social media companies. After discussing Snowden's warning with the class, I use the open source, open access tool *TAGSExplorer* to scrape the *Twitter* API (the application interface that allows two programs to communicate with each other) and collect data about their online activity using our course hashtag with very little effort or technical prowess. As a scholar of digital humanities, my priority is to use tools that are open and accessible in my teaching so students can learn transferable digital literacy skills. Martin Hawksey's tool allows the user to put in any hashtag and almost instantly sort the resulting data into an easy-to-use *Google* spreadsheet. In addition to the searchable database, the archive also provides a summary of engagement, which may assist in assessing student participation.

The aspect of *TAGSExplorer* I find most compelling is the interactive data visualization. In courses on digital humanities theory and practice, we use this dynamic network visualization to engage in discussions about the value of data-driven analysis in the humanities. A bar graph of the "top tweeters" indicates the total number of posts by each student, and a network graph shows the interactions between each student and the members of the community who joined the conversation. Students whose posts received many replies, as well as those who replied to many other people in the conversation, appear larger and more central in the visualization. They become nodes with greater force in the dynamic version of the visualization, with a magnetism that draws other members of the conversation around them, which is apparent when we play with the network visualization in class. Presenting the conversation in this way demonstrates the power of frequent posting in social media spaces. I ask students to consider a number of challenging questions that may lead to future research projects: What can we learn by sorting the data in these ways? What patterns emerge? What is hidden? If your English professor can do this level of dataveillance easily, what might "Big Tech" companies be learning from the data you produce on social media platforms? What might the government do with this data?

Asking these questions of students does cause them to feel their privacy has been invaded, and that represents a significant shift for many of them. As David

Lyon argues in *The Culture of Surveillance*, "[T]here is a potential to observe or monitor others and ourselves as never before. Things like social media surveillance often seem like a soft set of activities, seemingly inconsequential, but as I shall insist, they actually contribute to a social-cultural transformation. Watching has become a way of life" (4). Students move from feeling that they are being watched to feeling as though they are being controlled. I believe that resonates with the intention of Atwood's novels and aim to demonstrate that theme across multiple texts.

The Handmaid's Tale

Thanks to the immense popularity of the television adaptation produced by Hulu beginning in 2016, *The Handmaid's Tale* is experiencing a renaissance corresponding with a particularly tumultuous time in American politics. Both the television version and the original text have been used as the inspiration for political protest in the form of memes, GIFs, and a cascade of viral images of people dressed as Handmaids across social media. There is even a picture of the book on a store table in 2011 with the label "Books We Pretend We've Read" that is still actively circulating more than ten years later, indicating that there is cultural pressure (in some circles, at least) to be familiar with the text. Therefore, when introduced to *The Handmaid's Tale* as a literary object for analysis in a course, students may have preconceived notions about the storyline or, more significantly, about the thematic concepts represented in the book. Rather than resisting the work's popularity, I embrace and incorporate the online community into our discussion of the book.

To begin, I ask students to list on the board (or in a shared online space) thematic concepts they are aware of being present in *The Handmaid's Tale* from previous exposure, and we group them by commonality. A sample list might include sexual violence, government surveillance, feminism, religious oppression, and more. I then ask them to track three of these themes in their journals by writing down examples as they read in the form of a brief summary or direct quotation documented in MLA style. This way, no matter what format (such as e-book, paperback, or audiobook) meets their needs in consuming the content, they have a log of textual evidence to refer to when completing assignments for class. By tracking examples across a text—or across multiple texts that have a shared theme—students learn the process of close reading. Although they may default to skimming for specific concepts, giving them a variety of ideas to look for and strategies on how to trace these patterns may help guide them from shallow to deep reading. I suggest using highlighters or Post-it tabs in different colors or dividing a notebook or digital document by theme to help them organize their thoughts. Sharing examples in class crowdsources the content analysis but also alerts students to sections of texts they may need to revisit.

I ask students to gather their own textual evidence around the theme of surveillance, and we share their findings using several digital tools. For example, each group is assigned a set of chapters for each novel, and on their designated week they post a "provocation," which must include a quotation, a brief analysis of that quotation, and a question for discussion. Students who are not members of the group must respond to a set number of the posts with substantive answers citing direct textual evidence in MLA style. The posts and responses are due before the in-class discussion, which includes a fifteen-minute fishbowl exercise in which the group leaders talk among themselves about the scenes they chose and the responses they received, and the other students observe and take notes. This allows every person in the class a chance to compose a thoughtful thread, lead an in-class activity, and respond to their classmates through a variety of modalities, creating a distributed labor system.

Each week I also gather a set of scenes to analyze in depth to demonstrate how a literary critic might perform a close reading and connect analysis to literary theory. In my slides, I interweave quotes from the students' posts with my own selections. In the case of *The Handmaid's Tale*, students point to the "Eyes of God" (Atwood, *Handmaid's Tale* 193), commonly referred to as "Eyes," as a dominant figure of surveillance in the text.[3] An Eye in Gilead is always male, always covert, and always trained to watch citizens to ensure they are complying with the theocratic rules meant to control and contain everyone living in Gilead. As Pamela Cooper writes, "In Gilead this male gaze, detached from the specificity of a body and so freed from any humanizing context, is rendered mechanical, impersonal, bureaucratic. Identified with political authority figured in traditional terms as all-seeing, the eye becomes the Eye" (50). One unique quality about the Eyes is that, unlike Guardians, Angels, or Aunts, all of whom are subservient to the Commanders and their wives, Eyes have a higher power that allows them to surveil even the upper echelon of society, making them a source of fear for even the seemingly untouchable. As Cooper asserts, the Eyes become a technology of surveillance, the tool of an all-powerful theocracy that collects data on the citizens of Gilead while also limiting access to information through shrouded secrecy. In this way, the Eyes evoke Donna Haraway's notion of "the conquering gaze from nowhere," able to "represent while escaping representation" (qtd. in Browne 49). While students consistently highlight the Eyes and Nick (Offred's lover) as a symbol of surveillance, I complicate the topic by discussing Mayday as a system of sousveillance and Nick's role as an agent of both networks. The term *sousveillance* was coined by Steve Mann (see Mann and Ferenbok) but is complicated and racialized by Simone Browne in *Dark Matters*, which is the context through which I introduce it to students.

I use this quotation from the end of the novel to demonstrate this connection between the Eyes as surveillance and Mayday as sousveillance: "I expect a stranger, but it's Nick who pushes open the door, flicks on the light. I can't place that, unless he's one of them. There was always that possibility. Nick, the private Eye. Dirty work is done by dirty people. You shit, I think. I open my mouth to say it, but he comes over, close to me, whispers. 'It's all right. It's Mayday. Go with them'" (293). In this passage, Offred comes to the realization that Nick, who is employed in her Commander's household as a driver, is in fact an Eye. At the same time, June must decide if Nick is also acting as an agent of Mayday, the underground network of rebels working against the theocracy. June's path to freedom relies on the relationship she has formed with Nick and her willingness to trust Ofglen and the other Handmaids, both tenuous connections based on glimmers of hope rather than tangible facts. This scene cracks open a line of inquiry about the power of the oppressed to resist the oppressor through sousveillance.

Browne's theory of "dark sousveillance" brilliantly demonstrates the historical use of surveillance technologies to enslave Black Americans (12). Browne investigates how early technologies of identification and border-crossing documentation helped white plantation owners restrict the mobility of enslaved peoples and how control was maintained by limiting access to forms of education and communication, specifically concerning literacy. As Atwood has attested in interviews repeatedly, the means of oppression in her fictional depictions are all historically derived, which lends to the haunting realism of novels like *The Handmaid's Tale*. In this text, Offred narrates the use of multiple forms of identification, from a card she carries in her sleeve to a branding on her skin, and in the television series there is a homing device attached to her ear. Offred, like other women, is banned from reading and writing in Gilead, and she craves any news, even if it is untrue. Placing these examples in the context of Browne's work resonates with many students, providing a conduit through which they can explore intersectional readings of Atwood's work, which has often been criticized for lacking representation (see, e.g., Khuram et al.).

In my lectures, I introduce dark sousveillance to draw attention to the power of the Mayday network and how the Handmaids and Marthas create a subculture through which they share information and resources even under extreme oppression. I strengthen that connection to intersectionality through the work of Kimberlé Crenshaw, who explains: "Over the last two decades, women have organized against the almost routine violence that shapes their lives. Drawing from the strength of shared experience, women have recognized that the political demands of millions speak more powerfully than the pleas of a few isolated voices" (1241). By emphasizing a shared experience, Crenshaw invites us to consider how women of all racial backgrounds can come together to fight for a common cause. Connecting the concept of *intersectionality* as defined by Crenshaw to the efforts of Mayday provides a foundation through which we can complicate the term using selections from Judith Butler's "Imitation and Gender Subordination" in the next unit of the course.

Moving from Low to High Stakes

These low-stakes assignments are scaffolding to support a public-facing multimodal project through which students explore the connection between the fictional texts and current events. This project focuses on intertextual analysis of one thematic pattern in Atwood's work. For an upper-level undergraduate course, I provide an assignment sheet to help students navigate what may be an unfamiliar genre, instructing:

> Using Judith Butler's argument that there is no pre-given distinction between "theory, politics, culture, and media" (308), please construct an intertextual analysis of one thematic pattern in *The Handmaid's Tale* across presentations of that theme in current cultural and political artifacts. Identify one thematic concept you have been tracking throughout your reading of the novel and find present-day corollaries in the media, including but not limited to news articles, political campaigns, movies, television shows, advertisements, fashion statements, music, protests, social media posts, memes, GIFs, and viral online content.

The formatting of the assignment evolves with technological advancements but generally asks students to present, in the form of a video, interactive game, animation, dynamic infographic, or another digital creation, a digital mash-up that highlights the connections between Atwood's novel and the trend they have traced in popular culture and politics. The final product must include a framing narrative that defines the theme and connects it to literary theory, including Butler's argument.

The results always exceed my expectations. Students pick up on the thread of intersectionality and sousveillance in their multimodal research projects. For example, one student demonstrated how violent acts of cyberbullying devalued the expertise of women in positions of power. The student adeptly interspersed these images with examples from the texts we read in class, providing analysis of how female characters were stripped of their professional positions and authority, relegated to subservient positions, and given only menial tasks to keep them busy. Another student created a fake *Instagram* influencer account of a young white woman who transformed from a typical American college student to a Handmaid-in-training by embracing domesticity, rejecting materialism, and accepting a life of surveillance. In a parody of the recipe video, an extremely popular genre on *Instagram*, the student played the part of a young woman guiding the viewer through the process of making brownies with traditional ingredients and overlaid a voice dub replacing the food items with conceptual elements of oppression and control. At the end of the multimodal composition, the character dons the iconic red cloak and white bonnet of Atwood's Handmaid while music about being watched blares in the background.

These projects exemplify the connections students make between the texts, theory, and current political issues using popular social media sites. As Julia Kristeva argues in "Word, Dialogue, and Novel," texts "cannot be detached from the social or cultural textuality which is the backdrop in which a text is created" (Kristeva and Moi 37). In lower-level classes, these multimodal research projects serve as the final project, submitted with an "artist statement" that frames the student's thesis and provides context for their research. In the upper levels, this is a precursor (often turned in at midterm) to the mandatory departmental showcase presentation, which includes a research paper, a poster, and an oral presentation. While students sometimes express anxiety about the format of this project, their reflection letters convey an appreciation for the chance to learn or further develop their skills, especially as they directly relate to most internship and job applications students are pursuing. This assignment sequence not only leads students to be more critical consumers of social media but also teaches them how to be thoughtful creators of digital texts.

My use of social media to teach Atwood's works is not a technology-for-technology's-sake approach; rather, it intentionally marries the themes of the texts with Atwood's presence on these platforms to amplify the connection to surveillance culture. In the eerily relevant Netflix drama *The Chair*, Nana Mensah as Yas McKay, the only Black female junior scholar in the English department, explains her use of *Twitter* in teaching to Bob Balaban as Elliot Rentz, an older white male senior scholar. When Professor Rentz snorts that this activity is "low-hanging fruit," Professor McKay replies, "It's a way of connecting with them. And I find that it mobilizes the skills of close reading" ("Brilliant Mistake"). There will always be skeptics, and rightfully so, since social media is evolving and uncertain. I am constantly revamping and revising not only this unit but also my entire approach to teaching as the digital landscape changes. But at the heart of my approach remains my dedication to a student-centered learning environment that meets students where they are and connects the content of the curriculum to their lived experiences so that the humanities resonate as a relevant and vibrant part of their lives.

NOTES

1. Dataveillance, Simone Browne explains, is conducted "through data collection as a way of managing or governing a certain population, for example, through the use of bar-coded customer loyalty cards at point of sale for discounted purchases while also collecting aggregate data on loyalty cardholders, or vehicles equipped with transponders that signal their entry and exit on pay-per-use highways and roads, often replacing toll booths" (18).

2. This essay was composed in 2023, before Elon Musk purchased *Twitter* and redesigned the platform as *X*. After the essay was completed, many people in the academic community left the platform due to the structural and political changes enacted by Musk. I would now recommend using *Bluesky*, which is a decentralized network, for this assignment.

3. This essay cites the 2017 Anchor edition of *The Handmaid's Tale*.

FOSTERING ECOLOGICAL UNDERSTANDING

Considering Nonhuman Animals in World Literature: *The Complete Angel Catbird*

Danette DiMarco

The twenty-first century has seen a rethinking of the disciplinary purposes of world literature. Gayatri Spivak, Waïl Hassan, and David Damrosch, among others, have given sustained attention to theoretical approaches behind curriculum design and pedagogy. Karen R. Smith published her useful historical review of the field's evolutions: from emphasizing a "postwar ethic of global understanding" to "the benefits of multiculturalism" to "new global programs" borrowing their "educational ideals" from both camps in the face of massive budget cuts. Ultimately, Smith understands world literature courses as narratives of ideal pursuits of "global coherence and connectivity" that help students sharpen their "rhetorical tools for articulating the nature of the world crisis in which we find ourselves today" (601).

This essay situates itself squarely in the middle of Smith's claims as it imagines expanding world literature's vision to include approaches to teaching works where nonhuman animals figure critically. Taking as its focus the pedagogical uses of Margaret Atwood's *The Complete Angel Catbird* in world literature, the chapter argues for teaching students about interpretive reading through an entanglement lens as shaped by Thom van Dooren's work on shared worlds in *Flight Ways: Life and Loss at the Edge of Extinction* and *The Wake of Crows: Living and Dying in Shared Worlds*. Human-nonhuman literary entanglements are often reserved for environmental literature courses; I propose not separating them from but instead including them in world literature courses, offering students a refreshing path for expanding their understanding of the value of world literature. Doing so gives students a rhetorical means for learning to better articulate "the nature of the world crisis in which we find ourselves today" (Smith 601).

Nonhuman animal imagery has always had a presence in Margaret Atwood's poetry and fiction. However, it is her young adult graphic novel *Angel Catbird* that offers students a new way of reading with entanglement at the forefront. Giving story to a hybrid human-nonhuman protagonist, Atwood's novel offers instructors an avenue for discussions about human and nonhuman entanglements.

This essay discusses the value of introducing students to van Dooren's reflections on *wake* and awakening, laid out best in *The Wake of Crows*. It offers ideas for low-stakes research on Atwood and close analysis opportunities for *Angel Catbird* with van Dooren's ideas in mind. It also provides examples of student-created image-text projects (taking up Atwood's in imitation) and supplemental metanarratives about select animals and human-nonhuman entanglements. Finally, it shares one especially astute student's revised elaboration on the uses and value of studying world literature after being exposed to an entanglement approach to reading. In my world literature course, students are asked to consider the value of world literature at the beginning, at midterm, and at the end, and this student's revision reflects his midterm thoughts, since Atwood's novel is completed around that time.

A Wakeful World

Van Dooren's reflections on *wake* and awakening and multispecies entanglements are like Atwood's own long-standing knowledge of the interconnectedness of all living entities. Both authors believe that humans must stay awakened to the power of diverse forms of life and their agency, to engage others not just as subjects "but as beings who are themselves shaping our shared worlds in consequential ways" (3). While *The Wake of Crows* is based in fieldwork, and so is notably divided from the general classroom experience provided in the humanities, it nonetheless provides a helpful framework, especially because van Dooren employs strategies for "think[ing] through the complexity of our *world*-remaking epoch" (6, my emphasis). Since I teach *Angel Catbird* in conjunction with Kazuo Ishiguro's dystopic novel *Never Let Me Go*, it is helpful to use van Dooren's notion of a wakeful world in transition between the texts, although instructors not wishing to teach Ishiguro can still appropriate van Dooren, since he provides excellent framing for students to reflect upon processes of worlding. Instructors who include Ishiguro can supplement his work with Atwood's review of the novel (Atwood, "Never").

Prior to beginning *Angel Catbird*, I ask students to look up denotative definitions, with concrete examples, of the words *wake* and *woke* as homework. In class, in pairs or small groups, they compare their discoveries. The conversation typically elicits connections between woke culture and the Black Lives Matter movement and sometimes leads to student observations about the use of *woke* for political purposes. Discussion of *woke* in juxtaposition with definitions of *wake* pushes students to rethink what they may have understood as the static nature of language. This is where van Dooren's own explanation of the term *wake* can be introduced. Students will likely have discovered that a wake is "a gathering, a pause to reflect in the presence of death" (van Dooren 7). They may be less likely, however, to focus on how a wake is both "an opportunity to grieve and to learn" (7). When pairing *Never Let Me Go* with *Angel Catbird*, it is worth asking students to look back to that narrative and consider how it might be a kind of written wake, one where the narrator, Kathy, uses the authorial space to learn about herself and society, one where she tries to celebrate her friends' lives while trying to move forward with those left behind.

Besides understanding *wake* as a noun, students may have also learned that *wake* is a verb, as in "to awaken" (literally and figuratively). In this second way, *wake* is a concept for considering what it means to be mindful in a shared world. But it is van Dooren's third definition that may be most helpful, because it is the one that students either miss or ruminate on the least: *wake* as a "disturbance . . . a dynamic unfolding, emerging as movement takes place" (van Dooren 7). Some might recognize this idea in a boat's creating a wake; however, those same students will tend to focus more on the possible negative repercussions of the wake as opposed to the relational aspect. Focusing on wakes' relational aspects "as dynamic unfoldings" reminds all that both the body creating the wake and the atmosphere through which it moves are transformed. This additional definition helps cement the idea that an interpretative approach using a multispecies ethic lens "takes seriously the fact that all life, including human life, occurs within fundamental and constitutive relationships with other kinds of beings, living and not" (van Dooren 7). Van Dooren's use of the word *not* in the aforementioned quotation alludes to extinction, and a return to *wake* as a celebration of life while moving forward with those who remain behind enriches our reading of van Dooren's work on the shared worlds of living and dying.

An Entangled Hero

Introducing students to Atwood and helping them educate themselves on her lived attention to shaping a wakeful world serves as preliminary framework for reading her fictional yet polemical *Angel Catbird*. To do this, instructors might reserve a day for students to present on a magazine or newspaper article that deliberately positions Atwood in her environmental advocacy. If there isn't enough time for students to do that work, professors might provide synthesized background information for them. However, it is my experience that the hands-on experience of reading and discussing an article with peers and then briefly presenting a summary to the class gives students a low-stakes opportunity for understanding Atwood's personal commitment to environmental sustainability. Helpful and short publications that students might report back on include, but are certainly not limited to, Jennifer Bain's "Atwood's Coffee Is (Literally) for the Birds," Jonathan Carey's "What's Part Cat, Part Owl, and Out to Save the World? Meet Angel Catbird," Deborah Dundas's "Birdwatching with Margaret Atwood," Jessica Leber's "Margaret Atwood Insists Birds Matter to Everyone—Whether They Realize It or Not," Grant Munroe's "How Margaret Atwood and Graeme Gibson Built a Bird Sanctuary," Anita Sethi's "Birdwatching with Margaret Atwood," and Atwood's own "Act Now to Save Our Birds." Once armed with helpful background information about the author's woke sensibilities, students are ready to read and analyze *Angel Catbird*.

To familiarize students with *Angel Catbird*'s hybrid form, I slow down the reading and analyzing process, asking each student to select just two passages from a list (one from the first half of the book and one from the second) and to share their interpretations on a discussion board. The first list might offer students a chance to analyze pages 21–23, "Three days later," or 39–40, "Wow, this is rich!," while the second list invites them to consider pages 123–27, "The wives were giving him a hard time," or 146–54, "Faster." I give directions that remind them of our discussion of van Dooren's notion of multispecies entanglements and a wakeful world, cue them to recall what they have learned about Atwood's avian interests already, and offer them some prompts to get them going. For example, a general statement about Atwood's work could read as follows:

> In *The Complete Angel Catbird*, Margaret Atwood (writer), Johnnie Christmas (visual artist), and Tamra Bonvillain (colorist) pursue the notion of multispecies entanglements through its human-cat-bird hero, Strig Feleedus. Strig is literally entangled within himself—a person, a feline, and a bird. The graphic novel uses Strig's story to complicate subjectivity—to pluralize it across species—and to educate young adult readers about human "accountabilities" and "obligations" (as Thom van Dooren might say) to animals (i.e., cats and birds). Atwood is on record as having said that there is nothing more useful (and more annoying to families) than having ten-to-twelve-year-olds hounding adults to take better care of their environment. To capture the power of that audience, Atwood partnered with the Nature Canada organization (naturecanada.ca), Christmas, and Bonvillain to write a humorous but sobering graphic novel that tried to teach younger readers that humans might behave better in their relationships with cats and birds.

Helpful guide questions to support analysis might include: What do you notice about how Atwood defamiliarizes the human story, so readers are forced to "wake up," to have to think about multiple species (human, cat, bird) simultaneously? What strategies or elements (i.e., printed words, visual images, color, etc.) used in the portion that you have selected make you work, as a reader, to put together different worlds? How hard is it to isolate these worlds? What do the black cat marginalia offer the reading of the plot? Do they serve to contradict, elaborate upon, or perpetuate anything? In what way do the black cat stamps disrupt the story as a linear narrative that we might be used to? When we revisit the student analyses in class, authors serve as discussion leaders and peers elaborate upon points. If students overwhelmingly select certain passages over others, class time could also be used to discuss the portions not selected and consider why they were passed over.

One student reflected upon the "Wow, this is rich!" scene, using an inductive and reader-response approach, walking readers through his thoughts as he looked at the distinct aspects of the image-text segment. Even as he notes how the image draws a "vertical division" between species, he observes a blurring of subjective roles:

> This scene comically starts with Strig leaning over a trashcan and drooling over some rather disgusting-sounding rotting proteins, which right away is cause to remember the half animal side of him, as his behavior is more catlike than manlike. However, as the scene progresses, he rescues a baby bird from three dastardly street cats, which confuses not only the street cats but also Strig, who isn't sure why he didn't just eat the bird when he had the chance. What is unique in this scene, that I believe separates the worlds of cat, bird, and man, is the vertical division between the characters in this scene. There [are] the cats who are clinging to Strig's legs and begging for the bird to be eaten . . . , the birds who are pleading for the safety of their child [and who] are perched in a nest above all other characters, and in the middle is Strig who is facing the moral decision [of] acting as the mediator demonstrating the human ability to make decisions based on ethics and not instinct. The black cat marginalia on these pages provides detailed statistics on the role of pet cats and feral cats in the killing of birds[,] and in this case it simplifies the purpose of a complicated metaphor that might soar over the heads of a younger audience. I believe the marginalia here helps elaborate the responsibility people have in aiding birds by being responsible pet owners.

While the student does not invoke the term *wake* in his response, it is suggested in his invocation of "responsibility," an effect of wakefulness.

Another student reflected upon *Angel Catbird*'s strategy of constructing multiple worlds—human and nonhuman animal—simultaneously so as to demonstrate those worlds' interconnectedness:

> On pages 30 and 31, Atwood defamiliarizes the human story by showcasing differences in Feleedus's daily routine that are closely related to cats and birds. For example . . . Feleedus spits out his coffee, and he thinks to himself that he was poisoned. This defamiliarizes the human story because . . . coffee is a staple in many humans' lives; however, it is poisonous to cats. Thus, Atwood includes this to make the reader think of both cats [and] humans. Additionally . . . a bird is chirping, but Atwood indicates that Feleedus understands what the bird is saying by using a text box with an asterisk, [translating] what the birds [are] saying [in a human language, English]. The bird is calling Feleedus a "rotten predator" because Feleedus is part cat. Not only does this defamiliarize the human story but it also showcases the species' entanglement between cats and birds. Although Feleedus is both a cat and a bird, the bird only recognizes the cat part; therefore, the bird is insulting him. Further, . . . Feleedus is waking up from sleep, and he is stretching. In the illustration, Feleedus is in a dramatic cat-like stretch, and his fingers are gripping tightly into the sheets. [Although] Feleedus physically appears as a human, . . . he is engaging in cat-like behavior. [I]t is not too difficult to isolate the different

worlds because Atwood utilizes common facts and behaviors from cats and birds that are relatively easy for a reader to pick out.

Multispecies Entanglements

Following our close analysis exercise and discussion, students begin a course project called "Multispecies Entanglements—Image-Text Storyboard and Accompanying Narrative," employing Atwood's hybrid graphic novel as a model. The three-part project continues the discussion of how our understanding of the world changes when we open ourselves to the idea of multispecies entanglements. In this project, students have an opportunity to learn more about multispecies thinking. The project can be done with a partner or alone. Part 1 is research-based and—much like Atwood's own research with Nature Canada on birds and cats—asks students to consider their personal relationship with nonhuman animals, brainstorming about the nonhuman animals that intrigue them and studying the animal that they are most curious about, want to learn more about, or have a passion for. Guide questions for their research include: What sort of world does the chosen animal live in (i.e., what habitat do they require and how do they relate to animals of their own and other species)? What are that world's expectations and customs for its species, separate from the human world? How have humans interacted with this species? What is the current relationship between humans and this species? Have humans imposed their own ideas of worlding upon this species in particular, observable ways? Have humans interrupted or interloped in this species' habits and habitats? Have humans found ways to live beside or even within this species' world in positive ways? Are there human programs or organizations that seek to protect this species or to care for this species and its worlds?

After students complete their research on one nonhuman animal, I provide them some version of these instructions for part 2:

> With Atwood's *The Complete Angel Catbird* as a blueprint for your project, construct a four-to-six-frame image-text that educates but still provides pleasure for your reader. Imagine that your audience is a younger person. In other words, you are to create a fictional storyline interwoven with a nonfictional one—a hybrid text like *Angel Catbird* that teaches readers about the animal you have chosen as well as about the animal-human entanglements in which they participate. Creating a polemical and pleasurable read brings attention to multispecies entanglements—or the way humans and nonhumans' worlds blur, connect, depend on, and interfere with one another. Will you use an Atwood-like marker to identify the educational information (you will recall her black cat stamp)? Will you create the educational parts as marginalia in the text? If so, where? In the box next to the story? Will you create a character who educates the readers? Make this interesting or fun or sad or scary (or all the

> aforementioned) to read. Draw upon rhetorical strategies of pathos (emotion), ethos (as the author, I know this because—or as the character, I know this because—or as the animal, I know this because), and logos (use logic and evidence to support your claim) as needed. You may draw, paint, use free Internet art, or do whatever works to help you convey the message.

After students have completed their image-text design, they are asked to write a narrative, with a works-cited list attached. The goal is for their image-text portion of the project to serve as part of a larger conversation about a wakeful world and for their narrative to analyze their own choices. With their peers as their audience, they are to explain what they researched and why, using the following questions as a guide: Why did you make the decisions that you made in creating your image-text? Where do you see your image-text being most effective? Least effective? Why? How did *Angel Catbird* specifically influence you? What did you learn from this assignment? Once the visual and narrative requirements are complete, students upload both to a discussion board in our learning management system so that everyone in the class can see and read their work. This task is especially important because students will be asked to draw upon various peer image-text projects in their midterm and final assignments, which are elaborations of the question that we began with in the course: What are the values and uses of world literature?

Three examples of student work are included below: the first as evidence of background research, the second as one example of the image-text portion of the project, and the third as a cohesive illustration of how the accompanying narrative sheds light on the image-text work. I have been surprised at the quality of student work imagined through this multimodal opportunity. While differing in type, both the image-text and narrative portions frequently reveal authentic understanding of animal-human entanglements, good and bad. One student, writing on the history of the relationship between humans and cattle, indicated that while "[c]attle have been a fundamental part of human and cultural development [and] [i]n Europe and present-day America have been used to nourish and clothe humans," she recognized that the "relationship is capricious and depends on economic and technological development, and the multispecies entanglement between cows and humans has been altered due to animal commodification." Her research revealed how, today,

> [t]here is an important history of the relationship between the mistreatment of animals and the development of capitalism, and [how] it is centered on "alienation." In other words, most consumers do not come in contact with the production of what they are consuming. Therefore, they are separated from the capital, which allows for the overconsumption of meat and other animal products because the ceremonial tradition of eating animals is removed from the actual process of eating it.

The student's attention to separation and removal for purposes of exploitation and profit provided her some grounding to consider an entanglement doing more harm than good, in terms of the cattle's world, which is also our own.

A second student researched the relationship between beluga whales and humans. Her imitation of Atwood's animal symbol, here in the form of a whale instead of a cat, provides a way to offer readers factual knowledge within the fictional narrative. The five frames emotionally elaborate upon this fact and fictionalize humans as unable to see their own entanglement in whale life (fig. 1).

Figure 1. Student image-text sample, World Literature, Slippery Rock University.

"Dad, look! What kind of bird is that" / "Oh, that's not a bird." I say "That's my grandfather." / "Pap?" / "No not Pap, Pap's an eagle now, that's Bumpa, and he's a Heron."

"The Great Blue Heron eats mostly fish, but will also feed on insects, amphibians, crustaceans, and other small animals. It silently stalks its prey in shallow waters, then plunges its bill into the water to capture it. It will spend about 90 percent of its waking hours hunting for food."

Goodbye's are hard. No, we won't say goodbye, we'll work together so we can stay together. There's other people who feel the same way. Grandparents are important, even the ones we never met. I've met you though, even though to me you've always had wings.

"Wetland destruction has caused a decrease in heron populations from their historic numbers. Since the 1950s, habitat loss has occurred at an alarming rate, destroying wetlands critical to breeding herons. Protecting great blue herons is closely tied with protecting their wetland habitats."

Feather Facts

✎ Great Blue Herons reside in North America and can be found as far south as Panama and Columbia (iucnredlist.org).

✎ "The Great Blue Heron eats mostly fish, but will also feed on insects, amphibians, crustaceans, and other small animals. It silently stalks its prey in shallow waters, then plunges its bill into the water to capture it. It will spend about 90 percent of its waking hours hunting for food" ("Chesapeake Bay Program").

✎ Great Blue herons nest in large colonies and they nest where they will be able to find the most food (wetlands, swamps, and bodies of water) (Gibbs and Kinkel 1).

✎ "In the 1600s, over 220 million acres of wetlands are thought to have existed in the lower 48 states. Since then, extensive losses have occurred, and over half of our original wetlands in the lower 48 have been drained and converted to other uses" (archive.epa.gov).

✎ Wetland destruction has caused a decrease in heron populations from their historic numbers. Since the 1950s, habitat loss has occurred at an alarming rate, destroying wetlands critical to breeding herons. Protecting great blue herons is closely tied with protecting their wetland habitats (Davenport).

Figure 2 (left and above). Student image-text sample, World Literature, Slippery Rock University.

A third student challenged Atwood's use of the black cat stamp because, as he noted in his follow-up narrative, many students thought that the black cats interrupted the flow of the story. Thus, while he imitated *Angel Catbird* by including his research on the great blue heron as a footer below his images, he used a small font and created a concluding section to share additional facts. This student engaged in "a personal retelling of a family mythos," sharing with his daughter the story of his grandfather's reincarnation. He wrote, "I wanted to associate the feelings of having a grandparent you never met with extinction, as well as use reincarnation as a framework for human/animal hybridization." The select images from his project are frames 1, 3, and 7 (fig. 2). To capture the entanglement ideas, the student wove three different stories, as he describes them: "the main text . . . that is thought and not spoken, . . . the interjection of dialogue when the Great Blue Heron is spotted, [and the] message to the Great Blue Heron, who acts as my grandfather." His choice to color little, using only light browns and greens in the depiction of the landscape, is an effort "to illustrate the connection between human development and habitat destruction, the connection between humanity and death to animals." As he explains in his narrative, humans are to blame for "the colorless world we create, emotionally and physically." While the lack of color depicts the negative in human-heron relations, his "Feather Facts" section stresses the positive—he had learned that great blue heron populations are increasing thanks to beneficial human interactions through wetland population. Ending with the Feather Facts gives this student the agency to offer readers a more hopeful conclusion.

A goal of this project is for students to better understand the relational insights that emerge when reading through an entanglement lens. Atwood's work opens doors to this way of thinking. When the project is complete, which is around midterm in my class, students are asked to revisit their elaborations on the value and uses of world literature that they wrote at the term's start. Since *Angel Catbird* is taught alongside the novel *Never Let Me Go*, students are encouraged to draw out comparisons and differences as they reimagine their definitions of the value and uses of world literature and what, exactly, worlding even means. One student revised accordingly:

> Reflecting on my initial pre-course reflection, I cannot help but become blatantly aware of a major flaw in my initial evaluation of the importance of international literature. My view was not wrong, but was still narrow, given that it was very human-centric. When I referenced the connected struggle of the global man, I had taken a somewhat Marxian stance in regard to the common difficulty, but I completely failed to regard the fibers of nature that combine all of us. I had alluded to international struggle but failed to illustrate the international crisis that is global climate change and habitat destruction. Through the work of Margaret Atwood and Kazuo Ishiguro the shared responsibility that humanity has towards the Earth became more and more apparent. . . . Margaret Atwood's work with *Angel Catbird* portrays characters that are actively engaging in ensuring their survival. There are multiple times where the cat hybrids engage in literal battle with the threat to their survival, which is a testament to Atwood's belief that there is a fight to be had against environmental collapse. One of the main characters, Cate Leone, is especially intriguing in the context of a global catastrophe because of her refusal to be idle when Angel (Strig) is kidnapped. She insists, regarding Strig's rescue, that "It has to be now! Every minute we wait, terrible things could be happening to Angel," a sentiment that is shared by many environmental activists especially given the growing intensity of environmental destruction. So, when there's Atwood, urging for action against the injustices suffered by animals at the hands of humans, and Ishiguro, who makes it blatantly clear about who the innocent party is [in the clones], it becomes transparent that there is purpose, meaning, and urgency in an environmental movement that protects global interests.

Ultimately, this student, like others in the class, concluded that studying world literature shows readers that despair and cynicism are not the only options: there are those who try, through literature and other art forms, to provide hope in turbulent times. As one of my students surmised, we must seek out works of those who "steadfastly remain optimistic in humanity's ability to correct their sins and irresponsibility and provide care and protection for the innocent ward that is Earth." In this way, the entangled world can be awakened.

Lessons in Teaching and Living *The Year of the Flood*

Shoshannah Ganz

Margaret Atwood concluded her book-launch tour for *The Year of the Flood* by narrating a dramatic and musical performance inspired by the novel in Sudbury, Ontario, on 19 November 2009.[1] According to Atwood, this was an appropriate place for the final performance and reading because Sudbury is a model community in demonstrating how together we can reclaim, rebuild, and regreen an ecosystem following human-made ecological disaster ("Sudbury"). Part warning, part celebration, and part survival guide, *The Year of the Flood* models ecological community education and lifestyle through the God's Gardeners eco-cult. The survivors of the coming "flood" (i.e., human-made disaster) are almost exclusively God's Gardeners and the children of the God's Gardeners, who have been brought up recycling, learning how to forage, eating vegan (save honey and the occasional pigeon egg), and celebrating the environmental saints who have attempted to protect planetary life. A careful reading of this text will educate the reader and provide potential lessons about a variety of edible plants, gardening techniques, water treatment, natural medicine, bio-arts and -crafts, and ways to honor and protect fellow life in all its forms. While fictional, *The Year of the Flood* also serves as a beginners' guide to living ecologically conscious lives in community and maps various aspects of surviving the results of climate change.

Atwood's recommendation of Sudbury as a model of the principles espoused in her fictional work *The Year of the Flood* suggests to me that Sudbury is an appropriate place to begin our discussion of the central and moral message of this text. As such, and as a former member of the Sudbury community, I had to look no further than the many lakes where people swim and fish, the landscape of trees and rich vegetation hiding the occasional sites of blackened rock and wasteland, to see the results of resource extraction and the efforts of the community to detoxify the land. *Healing the Landscape: Celebrating Sudbury's Reclamation Story* details how the Sudbury community, working together, healed at least some of the damage wrought by human greed and avaricious consumption (Ross). Atwood likewise celebrates the evidence of collaborative community restoration in *The Year of the Flood*. There is, however, another and parallel story of Sudbury, a much sadder one of lakes that are still crystal-clear acid pools, of lakes choking with algae, of the strange grass growing over slag heaps, and of the bright-orange pools that are fenced off to protect all life against the deadly poisons that remain.

The Year of the Flood opens with Toby, a member of the God's Gardeners, describing the vista of the devastated unnamed setting of the text: "As the first heat hits, mist rises from among the swath of trees between her and the derelict city. The air smells faintly of burning, a smell of caramel and tar and rancid barbecues, and the ashy but greasy smell of a garbage-dump fire after it's been raining" (3). The descriptions I have given of Sudbury, Ontario, are eerily mirrored in the fictional landscape that begins the story of *The Year of the Flood*, which provides a bounteous spread of useful and nonfictional information to begin the process of educating people on the practices of living in sustainable community. From the terrifying not-too-distant world of the future, Atwood cobbles together a band of survivors. The survivors of this quite literal meltdown of humanity are members of a purposeful and peaceful community of rooftop gardeners. The leader of the God's Gardeners urges at the beginning of the text that "if all were to follow our example, what a change would be wrought on our beloved Planet!" (11). The Gardeners in many ways do serve as a model for sustainable living. They educate the reader on the damaging, disgusting, and dangerous habits that are a part of today's culture and model the change necessary for remediation.

Arguably, one of the most central issues to the God's Gardeners and Atwood's text is food—growing food, harvesting food, foraging for food, preserving and storing food, and healing with food. The Gardeners keep bees, grow mushrooms, garden, preserve their food, and know how to use the various plants, mushrooms, and animals for medicinal as well as food sources. In our own world, food is one of the growing issues facing the planet as climates change and populations grow. Ultan McCarthy and colleagues have shown that food security is central to our education and preparation for the future. Currently, one billion people, or sixteen percent of the global population, goes hungry despite there being enough food to feed everyone. To avoid mass starvation, humans need to increase food production by seventy percent by 2050. A survey of key findings and studies on global food security reveals that "Food experts indicate that no single solution will provide a sustainable food security solution in the future." Rather, "collective stakeholder engagement will prove essential" (McCarthy 11). Thus, literature and education on sustainable food practices are key to bringing about the necessary changes to create sustainable global food security.

Literature has always provided a forum for critique of culture and practice and for the picturing of something better for the future. According to Emma Parker (writing prior to the publication of *The Year of the Flood*), in Atwood's novels, "eating is unequivocally political," and, in fact, "consumption [of food] embodies coded expressions of power" (349). Moreover, Parker points out that Atwood's definition of politics is "who is entitled to do what to whom with impunity; who profits by it; and who therefore eats what" (349). Parker's observations, published in 1995, still hold true for *The Year of the Flood*, which has the politics of food at its heart.

For example, food is used to show Toby's power and lack of power at various moments in the text. In the time before the CorpSeCorps had taken full control of all or most food sources, Toby's family was able to eat well in part through hunting. Toby remembers that "[t]hey'd been living in the semi-country. . . . They'd eaten deer stew, and her mother had made soup with the bones" (Atwood, *Year* 24). As Parker has observed of other Atwood characters, the family's power and health are "symbolized by . . . hearty eating" (352). After the death of her parents, Toby is only able to eat a "sparse breakfast" before she flees the clutches and control of the multinational CorpSeCorps for the pleeblands (28).

In *The Year of the Flood*, control of food sources, food security, and sustainable growing and harvesting practices are contingent on knowledge and power, and the novel offers readers knowledge and thus power over the food practices they participate in through how they live and eat. Why else would Atwood dedicate chapter after chapter to detailed explanations of how to plant in season, how to preserve food, how to eat as a vegetarian, how to select edible wild plants, and how to glean food at times of crisis and as part of the local foodshed (the food produced in a specific geographical region for the people of that place)? I will not here make an in-depth textual study of the novel's treatment of natural medicine, beekeeping, mushrooms, gardening, and hunting, but all these subjects instruct and empower the reader to take control of their local foodshed.

Following a semester of teaching *The Year of the Flood* among other texts focused on environmental topics, I decided to try to build a course that would ground students in the place they live and in projects for sustainability that can and will impact the community. This is not what literature courses have historically been about, but a literature course focused on environmental issues must engage with the intersection of fiction and nonfiction. To locate a course in the particulars of the place and find the corollary problems, and, hopefully, solutions is perhaps one way of moving beyond the fictional world to practical applications for the natural world.

Emerging from a textual study of *The Year of the Flood* and inspired by Atwood's relentless education in sustainability as part of this work of literature, I wanted to fuse practical life skills and action with the study of the novel. The ongoing course-length project asked students to find people in the community who make and grow various kinds of food and listen to their stories and learn from their practices. The second part of the project would involve contributing to the local foodshed.[2] This practical project suggested by the novel would be an interesting application of the survival recipes in *The Year of the Flood* and hopefully, through students' interactions with the community, would make people more aware of their local foodshed and inspire students to contribute to the growing, gathering, and preparing of local foods. This activity would also empower students to know and in some small part take control of their food security.

Much of the nonfictional information from *The Year of the Flood* could lead to students' changing their lives in simple or more significant ways to be more sustainable. *The Year of the Flood* engenders projects that are focused not on writing papers but rather on living purposefully and taking action—whether it be growing vegetables, learning how to recycle certain materials, attempting to make vegetarian dishes, or finding ways to reduce the consumption and waste of water and other precious resources. I believe this project in living can bridge some of that cavern between practical "real-life" knowledge and the world of fiction. Not only would students be participating in promoting sustainability in the community, but also their writing about the experience would be the first step in contributing to the literature of sustainability and survival.

Several of my students at Laurentian University in Sudbury took the lessons from *The Year of the Flood* and designed final research projects out of the literary material that addressed both the fiction and the reality of the story of environmental destruction and rebuilding.[3] One student took the idea of reclaiming past knowledge as an incentive to ask her grandmother about the gardening practices she had learned as a child in Italy. Under the tutelage of her grandmother, this student planted and tended her first garden and committed to eating only what she could grow or gather. Subsequently, this student presented what she had learned from this project at the inaugural national conference for the Association for Literature, Environment, and Culture in Canada (ALECC).[4]

One of the important food texts that I incorporated into the reading list and teaching both in Sudbury and later, when I moved to Corner Brook, Newfoundland, was Sarah Elton's *Locavore*, which notes that "[i]n Newfoundland, less than 10 percent of the food people eat is grown on the island" (3). Since this province in many ways still holds on to a variety of traditions, it seemed that some of these traditions must involve food—the growing, gathering, fishing, preserving, and eating of it—so the local foodshed was a meaningful focus in adapting the course.[5] I again focused the discussion, outside readings, and final research projects on the central questions of food, sustainability, environmental rebuilding, and community. I challenged the students to look outside the text for real-life corollary examples and to focus on the possibility of applying the lessons of the text to their own life and the protection and rebuilding of the environment.

There were several final projects relating to *The Year of the Flood* that grew out of this assignment. One student decided to pursue a project she had long considered: keeping bees. There are local beekeepers in the area, and this eventually (and independently) became a project that the university was involved in as one of many on-campus food and sustainability projects. There are now dozens of hives kept on university property that faculty members tend and gather honey from on a regular basis. The student conducted a great deal of research into local beekeeping practices and eventually began keeping bees on her property. In class, we read the beekeeping portions of the text and then discussed the uses of honey from the text and from our own experience. In *The Year of the Flood*, Pilar explains the bees to Toby: "They need to know you're a friend," "They can smell you. Just move slowly," and "They'll know you next time. Oh—if they do sting, don't slap them. Just brush the sting off. But they won't sting unless they're frightened, because stinging kills them" (99). The instructions in the text serve as a beginner's guide to contact with bees and beekeeping. The text also supports a discussion of the uses of honey beyond simply as a food source and sweetener ("Honey helps an open wound" [99]). I brought many bee products, including beeswax candles, which purify the air and create a positive atmosphere, to class when we spoke about this portion of the text.

Another student was very interested in wild edible foods, and we discussed as a class our previous experiences with mushroom gathering, including its dangers and challenges. I recalled how every year my family would gather morels in the woods, and this would be a special treat. A friend, who explained the properties of edible and dangerous mushrooms, took us to the woods to gather and then cook some of the many edible mushrooms found there. As Pilar teaches in the text, "There were mushrooms for eating, mushrooms for medicinal uses, and mushrooms for visions" (100). Students shared their own experiences of collecting mushrooms such as chanterelles, a local delicacy that many people in Newfoundland gather, dry, and use through the year.

Other students likewise focused their projects on local and wild food sources. These included the many berries that could be collected in different seasons and the associated preserving and canning processes. The introduction to "Saint Euell of Wild Foods" and the hymn in his praise, "Oh Sing We Now the Holy Weeds," name the wild plants that can be eaten and give details about how to prepare the wild foods, what parts to use, where to find them, and when to gather them (123–28). This useful information can form part of a lesson on wild foods or the basis for a larger project that involves the finding, gathering, and preparation of wild foods. For many students, this book was the beginning of a change in their lifestyles or a moment of becoming more aware of the way they were living with local food sources and the ways in which they could live more sustainably.

Teaching *Oryx and Crake*, the first volume of the MaddAddam trilogy, in 2006 brought a remarkably different response than teaching it after the March 2020 onset of the COVID-19 pandemic. In the interlude of fourteen years, general knowledge of climate change and the sense of urgency had changed. In 2006, only a couple of students raised their hands when I asked who in the class was concerned about climate change (or even believed it was real). I now tell this story to students who are well acquainted with the threats of climate change. In the weeks leading up to the declaration of a global pandemic, I watched in horror as more and more people around the world were infected with and then died of COVID-19. I spoke to my class of the feeling I had that we were living in *The Year of the Flood*. Teaching *The Year of the Flood* online during the pandemic only highlighted students' growing fears around climate change and confirmed the urgency of systemic and personal change to the way we were living. In 2021, back in person and wearing masks and distanced, I again taught *The Year of the Flood*. In this case I offered students the opportunity to write a personal essay about reading *The Year of the Flood* during the global pandemic. The question read: "Discuss how you read *The Year of the Flood* in the context of the global pandemic. You may refer to your personal experience and parts of the text that resonate with you. Please be sure to relate how and why if you are writing from a personal perspective." Many students chose to write about the connections between their experience of the pandemic and the way it was represented in *The Year of the Flood*. Students discussed how the God's Gardeners emphasized handwashing and wore nose cones to protect them from viruses. They also noted the lessons in dealing with isolation and how they themselves dealt with the various government-mandated periods of social isolation, which in Newfoundland were lengthy and numerous.

Although I have been teaching Atwood's work in university classes for seventeen years, in the fall semester of 2023 I offered my first full course on the subject. This year was also the inaugural year for a new master's program I developed at our university, the master of applied literary arts. My undergraduate teaching and the new master's program are both dedicated to experiential and applied practice both inside and outside the literature classroom. Also key to my pedagogy, the master of applied literary arts, and the strategic plan of the university are decolonizing and then Indigenizing.

The question I had as I set out to teach the Atwood course was how I could do this challenging work of undoing the colonial legacy through works written by Atwood. As part of Atwood's birthday celebration years before in Sudbury, I had witnessed a local Anishanaabe chief give Atwood a sacred Eagle Feather in recognition of her work for Indigenous people and the environment. Thus, I knew that there was a connection between Atwood's work and decolonizing. I decided to create applied assignments in the Atwood class and ask the master's students in the arts management class to work as the arts managers for small groups of students. A Mi'kmaq student in the class, a man working on his master's but also employed by the university as the Indigenous education specialist in the Office of Indigenous Affairs, immediately suggested that I was going about the exercise in the wrong way. What needed to happen first, from an Indigenous and community empowerment perspective, was discussion with the students who would be working on the project about what they wanted to create in the class. I readily recognized the problems with imposing my creative vision on the class and revised the way the course was being taught.

In the revised version, master's students went to the Atwood class and discussed with the students what they would like to do as applied activities on the three novels: *Oryx and Crake*, *The Year of the Flood*, and *MaddAddam*. The master's students worked with the second-year students to create applied activities that reflected their ideas and abilities. The students thus collaborated in coming up with four different applied activities. One group of students made a survival guide from the perspective of survivors in the early days after the flood. This involved sketches of the hybrid animals, maps, descriptions of survivors, and various other observations about the world after the flood written from an insider perspective. Another group repurposed old books to create a 3D representation of the postapocalyptic world. A third group created activities for children, including coloring sheets, word scrambles, a scavenger hunt, and an animal-splice dice game. The last group created a *Year of the Flood* world role-playing game modeled after Dread, a horror role-playing game. Dread is built around the idea of exploring hostile worlds where there are few rules and thus is ideal for exploring and experiencing the world of *The Year of the Flood.*

The students noted how immersion in Atwood's postapocalyptic world of *The Year of the Flood* and imagining their place in that world increased their interest in the texts and forced them to keep going back to the books again and again to get the details right. While each student wrote at length about what they learned from the project, I would like to share how one student came to understand the lessons offered by Atwood's text and their own participation in the class. The student first wrote about the choices made in Atwood's world to either help or abandon animals and humans. The student wrote, "Usually, I would write a paper about how Margaret Atwood emphasizes the value of leaving no one behind, and how she argues that even in the direst of circumstances, co-operation and empathy is the way forward. However, by making a group survival guide, I was able to experience this theme firsthand." The student goes on to explain how at the start of the project they were of the mindset "every person for themselves." The student describes dividing up the work and then meeting together shortly before the class to assemble the book and present on the work. There was a problem, however, and the student goes on to describe what happened:

> Two days before we were due to present, we met as a group to put our project together. The drawings all looked fantastic, the descriptions were detailed and informative. This project was a resounding success. However, one aspect of the project was not up to snuff. As a group, [we] had to make a decision. We could hang a group member out to dry, while those of us who had completed our share of the work presented a solid project, or we could band together and work as a team to help our group member. Just like Toby in *The Year of the Flood*, we could take the easy way out and keep surviving as individuals, or we could band together and help a vulnerable person. In Toby's case, this person is a badly injured Ren, and ultimately, we made the same decision as Toby.

The conclusions this student drew from both the text and the group project encapsulated for me the work of decolonizing. The students realized the problem with the neoliberal mindset of personal achievement and progress at the expense of others and instead worked with empathy and care to help a fellow struggling student. The student concluded:

> It can be easy in life, to have an every-person-for-themselves attitude. In an environment that is so hyper-competitive, we often are not only trying to perform to the very best of our own abilities, but also outperform our peers. However, this is not the mindset we should have. After participating in this group project, like Atwood herself, I firmly believe that this project benefitted by leaving no one behind, and that even in the direst of circumstances, co-operation and empathy is the best way forward.

The conclusion of this group and this student illustrates the challenges and successes of attempting to decolonize the classroom. As the student observes, one of the problems that must be addressed is the competitive marking system and the competitive model of education where success only comes with the failure of others. However, emphasizing cooperation and care, as Atwood models in *The Year of the Flood* and other works, can demonstrate practices that can contribute to decolonizing the literature classroom through the practice of empathy and care.

Unlike earlier applied projects, which focused on reading the text in the real world through activities such as collecting mushrooms, gardening, and beekeeping, these current students living in a pandemic-era world decided to imaginatively enter the text and create activities that immersed them in Atwood's world. This was a different approach to the one I had envisioned and brought about real challenges to systemic educational practices and rewards for competition and personal success at the expense of others. The lesson of the necessity of working together with empathy through actual practice in the group project is perhaps the best application of Atwood's work to the current global climate crisis.

The students also decided on an ungraded activity to show the community their creations and invite community members to play in a day dedicated to Atwood activities at the local public library. The students 3D-printed glow-in-the-dark bunnies as prizes for a scavenger hunt, led role-playing games of Atwood-inspired Dread, and took the community into the world of *The Year of the Flood* and other Atwood texts, sharing the lessons they had learned along the way in short talks and in discussions of the activities.

The lessons offered in *The Year of the Flood* allowed for many different classroom discussions of a practical nature from within the literary context. The pairing of literature with practical applications was often a new experience for students. These applied lessons could also lead us back to the beautiful language and engaging characters and stories of *The Year of the Flood*. The text's interweaving of story and lessons for the real world demonstrated to students the power of literature to change them and potentially impact the material world. The individual and group projects and class discussions that grew out of Atwood's work changed people's lives in ways that enriched the place they lived and the lives of the people of the community.

NOTES

1. Sudbury is the largest city in Northern Ontario, with a population of 166,000. Mining is the main employer in the area, and the Sudbury region boasts eight base metal mines and is home to Canada's oldest and deepest mines. Sudbury is colloquially known as "The Big Nickel" or "Nickel City" on account of the ubiquity of the nickel mining industry. Starting late in the nineteenth century, the smelting of copper had led to the local landscape's being entirely devoid of vegetation, such that astronauts for the Apollo 16 and 17 missions trained there on what came to be called the "moonscape." After stronger regulatory processes were introduced in the 1970s, the 1980s saw the regreening of the landscape. For further discussion of this process, see Ross; Monet and McCaffrey.

2. Working with human subjects in the context of a class does not require consultation with the ethics committee at Laurentian University or Memorial University of Newfoundland and Labrador. Both universities are public Canadian institutions. However, I suggest that professors and educators contact the ethics committee at their university for regulations around teaching and using teaching for research purposes. In standard literature classes when there is a community or applied project as part of the course, I give the students the option to engage with the community or complete a standard research essay. I also ask students to sign consent forms to allow me to write about the class and include their written responses. As increasingly practical and applied projects and community engagement are a required part of English curriculum in Canada, many universities now have standard procedures in place for assessing these projects at the program, faculty, and school levels. At Memorial University our courses go through assessment at the program and faculty level, and ethics committee members are a part of the process. The courses then go through two more governing bodies, one of which includes members of the ethics committee. If there is any question about the safety of students, at our institution, there will be a suggestion to go back and get approval from the health and safety committee.

3. The students who made up the class were mostly from Northern Ontario, and many were from the Sudbury area. Many of the students who participated in the applied activities in response to the text were first-generation university students and in their third or fourth year of study for a Bachelor of Arts in English.

4. Cara Durigan presented a paper on her research at the inaugural ALECC conference at the University of Cape Breton, held 19–21 August 2010 and organized around the theme of "the ecological community."

5. In 2010, when I first taught *The Year of the Flood* in Newfoundland, the student body was almost entirely Newfoundlanders from western Newfoundland. Most of the students were first-generation university learners, and many of them were undeclared or general arts students.

Song That "Goes On Calling": Teaching Atwood's Poetry

Lauren Rule Maxwell

"Can poetry save the earth?" is the question John Felstiner investigates in his 2009 field guide to nature poems. That was not a question I asked my students the first day of Poetry, Landscape, and Identity, my 2022 graduate poetry seminar for MA and MFA students, though the students eventually came to pose that question themselves. I began more broadly with the questions "What is poetry?" and "What can poetry do that other genres can't?" As I explore in this essay, when students considered the qualities that distinguish poetry from other forms of art, they more deeply understood why poetry matters even now in our age of instant messaging and artificial intelligence. "So much depends," Felstiner posits, "on seeing the things of our world afresh by saying them anew" (3). This essay charts our exploration of poets' ability to reframe our points of reference and explains how the study of Margaret Atwood's poetry fostered a better understanding of how poets' "saying" inspires our "seeing" the world around us in a new light.

During the first class, we used the introduction to W. J. T. Mitchell's *Landscape and Power* as a starting point for conversations about what it means to understand landscape as "a process by which social and subjective entities are formed" and "what it *does*, how it works as a cultural practice" (3). We then turned to questions about the relationship of language to landscape and how authors created worlds with words. Opening this inquiry to other types of art and media, we then considered painting, the genre most traditionally associated with landscape, and discussed W. H. Auden's "Musée des Beaux Arts" and William Carlos Williams's "Landscape with the Fall of Icarus" in the context of Pieter Bruegel the Elder's sixteenth-century painting of the same name. Students talked about possible aims of ekphrastic poetry as we viewed Elisa Gabbert's *New York Times* multimedia feature "A Poem (and a Painting) about the Suffering That Hides in Plain Sight," which is a great resource for walking students through the close reading of a poem and for encouraging students to think about how audiences interpret and aesthetically appreciate different forms of art. Gabbert acknowledges and then discredits the line from Auden's "In Memory of W. B. Yeats" which says that "poetry makes nothing happen"; this poem does important work, she argues—it creates "a space for moral work, and for moral possibility." In comparing "Musée des Beaux Arts" to other famous poems, the class members agreed that poems open up many different types of possibility, that they create space for us to reconsider what we see and experience. At the end of class, we read and discussed Adrienne Rich's "Diving into the Wreck," a poem about exploration of language, identity, and place, which represents the aims of the course itself.

In her *New York Times* review of Rich's volume *Diving into the Wreck*, Atwood writes that it "forces you to decide not just what you think about it; but what you think about yourself. It is a book that takes risks, and it forces the reader to take them also." Atwood describes "the quest beyond myths," a journey for truths about relationships of self with other. "At their most successful," Atwood explains, "the poems move like dreams, simultaneously revealing and alluding, disguising and concealing. The truth, it seems, is not just what you find when you open a door: it is itself a door, which the poet is always on the verge of going through" (Review).

The most challenging aspect of designing this course was choosing poems to compel each class member on this type of journey where "the words are purposes / the words are maps" (Rich, "Diving"). Ultimately, I oriented the class toward modern and contemporary poetry: units focused on William Wordsworth, Walt Whitman, Emily Dickinson, Robert Frost, Langston Hughes, Elizabeth Bishop, Robert Lowell, Gwendolyn Brooks, Margaret Atwood, Natasha Trethewey, and Kevin Young. For each unit, the students read a few critical essays and theoretical selections. From "The Lucy Poems: Wordsworth's Quest for a Poetic Object" (Ferguson) to Dickinson and *The Undiscovered Continent* (Juhasz) to "Frost's Crossings" (Costello 19–52) to "Roots, Routes, and Langston Hughes's Hybrid Sense of Place" (Hogan) to "Reframing Exposure: Natasha Trethewey's Forms of Enclosure" (M. Jones), I tried to provide students with a range of critical and theoretical frameworks to examine depictions of space and place within these works. As I will discuss later, students tended to read Atwood's poetry alongside the course's other works, and it is in this context that we delved into her ecopoetics. Interestingly, although I did not assign readings from Felstiner's *Can Poetry Save the Earth?* in the course, that book does feature several poets we studied, including Wordsworth, Whitman, Dickinson, Frost, Williams, Bishop, and Lowell, but it does not include Atwood.

Given the broad scope of the course, we could not read all of Atwood's poetry in the unit dedicated to her work, but we did cover a sampling of poems from several of her collections, including *The Circle Game*, *The Animals in That Country*, *You Are Happy*, *Selected Poems, 1965–1975*, *True Stories*, *Morning in the Burned House*, and *The Door*, and we read her 2020 collection, *Dearly*, in its entirety. The students were knowledgeable about Atwood's fiction—several of them had read *The Handmaid's Tale* during their graduate studies—and most of them had some familiarity with her poetry. They were excited to delve into *Dearly*, a work so recently published that at that time there was little literary criticism about it. As one student reflected after the semester ended, this allowed the students to more independently develop their own responses to the collection: because there was "not a lot of scholarly source material on the text," she explained, "I had to focus primarily on my close reading and use past criticism of Atwood's work for interpreting something new, which helped me even more in developing my voice." In addition to the poems, I asked the students to read two critical pieces for the Atwood unit: Eleonora Rao's "'It Always Takes a

Long Time / To Decipher Where You Are': Uncanny Spaces and Troubled Times in Margaret Atwood's Poetry" and Richard Hunt's "How to Love This World: The Transpersonal Wild in Margaret Atwood's Ecological Poetry."

Within each unit, students had choices of possible assignments to post to the course's *Canvas* site the evening before the next class. The Atwood unit included several options:

> Discuss place, space, or geography in *Dearly*.
>
> Analyze the politics of location in two of the assigned poems.
>
> Write a poem in which "cowboy" addresses "backdrop" ["Backdrop Addresses Cowboy" (*The Animals in That Country* 50–51) was one of the assigned poems].
>
> Give your own definition of ecopoetry and, with close readings, explain how Atwood's poetry relates to it.
>
> Select an Atwood poem that was not assigned for the reading and explain how it relates to the themes of this course.

Here, as in the other units, the students created rich, thoughtful responses that exceeded the requirements of the assignment; they also responded to and commended their classmates' posts within the discussion thread.

Perhaps in response to the assigned Hunt essay, many of the posts addressed ecological themes even if they did not focus specifically on the ecopoetry prompt. One student who did write on the ecopoetry prompt applied Hunt's essay in a close reading of *Dearly*'s "Princess Clothing" (19–21). In this post, entitled "Ecopoetry and the World of Ethics," the student argues that "the role nature plays in Atwood's poetry is [not merely] figurative [or] decorative. . . . Atwood routinely brings nature, both the habitat and its various inhabitants, to the front stage of her poetic scenes . . . [raising the] question of ethics and responsibility when it comes to humans' relationship with nature." Turning to the poem, she writes:

> In the last two stanzas of "Princess Clothing," the poet shines a light on the life of silkworms:
>
> > Silk, however,
> > is best for shrouds.
> > That's where it comes from, silk:
> > those seven veils the silkworms keep spinning,
> > hoping they will be butterflies.
> > Then they get boiled, and then unscrolled.
>
> The poet describes the making of silk in a matter-of-fact, plain language that does not evade cruelty. It serves as a stark reminder that silk, like so many other luxury items, comes from the exploitation of living beings.

> The deliberate lack of sentimentality in Atwood's language confronts the reader with questions of ethics in its full impact.

"The last stanza," she goes on to explain, "takes it a step further, transcending the dichotomic relation between the princess and the silkworms, the relation of human vs. nature. Rather than pitching one against another, Atwood reveals that the pattern of deceitful exploitation does not stop at how we treat animals. It is also how we treat each other." After gesturing toward another commonality between humans and other living creatures, the inevitability of all living things' dying, she concludes by returning to Hunt's essay to emphasize how the close of "Princess Clothing" leaves the reader to ponder what a "renovated relationship" between human and nonhuman beings would look like.

Because the class included not only MA English students from our joint program with the College of Charleston but also MFA poetry and fiction students, it was not surprising to me that about a third of the students chose the option of writing a poem from the perspective of the cowboy. One of the MA students, a talented poet, chose to "create a dialogue of the cowboy speaking to this backdrop as if it's a relic" to explore the effect of our increasing reliance on devices on our experience of art and on the digitization of art itself. These present-day concerns relate more closely to poems in *Dearly* than to Atwood's 1968 "Backdrop Addresses Cowboy," where the cowboy is "Starspangled" (50) and the backdrop is "the horizon / you ride towards" and "the space you desecrate / as you pass through" (51). The cowboy in the student's poem questions how backdrop, "Sitting there almost forgotten" yet "always seen," "make[s] your presence / Known." Like Atwood's "Backdrop," the student's poem underscores a threat of violence as it blurs lines between human and inhuman, artificial and natural. With a nod to 1980s popular culture and film, the cowboy displaces emotion onto the object as he muses, "Perhaps my full metal jacket might / Miss the acid wash portion of your canvas" and then asks, "What does it mean that I haven't forgotten you?" The poem ends with two questions: "In the vast expanse of technology, / Have you lost your importance / In the binary code of algorithms" and "When computers fail, / Will they be able to paint another as beautiful as you?"

These last lines with the notion of failed computers evoke the "Plasticene Suite" of Atwood's *Dearly*, particularly the "little robot" that is "designed to learn like a child" and "plays with [objects], absorbs. / Then it gets bored / and drops things on the floor" (91). "Where," the speaker asks, "will you bestow yourself / when you are obsolete? / On what cosmic trashheap?" (92). While pointing out planned obsolescence of many of our devices and our quest to distance ourselves as much as we can from our junk, the speaker of Atwood's poem considers the consequences if the little robot were to "live forever"—would it "erase us"—"[w]ould that be better?" (92). Examining the student's poem alongside the "Plasticene Suite" led to in-class discussions about art and innovation, the relationship of nature to beauty, and the impact of digital tools and artificial intelligence on the production of art. We concluded that despite the recent advances of AI programs, the attempts to parrot human patterns of speech lack the humanity, warmth, and ability to connect that we associate with good writing. Among writers, it is the poet who most compellingly inspires us to see anew the world around us. It is the poet who makes the backdrop in the student's poem, "[s]itting there almost forgotten," "always seen." The poet "make[s that] presence / Known."

Months after the course ended, Atwood herself addressed AI programs' using pirated copies of her works in "Murdered by My Replica?" "Beyond the royalties and copyrights," Atwood writes, "what concerns me is the idea that an author's voice and mind are replicable." She deems these programs' attempts to write an Atwood story "pedestrian in the extreme. . . . The program, so far," she explains, "does not understand figurative language, let alone irony and allusion." While conceding that AI's capabilities undoubtedly will advance, Atwood argues that the power of the writer rests in the ability to delight by making the song come alive: "The clockwork bird can sing, but only the song with which it has been programmed. It can't improvise. It can't riff. It can't surprise. And it is in that surprise that much of the delight of art resides . . . Only the living bird can sing a song that is ever renewed, and therefore always delightful."

Like Emily Dickinson, who famously wrote to Thomas Wentworth Higginson asking, "Are you too deeply occupied to say if my verse is alive?" (qtd. in Higginson), Atwood judges art by asking the "only one important question to be asked of a work of art: 'Is it alive, or is it dead?'" Unlike the "dead" writing produced by AI, which "sort of looks like art [and] sort of sounds like art," the work of the poet stands the test of time ("Murdered"). Suggesting that poetry that stands that test is grounded in nature, Felstiner begins the preface to *Can Poetry Save the Earth?* with a quotation by John Keats: "The Poetry of earth is never dead" (xiii). This line comes from Keats's poem "On the Grasshopper and Cricket," which assures the reader that the earth will always supply a song "When all the birds are faint with the hot sun / And hide in the cooling trees, a voice will run." The next voice highlighted in the poem is that of the Grasshopper, who "takes the lead" in the "new-mown mead." Keats's poem suggests that the earth provides a continual soundtrack of voices that rise and fall with the seasons and natural cycles, but it also, to Felstiner's point, suggests that there is something everlasting about nature poetry itself, "poems [that] end up turning your eye and ear toward a world that is good to live in" (xiv). It is this relationship between the "eye and ear" that the poetry students investigated as they analyzed Atwood's poetry.

As we considered throughout the semester what made poetry poetry, we returned again and again to song. At the beginning of the semester, I focused on the importance of sound to poetry as we discussed form and qualities such as meter, rhythm, rhyme, repetition, assonance, consonance, euphony, cacophony, and alliteration that affect the musicality of poetic language. In the subsequent units, we applied a heightened attention to the sounds of words. When analyzing the Preface to *Lyrical Ballads* in the Wordsworth unit, we explored how Wordsworth's conceptualization of poetry related to music and song. We asked what was at stake in Whitman's titling his masterwork "Song of Myself" and considered the importance of sound to the poem: "Now I will do nothing but listen, / To accrue what I hear into this song, to let sounds contribute toward it." One student postulated that this poem had an ecopoetic design, that in creating this song, "Whitman makes it clear that we are not only intrinsically linked to each other but also to our environment." Furthermore, she argued, the aesthetic beauty of the song produces another sensory experience in which readers imagine or picture a scene in the mind's eye: the "Song" helps readers "see the importance of natural functions, both human [and] nonhuman, and discover a pleasure within."

To conceptualize what the pleasure of song has to do with reframing our view of the world, we took a bird's-eye view. In addition to the songs mentioned in the Keats and Whitman poems I've discussed, there were many other mentions of birds' songs in the works we studied over the course of the semester. Some of the most notable discussions about song arose from Marta Werner's "Sparrow Data: Dickinson's Birds in the Skies of the Anthropocene," selected by the student leading a critical discussion on Dickinson. Werner's article takes as its starting point the fact that "birds crowd Dickinson's work" and then delves into the form and content of her writings, ultimately claiming that "birdsong is arguably the most constant, evanescent sound she recorded through writing in an age before the technologies of recording had been invented" (45). To demonstrate how the article addresses what the student presenter termed our current "ecological crisis," the student quoted the following passage from the essay:

> Dickinson's birds—that is, the cloud her poems make—are not manifest to us . . . as a unity but rather as a mobile, ever-changing figure, an "emergent unreadability." Like the birds themselves, the bird-poems are without fixed abode: they offer a view of the earth from somewhere else. One possible stance in relation to Dickinson's lyric oeuvre, and the one practiced here, involves attending to, as in tending to and caring for, the sudden questions it stirs in and for our time as well as for the uncertain future. For while Dickinson's poems did not sing the ecological crisis we have named the Anthropocene—how could they?—by sounding the convergences between the lyric, birds, lateness, and precarity, they flew headlong from the nineteenth-century into the cataclysm of the twenty-first. (Werner 54)

When drawing attention to the crisis of human impacts on the earth, Atwood has pointed to birds as a gauge of our ecological impact on the life around us: "The birds have something to tell us again, and the truths are not comfortable ones" ("Act Now"). Atwood and her late partner, Graeme Gibson, the author of *The Bedside Book of Birds*, were named honorary leaders within BirdLife

International, a bird conservation and advocacy organization, and Atwood has for many years been an advocate and spokesperson for bird-related causes ("Act Now"). One of the students who focused on Atwood's poetry for her final paper noted the importance of considering Atwood's advocacy for bird conservation when reading her poetry; she claimed that knowledge of "Atwood's relationship with ecological preservation and bird conservation" helps us "understand what Atwood is saying about human connection and what is revealed about humankind's relationship with nature." In her final paper, entitled "Flightless Birds: The Nature of Hope in Margaret Atwood's *Dearly*," the student argues not only that "birds represent speech and communication through song" but also that Atwood's poetry stands as a "a song in and of itself," that the blurring of the lines between "poetry and birdsong" inspires "her readers to retain hope" and inspires "future generations to restore and maintain" the environment around them.

Birdsong in fact has many similarities with poetry, as members of the class noted at different points of the semester. The student quoted above cited a passage from Onno Oerlemans's *Poetry and Animals* to explain "the complications of hearing birdsong in real life":

> Birdsong [might seem] meaningless because it comes from another species and because it is merely music [but it is] meaningful because like language it is intentional and patterned, and we feel the effects of music as spontaneous meaning. Moreover, because Birdsong is normally apprehended not as the song of a single bird but as that of a particular species, it can be understood as conventional (something merely repeated, whether by instinct or learning) even as it appears deeply imbedded in the natural world, specific to a single bird singing in the particular moment. (93)

Like poetry, birdsong uses the meaning-carrying capabilities of language to convey a message to those beings that understand the grammar, but also, because of the euphonic combinations of sound, it appeals to us humans, and perhaps the birds themselves, as the music of life. Oerlemans's description of the "effects of music as spontaneous meaning" is particularly relevant when one likens birdsong to poetry, a genre in which words collapse into sound, because it captures the sentiment behind Atwood's contrasting of art to the output of AI, that "[o]nly the living bird can sing a song that is ever renewed, and therefore always delightful."

The student author of "Flightless Birds" concludes that "Atwood's bird poems become her own birdsong for the human species." Using "Siren Brooding on Her Eggs" as one example, she claims that "Atwood uses her poetry like the siren, to intrigue listeners into understanding the necessary interdependence between us and nature." In "How to Love the World," Hunt argues that "neither the intensity or the nor the direction of [Atwood's] environmentalism has yet been fully recognized," and I would agree (233). Hunt discusses nature as a setting and, more centrally, as the subject of Atwood's poetry, but in this paper, the student goes further in arguing that Atwood's birdsong acts not only as figure and subject but also as mode, that the poems themselves sound "birdsong for the human species." *Dearly*'s "The Dear Ones" references "the kinds of stories / we used to tell," ones that "were comforting in a way / because they said / everyone has to be somewhere," but it goes on to suggest that we have already forever lost so many—not only people we love, but species, birds, beings with lives outside our comprehension (40). This song strikes a somber chord as the poem closes:

> After a while
>
> You sound like a bird.
> You stop, but the sorrow goes on calling.
> It leaves you and flies out
>
> over the cold night fields,
> searching and searching,
> over the rivers,
> over the emptied air (40–41)

With its songs of shifting rhythms' calling readers to attention, *Dearly* fills the air that used to contain many, many more birds.

The songs of *Dearly* move us to change our frame of reference and see the world around us differently. One student explained that *Dearly*'s "'Bird Soul,' as part of a grouping of poems, positions the reader above the natural landscape looking at different aspects of the environment as the speaker questions the reader's [perspective]." Another noted that in Atwood's poetry, as in the paintings Atwood describes in her short story "Death by Landscape," "there [are] hardly [ever] any neat vista points or quiet backdrops. Instead, one sees a lot of foregrounds, going back further and further, embodying a never-ending, painstaking quest for agency, truth and meaning." Like Rich's *Diving into the Wreck*, which Atwood reviewed more than fifty years ago, *Dearly* "is a book that takes risks, and it forces the reader to take them also" (Atwood, Review).

The impact of this change of perspective can be seen in the fact that several students chose to write on Atwood's poetry for their final papers and that, in the following semester, two MA students who were graduating chose to make *Dearly* and its ecopoetics central to their capstone portfolios. One, who claimed that Atwood was the "ecopoet of [her] generation," writes that "Atwood makes it clear that man is not central to nature but ethically responsible for it [;] she . . . 'seeks to inspire a change in the way we perceive the relationship among all living things' (Hunt 240)." Highlighting the changing rhythms and the shifting line breaks in the poem "Aflame," from *Dearly* (52–53), this student observes, "The poem physically ends in this final stanza by appearing to be the hand of a pendulum clock, swinging back and forth as time continues to pass. Atwood reminds her reader not only through language but [also] through this image that change must occur or time will run out to replenish the Earth." Compelling us to see the world around us anew, Atwood makes us consider more deeply the possibilities of poetry and song and, as another student reflects in her final portfolio, "why literature matters." Her "future endeavors," she explains, will focus on the "necessity" of reading literature, on "its ability to provide readers with a shared human experience of empathy and compassion for everything, human and nonhuman." Perhaps poetry can save the earth after all.

CROSS-DISCIPLINARY APPLICATIONS

Testimony, Truth, and Judgment in *Alias Grace*

Melissa J. Ganz

"Should Grace Marks have been convicted of murdering Nancy Montgomery and Thomas Kinnear?" I ask students when I teach *Alias Grace*. "Was Grace's punishment just? Should she receive a pardon and be released from prison now?" These questions give rise to lively debates about the causes and consequences of criminality, the complexities of legal and moral judgment, and the unequal power relations between men and women. Through the discussions that follow, students gain a better understanding of Margaret Atwood's reworking of a sensational 1843 murder case while reflecting on the ways in which the novel can help us think through questions about gender and justice that remain of concern today.

I teach *Alias Grace* in an upper-level English course entitled Crime and Punishment in English Fiction, which examines the centrality of crime and punishment to the novel tradition from the early nineteenth century to the present day. The class meets twice weekly and draws students from across the university. *Alias Grace* works well at the end of the course because it both draws upon and revises the conventions of nineteenth-century crime writing. The openness of the novel's ending and its skepticism about truth and objectivity enable us to track a shift away from the certainties offered by Arthur Conan Doyle's detective fiction. The novel's focus on female criminality also makes for illuminating comparisons with Charles Dickens's *Oliver Twist* and Mary Elizabeth Braddon's *Lady Audley's Secret*, which we read earlier in the semester. In addition to situating the novel in this broader tradition, we read selections from contextual materials including Susanna Moodie's *Life in the Clearings versus the Bush*, which Atwood references in *Alias Grace*. I also show clips from Mary Harron's television adaptation so that students can compare Harron's portrait of female criminality with Atwood's. These materials help us analyze Atwood's brilliant and intricate text.

We begin our discussion by considering Grace's opening account of her incarceration in Kingston Penitentiary and the fragmented recollections she has of the moments leading up to and following Nancy's murder. I ask for volunteers to read the first few paragraphs aloud and then invite students to share their initials impressions of Grace. Students are immediately struck by her frank, confessional tone and her youth—just sixteen years of age—at the time of the crime. We also consider Atwood's lyrical style and use of flower imagery as well as the abrupt end of Grace's account when Nancy's smiling face dissolves into "patches of colour" and Grace has a vision of being trapped in a cellar (Atwood, *Alias Grace* 6).[1] We do not yet know what happened at the Kinnear residence or what role Grace may have played in Nancy's death. But Grace's account underscores the difficulty of accessing traumatic memories while offering a glimpse of the challenges associated with lifelong imprisonment.

We turn next to the ballad entitled "The Murders of Thomas Kinnear, Esq. and of His Housekeeper Nancy Montgomery at Richmond Hill and the Trials of Grace Marks and James McDermott and the Hanging of James McDermott at the New Gaol in Toronto, November 21st, 1843," which constitutes the second chapter. I ask students to take turns reading the stanzas. We begin the semester by discussing selections from popular crime narratives and execution ballads, so students are familiar with the ways in which such texts sensationalized crime. We consider how this ballad likewise oversimplifies the motives for and circumstances surrounding the deaths of Nancy and her employer, Mr. Kinnear. According to the ballad, the murders were motivated by jealousy and revenge on Grace's part and lust on McDermott's. In this account, Grace not only tempted McDermott to kill Nancy but also played a crucial role in her death: "McDermott held [Nancy] by the hair," while Grace held her by the head, "And these two monstrous criminals, / They strangled her till dead" (12). The poem goes on to recount their testimony at the trial, as well as McDermott's execution and the commutation of Grace's death sentence to life in prison. The final lines nonetheless hold out the possibility of redemption for Grace:

> But if Grace Marks repent at last,
> And for her sins atone,
> Then when she comes to die, she'll stand
> At her Redeemer's throne.
> . . . .
> And she will be as white as snow,
> And into Heaven will pass,
> And she will dwell in Paradise,
> In Paradise at last. (15)

We discuss the ways in which the ballad's rhyme scheme and simplified moral framework reinforce Grace's guilt even as the poem emphasizes the importance of confession and repentance. I ask students to consider how Atwood's retelling of the story complicates the version put forward by the ballad.

We begin to answer this question by turning to the account Grace gives in the next chapter of working as a servant in the residence of the governor of Kingston Penitentiary and the fascination Grace arouses in the governor's wife and her circle of friends. Grace is keenly aware of the conflicting judgments that have been made about her. The public views her alternately as an "inhuman female demon," an "innocent victim of a blackguard," and a naive youth who was "too ignorant to know how to act" (23). "And I wonder," Grace asks, "how can I be all of these different things at once" (23). We consider how Grace's reflections undercut the contradictory judgments about her while highlighting tensions in the idea of the female criminal.

Over the next few classes, we examine Grace's exchanges with Simon Jordan, the mental specialist hired by Reverend Verringer and his committee to help exonerate Grace. We discuss the power struggle that quickly emerges as Grace resists Dr. Jordan's efforts to access her knowledge of the past. We also examine Atwood's alternating use of first-person and third-person narration. As students note, the chapters that Grace relates are particularly compelling. Grace's account is direct and intimate; through first-person narration, Atwood invites readers to enter into Grace's perspective. We look closely at the description Grace offers of her initial meeting with Dr. Jordan, in which he brings her an apple and attempts to lead her through a train of associations concerning the biblical story of the Fall. (I ask students to read the characters' parts so that we can hear the different voices.) Grace understands the doctor's goals and methods but cannily refuses to answer his questions, and Atwood privileges Grace's point of view. We then turn to the end of the eighth chapter, in which Grace reflects on her exchanges with Dr. Jordan:

> While he writes, I feel as if he is drawing me; or not drawing me, drawing on me—drawing on my skin—not with the pencil he is using, but with an old-fashioned goose pen, and not with the quill end but with the feather end. . . .
>
> But underneath that is another feeling, a feeling of being wide-eyed awake and watchful. It's like being wakened suddenly in the middle of the night, by a hand over your face, and you sit up with your heart going fast, and no one is there. And underneath that is another feeling still, a feeling like being torn open; not like a body of flesh, it is not painful as such, but like a peach; and not even torn open, but too ripe and splitting open of its own accord.
>
> And inside the peach there's a stone. (69)

Through this series of images, Atwood undermines Dr. Jordan's efforts to penetrate Grace's mind and record her story, likening his efforts to violations of the body. We consider each of the similes in turn, noting the increasing violence that they suggest; we also consider how Grace's account of the stone at the center of the peach subverts the idea of any easy access to truth. We then view the opening scenes of Harron's television adaptation, including Dr. Jordan's initial meeting with Grace (*Alias Grace*, episode 1, 00:00:00–05:53), and skip to a scene that concludes with Grace sitting in her darkened cell, reflecting on her exchanges with the doctor (episode 1, 00:41:10–44:08). Students note how the lighting, music, and point of view in this scene amplify the threats that Dr. Jordan poses for Grace. We discuss, too, some of the other devices that Atwood uses to undercut the doctor's efforts. Early on, for example, Dr. Jordan writes to a friend that Grace will be "a very hard nut to crack" (Atwood, *Alias Grace* 54). When she later refuses to oblige him with an account of her dreams, he declares that "there is more than one way to skin a cat" (101). These metaphors highlight the dangers that Dr. Jordan presents for Grace's physical and mental well-being. What emerges is a struggle for access to Grace's unconscious mind and innermost self.

We consider how Atwood likewise uses third-person narration to undermine Dr. Jordan's character. The chapters that focus on the doctor's thoughts and actions position Simon, as he is called in these sections, at an ironic distance from readers. At nearly every turn, the doctor fantasizes about and objectifies women. He thinks of his maid, Dora, as a prostitute and a pig and of the governor's daughter Lydia as a "healthy young animal" (86). According to Simon, women are drawn to him because they crave "forbidden knowledge—knowledge with a lurid glare to it" (82). But he is himself obsessed with such knowledge. We consider the ways in which Atwood uses techniques such as free indirect discourse to expose and critique the misogynistic views of the supposedly objective medical professional.

At this point, I take a vote to see whether students think that Grace is guilty or innocent. Although some students are skeptical of her account and some are simply unsure what to make of it, many students are sympathetic to Grace. We discuss what it would mean for her to be "guilty" or "innocent" of the crimes. There are a range of possibilities: Grace could have instigated and played a material role in one or both of the murders, or she simply could have been an accessory before and after the fact, which—we later learn—is what the jury that convicted her concluded. Grace, we learn, was never tried for Nancy's murder; she and McDermott were sentenced immediately after—and based solely upon the evidence presented in—Kinnear's case. Grace may have participated willingly and eagerly in Nancy's murder, or she may have been coerced into providing assistance. These different possibilities prompt students to consider the complexities of legal and moral judgment.

In the next class, we consider the account that Grace gives Dr. Jordan of her family's difficulties prior to and following their journey from Ireland to Toronto. I divide the students into groups and ask them to jot down some of the themes and questions raised by Grace's account. When we reconvene, students comment on the ways in which Grace's narrative highlights class inequalities as well as power struggles between men and women. Students point to the challenges Grace experiences as a young girl living with an abusive father who charges her with caring for her younger siblings and earning money after her mother's death. We then look at Grace's description of her work at Alderman Parkinson's house, where she becomes acquainted with Mary Whitney. As students note, Mary appears to be at once a friend, mentor, and confidante, as well as Grace's alter ego; Grace frequently invokes Mary's words, which allows her to articulate "coarse" ideas and progressive views while distancing herself from them (150). (I show a clip from the television series to give students a sense of Mary's playful and defiant nature and the bond that develops between the two women [*Alias Grace*, episode 2, 00:03:20–07:00].) We look closely at Grace's devastating description of Mary's seduction, botched abortion, and death, considering the critique of men's infidelity that emerges from this account and the trauma that Grace experiences from the loss of her friend. Grace lays the blame for Mary's death at the feet of two men—the elder Parkinson son, whom Grace believes seduced and abandoned Mary, and the doctor who performed the abortion. In this way, Atwood establishes a narrative of male culpability and female victimization while inviting readers to sympathize with Grace.

We next consider how the sewing motif complicates Grace's reliability as a narrator. We look, in particular, at Simon's exchange with Reverend Verringer in which the two discuss Susanna Moodie's account of the case. (At this point, we read Moodie's narrative, with its sensational descriptions of the "celebrated murderess," whom Moodie saw in the prison and the asylum [215].) Simon notes that Moodie's report is filled with inaccuracies. Reverend Verringer is not surprised:

> "Mrs. Moodie is a literary lady, and like all such, and indeed like the sex in general, she is inclined to—"
> "Embroider," says Simon.
> "Precisely," says Reverend Verringer. (Atwood, *Alias Grace* 191)

As these synchronized sentences suggest, the men are in perfect agreement; in their view, women are naturally prone to exaggeration—to both literal and figurative fabrication. Their condemnation of "literary ladies," of course, has implications for Grace, who talks to Dr. Jordan in the sewing room, mending clothes and assembling quilts as she relates her account. On the one hand, students recognize, Grace might be stitching together her story—that is, creatively reworking, embellishing, or concealing the truth. On the other hand, the sewing metaphor highlights her agency as a narrator and her authority over the interpretation of her life experiences.

In subsequent classes, we consider the increasing liberties that Grace takes as a storyteller. We look, for example, at the beginning of chapter 27, when Grace admits for the first time that she has embellished her narrative. "Today when I woke up there was a beautiful pink sunrise," she observes, only to acknowledge in the next paragraph, "In fact I have no idea of what kind of a sunrise there was. In prison they make the windows high up, so you cannot climb out of them I suppose, but also so you cannot see out of them either, or at least not onto the outside world" (237). At the beginning of the next chapter,

Grace similarly explains that since Dr. Jordan "was so thoughtful" as to bring her a promised radish, she will "set to work willingly to tell [her] story, and to make it as interesting as [she] can, and rich in incident, as a sort of return gift" (247). We consider how this acknowledgment alters our view of her case. Students realize that Grace may be fabricating other parts of her narrative too. Indeed, as Simon notes, although Grace's account is suffused with details, there are no witnesses available who can "corroborate her testimony" (185). As Grace gets closer to relating what happened on the fateful day, Atwood increasingly hints at Grace's possible involvement in and responsibility for the murders.

We turn next to the account Grace gives of her tumultuous experiences after leaving the Parkinsons. Her attempts to fend off assaults by another employer, Mr. Haraghy, and the dealer in farm implements whom she meets en route to Mr. Kinnear's residence again underscore the threats that men pose to women's sexual and bodily autonomy. Grace's relationship with Mr. Kinnear, however, is more complicated. We review the dynamic at the Kinnear residence and Grace's tense relationship with Nancy, whom she discovers is Mr. Kinnear's mistress. Chapters 31 and 33 are confusing, and we look closely at them. Although Grace's relation is cryptic, it is clear that there is a good deal of jealousy and rivalry, as well as simmering passion, in the house. We examine the dream that Grace relates in which she finds herself outside the Kinnear residence being caressed by a series of men—a dream that culminates in her loss of consciousness. Grace explains that when she wakes up the next morning, she finds that the hem of her nightdress is damp and her feet are marked by the earth. (I show clips from the film to help students understand this sequence [*Alias Grace*, episode 4, 00:34:00–42:54].) Grace's description of her dream suggests that we are accessing her unconscious mind. But her relation is suffused with ambiguity. Was Grace asleep or awake at the time? Who caressed her? Were the embraces consensual or coerced? At the end of chapter 31, Grace coyly observes, "Dr. Jordan is writing eagerly . . . and I have never seen him so animated before. It does my heart good to feel I can bring a little pleasure into a fellow-being's life; and I think to myself, I wonder what he will make of all that" (Atwood, *Alias Grace* 281). Such reflections, of course, raise further questions about the veracity of her account. I give students a chance to weigh in on these questions.

In the next class, we turn to Grace's relationship with Jeremiah, the palm-reading peddler Grace meets at Alderman Parkinson's who later offers to take her away from the Kinnear residence. I ask students to consider how Jeremiah both resembles and differs from the other men in the novel. Some students suggest that, unlike Dr. Jordan, Jeremiah seems to be genuinely interested in Grace's well-being. But others note that, while Jeremiah offers to remove Grace from her threatening environment, he does not make her a proposal of marriage. Rather, he tells her that she can go with him and "be a fire-eater, or else a medical clairvoyant" at the fairs (267). As a young man, he explains, he used to team up with a woman: he "was the one who made the passes and also took in the money, and she was the one to have a muslin veil put over her, and go into a trance, and speak in a hollow voice, and tell the people what was wrong with them" (267). Jeremiah has a similar role in mind for Grace. But the novel suggests that Grace has already yielded her voice and agency too many times. "[T]here are always those that will supply you with speeches of their own, and put them right into your mouth for you too," she reflects not long afterward, recalling the constraints her lawyer, Kenneth MacKenzie, imposed on her at her trial. These sort of people, she thinks to herself, "are like the magicians who can throw their voice, at fairs and shows, and you are just their wooden doll" (295). We consider how this passage affirms Grace's concerns about Jeremiah while highlighting the connections between the courtroom and popular theater. We look, too, at Jeremiah's reincarnation as Dr. Jerome DuPont, a "trained Neuro-hypnotist" who convinces Grace's supporters to let him assist with the recovery of her memory (83). Grace appears to be at once shocked, intrigued, and afraid when she encounters Jeremiah in the governor's wife's parlor. We consider both the possibilities and the problems his presence poses for Grace.

We then turn to the chapters students have been eagerly awaiting, in which Grace recounts the murders. We begin our discussion of chapters 35 and 36 by recapping what Grace claims to remember about that day. Next, we take a closer look at the passage in which she recalls standing in the garden and hearing a "dull sound from within" after McDermott announces that he is going to kill Nancy (317). We read, too, her account of Mr. Kinnear's death, which, she explains, takes place while she is carrying a tea tray across the courtyard to the back kitchen. After McDermott commands her to open the trapdoor in the hall so that he can dispose of Mr. Kinnear's body, Grace runs back outside, whereupon McDermott fires his gun at her and she falls on the ground in a "dead faint" (320). With these and other details in mind, I ask students to work in groups to jot down evidence that serves either to convict or to excuse Grace. When we reconvene, I ask students in each group to share their evidence and arguments about the case. In defense of Grace, students emphasize that she appears to have been terrified of McDermott during his murderous rage and that he comes close to raping her before they leave the Kinnear residence and again during their flight to Toronto. Grace also indicates that she attempted to warn Nancy of McDermott's threats. But students point out that Grace had reasons to want Nancy dead, that Grace's kerchief was used to strangle Nancy, and that the boy next door, Jamie Walsh, testified to conversing with Grace when she claims to have been unconscious. Grace's references to McDermott as "James" also suggest a fondness and intimacy that Grace now disavows, and her flight in Nancy's clothes gives the impression of a cold and calculating criminal. Grace's description of the murders, moreover, is disjointed and incomplete, filtered through third-person narration; for the first time, we lose direct access to her consciousness. Students realize that they have not gotten closer to understanding what happened on the fateful day.

We consider, too, Simon's response to Grace's account, which further highlights the challenges posed by the case. Simon becomes increasingly frustrated as the truth continues to elude him. He cannot determine whether Grace has "a real case of amnesia" or whether "he is the victim of a cunning imposture" (321). But Simon's objectivity is itself increasingly undermined as Atwood emphasizes his misogynistic musings and sexist fantasies. Simon's desire for knowledge is linked to his desire to possess Grace's mind and body; he is determined to "pry" the truth out of her yet (322). After we look at these passages, I take another vote to see how students' views of Grace's guilt or innocence have changed. Although some students have become more skeptical of Grace, others continue to defend her, citing her account of McDermott's threats, which resonates with the novel's broader portrait of women's victimization at the hands of men.

In the next two classes, we continue to debate the role that Grace may have played in the murders and the justice of the punishment she received. Atwood raises further questions about the verdict through Simon's interview with Grace's lawyer, who gives a flippant account of his unsuccessful defense. When Simon asks MacKenzie whether he believes that Grace helped kill Nancy, MacKenzie asserts that Grace was "guilty as sin" (378), affirming the idea of women's fallen nature. But Atwood undermines the reliability of the pompous lawyer, who acknowledges that he fabricated Grace's admission of guilt in his statement to Mrs. Moodie and insists that his vulnerable, young client was infatuated with him when he represented her. The novel likewise calls attention to Simon's own erotic fantasies involving Grace. Even "professional" men—lawyers and doctors alike—cannot be relied upon to treat women with dignity and respect, Atwood emphasizes.

At this point we examine chapter 48, in which Jeremiah (aka Dr. DuPont) hypnotizes Grace. As in the chapters recounting the murders, in this chapter Atwood uses third-person narration; we remain distanced from Grace's consciousness throughout the episode. I ask students to read portions of the scene aloud so that they can better follow the dialogue. While in a trance, Grace confesses to killing Nancy, but her confession comes with a twist. The voice that Dr. DuPont unlocks claims to belong to Mary Whitney. We consider what it means for Mary—clothed in Grace's "earthly shell" (403)—to have strangled Nancy. The suggestion that Grace might be suffering from "double consciousness" (405) and might have two distinct personalities recalls our discussion of Robert Louis Stevenson's *Strange Case of Dr. Jekyll and Mr. Hyde*; students immediately draw connections with that text. Students are attracted to the idea that Grace might suffer from such an illness, as it would absolve her from criminal responsibility. But there is a good deal of evidence to suggest that Mary's "confession" is a masterful performance. Jeremiah is, after all, not only a charlatan and magician but also, we later learn, a ventriloquist. Still, it is unclear whether Grace actively and knowingly participates in the deceit or whether she is unconscious the entire time. Many students are surprised by this turn of events; they have been waiting for a definitive answer to the question of Grace's guilt or innocence. In the end, unlike in a Sherlock Holmes story or a Dickens novel, there is no revelation of "the truth." Atwood leaves us wondering about the extent of Grace's knowledge of and involvement in the murders.

In our last class, we consider Grace's pardon and release from prison many years later and her subsequent marriage to Jamie Walsh. After we read the novel's final paragraphs and review the key plot developments, I ask students to work together to come up with evidence that incriminates and exonerates Grace. As evidence of her potential guilt, students point to Grace's increasing admissions of her acting and deception. After learning she has been pardoned, it takes some days for Grace to get used to the fact that she will no longer be a "celebrated murderess"; she explains that it "calls for a different arrangement of the face" (443). She likewise explains that she forgives Jamie for his role at her trial even though in doing so, she is "telling a lie" (458). She confesses to embellishing the stories of her experiences in the prison and the asylum to captivate Jamie and prompt him to apologize yet again. She eventually encounters Jeremiah, too, after recognizing his picture in an advertisement for a "celebrated medium" (455). But, she cryptically explains, "I know my secrets are safe with Jeremiah, as his are safe with me" (456). All in all, it seems as if Grace may well have had a hand in the murders and may simply be telling others the stories they want to hear.

But there is also evidence suggesting that Grace deserves to be pardoned and released from prison. To support this reading, students emphasize the relentless misogyny at the center of the text and the novel's subversion of men's attempts to control and silence women. Others argue that, even if Grace played a role in the murders, she was extremely young at the time, appears to have been swayed by McDermott, and has already served a lengthy prison sentence. Still others underscore the difficulty of uncovering the truth given the vicissitudes of memory, the lasting effects of trauma, and the blurry line between fact and fiction. Other students point out that Grace's marriage to Jamie is far from ideal: they call attention to the ways in which Jamie's obsession with Grace's traumatic experiences reminds Grace of Dr. Jordan's own prurient interest in her case, highlighting Atwood's continuing concerns about the unequal power dynamic between men and women. After putting all the evidence on the board and debating the different interpretations, I take two final votes to see how many students think that Grace is guilty and how many think that her release from prison is justified. Most students answer "yes" to both questions, revealing a nuanced understanding of legal and moral determinations of responsibility and of women's constrained choices in sexual relationships. We look, too, at the end of Harron's adaptation (*Alias Grace*, episode 6, 00:30:25–43:50), which juxtaposes Grace's freedom with Dr. Jordan's debilitation and celebrates Grace's release even as it calls attention to the compromises she makes in marrying Jamie.

We conclude by looking at the final paragraphs of the novel, in which Grace describes the quilt she is making. Its pattern, the Tree of Paradise, diverges from the biblical narrative. "[The Bible] says there were two different trees, the Tree of Life and the Tree of Knowledge," Grace explains, "but I believe there was only the one, and that the Fruit of Life and the Fruit of Good and Evil were the same" (459). In another reversal, Grace places the signs and symbols of female sexuality at the heart of her paradise. Grace explains that she plans to stitch together pieces from Mary Whitney's white petticoat, her own faded-yellow prison nightdress, and Nancy's pink-and-white floral dress, which Grace wore on the ferry when fleeing Toronto. "I will embroider around each one of them with red feather-stitching, to blend them in as part of the pattern," she declares. "And so we will all be together" (460). Far from suggesting repentance, Grace's plans for the quilt testify to her continuing transgression. This ending represents a significant departure from the other texts we have read. Unlike in the Sherlock Holmes stories, in this text the criminal is eventually released and pardoned. And unlike the rebellious Lady Audley, who is silenced and written out of Braddon's novel, Grace gets the final word. In the last few chapters, she imagines herself recounting the latest developments in her life story to Dr. Jordan, who—unbeknownst to her—has lost his memory as a result of a gunshot wound in the American Civil War. In our discussion of the ending, we reflect on the ways in which Atwood reworks the conventions of nineteenth-century crime fiction while subverting men's efforts to control and objectify women. At the same time, we consider how the novel helps us think through questions about the causes and consequences of criminality that remain of concern to this day.

NOTE

1. This essay cites the Doubleday edition of *Alias Grace*.

Race and Reproductive Rights in *The Handmaid's Tale*

Rebecca S. Dixon

Before they embark on the study of *The Handmaid's Tale* in a women's studies course, students should understand the historical treatment of Black women in the United States and the appropriation of their bodies. Margaret Atwood borrows from the experiences of enslaved Black women in creating the futuristic dystopia of the novel, as does the Hulu series I teach in tandem with the book, yet the surprising absence of references to race in these texts opens up opportunities to incorporate a vital historical perspective. Although I have elected to use the texts to teach my students about sexual and reproductive rights, I guide my students always with an awareness of the importance of race in these conversations about contemporary issues and their historical precedents.

Angela Davis reminds us that the enslaved Black body was used as an instrument in the pursuit of wealth (89). This was especially evident during the nineteenth century. With the cessation of the British trade in enslaved people after Britain outlawed such trade in 1807, US slaveholders attempted a feat that other societies had yet to accomplish. They would increase their enslaved population through reproduction alone. The tremendous economic opportunities of cotton cultivation motivated slaveholders to seek out what they may have felt was the only viable means to continue to generate wealth (White 183; West 57). That American slaveholders were able to achieve their goal of maintaining and reproducing slaves is astonishing considering the problems of reproduction in the nineteenth century (Kolchin 39), a period of high infant and maternal mortality (Morgan 111). Reduced to her fecundity, the enslaved Black woman was dehumanized. Her pain, her suffering, and even her needs and desires were summarily ignored. The enslaved female body was a means to an end (Davis 96). This insensitivity to the pain and feelings of Black women continued beyond slavery.

After the abolition of slavery in the United States, Black women's bodies were commercialized for use in advertising and used as markers of white privilege. In addition to serving as domestics in wealthy Southern homes, Black women were featured in advertising for domestic products that evoked nostalgia for the days before emancipation, perpetuating the ideas that the labor Black women endured under slavery would continue, that the wealth and mythologized lifestyle of the white Southern planter class would live on, and that Black women, not white women or men, would have to do the work (McElya 7).

In addition to being commercialized, the Black woman's body was also and continues to be fetishized as source of sexual pleasure and objectification in Western society (Gilman 228). This is readily seen in the sexual abuse Black women incurred as domestics and the featuring of Black women artists in the entertainment industry (Litwack 124). In addition, because the Black woman has been seen as impervious to pain and easily expendable, her body has been a site of so-called scientific experimentation. Today, Black women's bodies continue to be contested spaces, as Sasha Turner discusses in *Contested Bodies*. Their pain when presenting for medical conditions is often overlooked, and in the media, they often are a source of ridicule or omission.

The goals of white slaveholders during the nineteenth century are the goals of the white men who govern Gilead in *The Handmaid's Tale*. The Handmaids' bodies are used as instruments to enrich the society, just as Black women's bodies were used. The children borne by the Handmaids are taken from them just as the children of enslaved Black women were taken from them for their masters' purposes. Other Black women had their children taken from them in the sense that they had to watch, unable to intercede, as adult responsibility and punishments were imposed on those children at an early age. The rights of Black women to own themselves and define their destinies were taken from them just as the rights of the Handmaids to make choices about their sexuality and reproduction were taken from them. In both cases, women's lives are defined by imposed sexuality and reproduction. While the similarities are clearly evident, Atwood virtually ignores race in her novel, and racism is not a major focus in the televised series.

This essay examines using *The Handmaid's Tale* as a tool for teaching contemporary issues within women's studies. Specifically, I examine the potential lessons gleaned by examining the intersections of women's identity, reproductive rights, and race. Initially, the novel and series appear ideal for the exploration of issues of reproductive rights. Both texts outline the major obstacles women have faced with respect to agency, especially regarding their lifestyles. The texts emphasize a lesson that I have imparted repeatedly to my students at Tennessee State University, which is a historically Black college or university (HBCU): Women must have autonomy over their sexuality and reproduction in order to have positive control over their life chances. However, when the issue of race arises in discussing the novel, my students, the majority of whom are of African descent, find a surprising absence of references to race in the text. That opens up opportunities for me to share other lessons. In teaching the novel and the series, in class discussions about gender, race, and reproductive rights, I have emphasized three additional lessons: what appears to be raceless is generally not; African American women, and other women of color, must take a decidedly educated and determined stance in approaching health care; and the government has a vested interest in controlling women's fertility and lifestyles.

Racelessness and the Importance of Race

In the opening scenes of episode 1 of *The Handmaid's Tale* series, the viewer witnesses an interracial couple with a mixed-race child fleeing from some undefined fate ("Offred" 00:00:00–04:45). This casting choice is an ironic twist given that the novel on which the series is based openly proclaims Gilead to be a white supremacist society, except perhaps for the "brown" Marthas (Atwood, *Handmaid's Tale* 9).[1] Although even in the 1980s, projections on race revealed that blackness and brownness would become more prevalent in society, not less, *The Handmaid's Tale* joined a wide range of media released post-1970—including blockbuster movies like *Star Wars*, *The Terminator*, and *Alien*—that project a future characterized by the dominant presence of white people. *Mad Max* did feature at least one Black character, portrayed by Tina Turner. Yet the US Census Bureau was gathering information on demographics that showed significant population shifts and evidence that suggested the near future would bring noticeable declines in what is understood to be the white population in the United States (N. Jones). The reporting showed that immigration patterns would play a significant role in the composition of America. Also at issue was fertility: white fertility, the rate at which children were being produced, was declining (on fertility trends tracked by racial and ethnic group, see Sandefur et al. 63–65). In presenting a whitewashed future, these productions point to an obvious question: Where are the Black people?

Atwood's novel explains the absence of Black people by stating that the "Children of Ham" have been sent to "National Homeland One" (83). The designation "Children of Ham" is an archaic, disparaging reference that suggests Black people are destined for oppression and suffering by aligning them with the figure of Ham, cursed by his father, Noah, in the Bible (Gen. 9.22–27). Jewish people are singled out in the novel as well. The Gileadans call them "Sons of Jacob," affirming in that Jacob is blessed by God (Gen. 35.11–12), but require them to either emigrate to Israel or convert to the specific Protestant form of Christianity enforced by the state (200–01). There are few other references to race, but the suggestion is that all the people of Gilead are white. Non-white characters are foreigners or visitors, such as the Japanese tourists that the Handmaids encounter (27).

While some audiences in 1985 might not have expected a direct acknowledgement of racial issues, those watching a TV series released in 2017 that opens with a scene depicting an interracial family expect some discussion about race. In Gilead there appear to be both Black and white people, but the racial differences are not acknowledged. Ironically, society seems to have progressed to a point where race is not a factor but survival in any form is. One exception occurs in season 3, episode 8, when Aunt Lydia tells a Black Handmaid that the Aunts are having problems placing her ("Unfit" 00:23:46). This is an opportunity for class discussion. Students should consider the problem that Black female presence poses in a white home and, in particular, the problem of producing a biracial child in a white society. This is an opportunity to explore the historical use of Black female bodies for reproduction and productivity and also how race is understood and defined in the United States.[2] Another important discussion to have here is about the history of Black female presence in white homes, about why African American domestics were favored in the past and how or why that might change.[3]

The first and second seasons of the *Handmaid's Tale* series relied on evolved understandings of sexuality and gender, highlighting restrictions imposed from an earlier and more oppressive period. This acknowledgment regarding sexuality and gender contrasts with the lack of recognition of racial difference. The story line proceeds, for the most part, as if race does not exist. Scholars such as Ellen E. Jones have addressed this. In the novel, the story belongs to June.[4] She is the narrator, and it is from her perspective that the reader learns about Gilead and the new world order. Given the social order described above, all the characters may be assumed to be white, with few exceptions. In the series, June, Aunt Lydia, Fred, and Serena form the central basis of the narrative, and the other characters' stories are told in relationship to them. Moreover, the Black characters in the series do not represent current racial attitudes or seem to have common experiences of racist hostility. Cultural attitudes and cultural dispositions are not truly acknowledged, meaning the Black characters may express themselves in ways that are racially and culturally specific, such as with hair or dress, but these expressions are neither seen as relevant to their characters nor are they explicitly discussed as signifiers of racial identity.

There is one element of the series story line in which race is significant, but its meaning is not fully realized: the origins of June's relationship with her husband, Luke. Luke, an African American man married to an African American woman, chooses to leave his wife for a white woman. Luke and June's relationship appears to be all-consuming and passionate. June ignores Luke's sexism, though her friend Moira, also an African American woman, does not. June also ignores her much more liberal and radical mother's disdain for her wish to be a wife. Luke dismisses his Black wife, Annie, in a demonstrative fashion, demanding that the Black woman never speak to his current white love ("Other Women" 00:32:30–55). This scene portrays a horribly painful experience for African American women—colorism, or preference for a whiter skin—without acknowledging that pain or its racial and historical resonance.

In fact, the infidelity committed by Luke and June in the series is more of an issue, in that it marks June and determines her fate as a Handmaid, than the racial dynamics of their relationship, which is surprising given the historical taboos against miscegenation and prejudice against children born of interracial unions (Alpert 210–11). Although sexual exploitation and rape of enslaved Black women was prevalent in the United States during and after the enslavement period, the laws of the time penalized and criminalized sexual relationships and marriage between Black men and white women. From the earliest periods of racialized slavery, the laws in the American colonies indicated that such relationships were taboo and subject to penalty, more for the white woman than the Black man in some cases (Alpert 195). Hence, the decision to make Luke Black in the series but to ignore the racial implications of his marriage to June seems bizarre. In the classroom, interracial relationships and their implications are generally a topic of curiosity among students, who discuss the reasons these types of relationships exist in a society that continues to perpetuate racial and ethnic segregation. In the classroom we explore both in conversation and in research-based writing the nature of interracial intimate relationships and their implications, historically and currently.

Another example in the series in which race has the potential to play a significant role but is ignored is the story of Moira. Moira is June's former classmate and best friend; in the series, she is Black and lesbian. Moira's sexuality and her choice to be a surrogate are of issue, but her race and even her dark skin are ignored. In the classroom, however, we discuss the intersection of race and sexuality. Students explore the ways in which race and sexuality inform identity and agency in the United States. They are asked how being Black and lesbian today would affect a woman's reproduction and her rights to claim ownership over her body.

In teaching *The Handmaid's Tale*, the two examples of Annie and Moira underscore one of the primary lessons imparted to my students: racial identity is paramount in issues of sexuality and fertility. The degree to which African American women's experiences are dismissed or ignored is suggestive of a larger problem in health care and in recognition—socially, politically, and culturally—of Black women. The stories of Black women, like Annie, are forgotten or "darkened," and the spotlight is cast upon white women. Thus, what appears not to be an issue is the central issue. This is evident in our current reality regarding reproductive and women's rights, which has been compared of late to *The Handmaid's Tale*.

The recent ruling by the Supreme Court that undermined the 1972 *Roe v. Wade* decision and the subsequent state laws restricting women's rights to make decisions about their reproduction have been the subject of intense media coverage and enter into our class discussion. Comparisons to *The Handmaid's Tale* have been made by newspapers and by Atwood herself ("I Invented Gilead"). The restrictive laws prevent women from making a choice: many of them indicate that once a heartbeat is detected, abortion is out of the question, yet the heartbeat is one of the ways pregnancy is confirmed.[5] Also ironic is the fact that the states restricting women's access to abortion have not proposed funding to support women through pregnancies and with childcare costs.

It is not surprising that in a time in which Western countries are becoming less white (Moslimani and Passel; Saenz and Johnson; Sheehey), laws restricting termination of pregnancy and encouraging motherhood abound. If keeping communities whiter is the goal, the mechanisms put in place by the Supreme Court and the state laws will not achieve this end. Since women of color are disproportionately affected by restrictions on access to reproductive care (Sutton), the restrictions have the unintended potential to increase unwanted pregnancies and births among women of color. These policies can have a devastating impact on women of color, who already experience inequities in health care: they could suffer further, and so, too, could their children.

Controlling Life Chances and Self-Advocacy

The treatment of Black women by health-care providers often has been less than adequate, if not negligent (Borrow; "Racial and Ethnic Disparities"). Experimentation on Black women's bodies and race-based standards that ignore real health problems have been prevalent in modern health care, and it has been established that Black women have not received the same level of reproductive care as white women (J. Taylor et al.). In the classroom, students are asked to consider what accounts for the differences and to be conscious of disparities. In the past few years there has been increasing media awareness of the disparities in adequate health care between Black women and white women, making clear that what may seem like just cultural bias or oversight can and does have deadly consequences for Black women and other women of color. Maternal death and loss of pregnancies have been consequences of this type of medical neglect (J. Taylor et al.).

The Handmaid's Tale reminds us that Black people will be silenced, ignored, and imposed upon. Both the novel and the representation of Annie's experience point to a problem African American women must continually navigate: unlike other groups of people who have the expectation that their health care providers will advocate for them, African American women and other women of color must be vigilant and educated about their bodies and health care. In teaching *The Handmaid's Tale* in the context of treatment disparities, educators should heighten women's studies students' awareness of this unfair but necessary burden Black women face in advocating for their own health care.

In the classroom, our discussions highlight the understanding of the past and present implications of reproductive rights for women of color. African American women, in particular, have been imposed upon with racist standards, especially with regard to pain, which is "often undertreated in Black patients" (Martin and Montagne; see also Sabin; Snipe). Recent media attention to trends of overprescription and abuse of pain medications has further reduced Black women's access to proper pain care. Moreover, African American women must negotiate the imposition of negative stereotypes regarding their race and drugs, for Black women are often, despite demographic evidence to the contrary (McCabe et al.), treated as potential drug addicts (Daniels). Systematic studies of media consistently find a connection between representations of addiction and narratives about race, and people who are members of racial and ethnic minority groups are more often portrayed as addicts. Pain can be an indication of larger health issues that if left uncared for can result in other, more serious complications. Therefore, in teaching women's studies, the navigation of the health care landscape is key. For African American women, it is not just access to abortion but also access to intelligent and compassionate health care that is at stake. African American women especially must be educated advocates for their own care. Classroom discussions of the historical and current problems that are definitive aspects of African

American women's experiences are crucial for highlighting racial inequities not spelled out in the texts under discussion.

Government Intervention and Control

In ignoring race, Atwood's novel and the Hulu series bring a hyperawareness to the fertility struggles experienced in almost all Western and "white majority" nations (lower birth rates or declines in fertility have been recorded primarily in Western countries, with few exceptions [Nargund 191; Clark; Santos and Easton]). What is driving the decline in white fertility is not clear (Frey). What is clear is that the governments, including the US government, have attempted to promote and even to impose fertility through policy. As an example of promoting fertility, Nordic countries have well-established policies that promote reproduction and provide support to both parents with maternity and paternity leave ("Modern Daddy"). Along these lines, in recent years, "the European Parliament approved a directive requiring member states to ensure at least two months of earmarked paternity leave" (Canaan et al.). Opting to take the path of imposing fertility, the US government has passed key legislation attempting to restrict and guide lifestyle choices for women. Of primary concern for this essay is the promotion of marriage.

Legislation such as the Defense of Marriage Act of 1996 and the Healthy Marriages and Responsible Fatherhood Act, proposed in 2004, was aimed at ending poverty through marriage (Lane et al. 405). This approach assumed that single-parent households were the key culprits in poverty and that the solution was marriage. The US government did not attempt solutions that might aid parents in raising household income, such as requiring states or employers to provide or fund day care. It did not seek to address major disparities in pay between men and women, even those who had the same level of education. It did not seek to promote education and training of women in higher-paying industries. It did not attempt to look at the discriminatory practices of industries toward women who have children or who have the potential to have children. Instead, those in power advanced the notion of solving the economic struggle of women with children by making them dependent on men. Women's abilities to shape their own personal lives and choose their lifestyles were not primary considerations. As pointed out by Lane and colleagues in their article "Marriage Promotion and Missing Men: African American Women in a Demographic Double Bind," policymakers have insinuated that women who do not marry are somehow defiant and choosing to be impoverished (406). In class, we consider what is at stake in claiming to help women by making them financially subordinate to their husbands and discuss how this affects the problems of generational poverty.

The Handmaid's Tale underscores and dramatizes the problems of promoting women's subordination to men as a solution to population growth, poverty, or any other societal problem. In season 1, episode 3, June and Moira discover that their bank accounts have been removed from their control and placed under the supervision of their closest male relative ("Late" 00:22:20–25:32). This parallels older laws that restricted women's economic independence, but it also is reflective of the same reductive and misogynistic attitudes that informed marriage promotion as a means of decreasing poverty rates. Atwood's work highlights this issue as one of which women must be cognizant. Too often, students express in discussion the confidence that they are making choices, especially about their bodies and economic choices, without imposition. In discussing this episode, students come to recognize that the relationship between reproductive choices and economic stability is affected by government policy. The interference depicted in Atwood's novel sheds light on present reality.

As students consider how the declines in birth rates might affect their life choices, *The Handmaid's Tale* makes it clear that such declines, if extreme enough, can produce radical and discriminatory behaviors. The prediction of white supremacy may not be a realistic goal, but it still may influence behavior. In a society that shows it values white lives more than Black ones, what are the consequences for Black women's sexual and reproductive rights and choices? Students must be aware of this issue and arm themselves with information not only in approaching health care but also when considering the decisions they make about their sexuality and their reproductive choices.

The decision not to consider race, and its importance to issues of gender, sexuality, and reproduction, in these popular texts is troubling but also provides opportunities for important real-world discussions. Atwood's novel reminds readers of the extreme imposition of heterosexist lifestyle, gendered binaries, and the normalizing of misogyny that can have oppressive and dire consequences for all women and for people with nontraditional gender identities. I caution my students that they must confront in real life the problems compounded by the intersection of racist and misogynistic practices. In teaching *The Handmaid's Tale* in the women's studies classroom, I advise that instructors acknowledge both the strengths of the novel, in terms of its stark depictions of issues regarding sexual and reproductive rights, and its weaknesses, in ignoring the complications presented by race in exploring women's rights—all of which makes for rich and thought-provoking discussion. These class conversations empower students with information that can help them navigate the convergence of racial and sexist oppression.

NOTES

1. This essay cites the 1998 Anchor edition of *The Handmaid's Tale*.
2. See, for example, Skloot; Gilman 223–61.
3. Rebecca Sharpless states that prior to the 1940s, African American women's primary opportunity for employment was domestic work (179). Studies of Black women domestics argue that the African American woman servant was thought of in nostalgic

terms as a means for white employers, particularly in the South, to reimage and act out their reimaging of the enslavement period, when they could openly proclaim themselves superior (G. Hall 125; McElya 3). Accounts by former African American women domestics describe an abusive and rigid work environment (185–87).

4. Atwood has commented that although she did not assign this character a name in the novel, "[s]ome have deduced that Offred's real name is June, since, of all the names whispered among the Handmaids in the gymnasium/dormitory, 'June' is the only one that never appears again. That was not my original thought but it fits, so readers are welcome to it if they wish" (Atwood, *Handmaid's Tale* xv).

5. Researchers have challenged the language of the "Texas Heartbeat Act" and other such laws as "contested and misleading. Medical and reproductive health experts argue that referring to a 'heartbeat' is medically inaccurate, as the embryo does not have a developed heart" at the earliest stage at which the laws apply (Haining et al.).

Teaching *The Blind Assassin* as a Representative Atwood Novel

Theodore F. Sheckels

This essay addresses a very real question for those who wish to teach Margaret Atwood's work. Rare is the case where an instructor can "teach Margaret Atwood," as in a seminar that surveys her work in multiple genres. More often, one is tasked with selecting one representative work for a survey or topics course, perhaps a course in Canadian writing, women's literature, or contemporary fiction. So, in most cases, the question is, Which work by Atwood do I choose?

Some instructors may be somewhat constrained in answering this question by the nature of the course. In the course focused on speculative or, more narrowly, dystopian fiction, then the choices are limited. The same might be true of a course focused on writing by women or environmental writing. In this essay, however, I am making three assumptions: first, that the course is sufficiently general—as on a topic like contemporary or Canadian literature—to allow for breadth of choice; second, that the goal in teaching a single Atwood text is to offer the reader a sense of what the author typically does in terms of genre, style, narratology, and theme; and, third, that the novel is the genre upon which Atwood's reputation rests.

An instructor can, of course, choose their favorite Atwood novel or select by length if that is a concern. However, in theory, if an instructor is offering students what might be their one exposure to an author, that instructor should try to choose a text that is typical as well as acclaimed. One should not, in Atwood's case, want students to think she is "just" a speculative fiction writer or a social commentator or an expert on women's perspectives. One should want students to grasp her range of work.

I will answer the question of which novel to teach, eventually, by arguing that *The Blind Assassin* is the best choice. But first I want to assess other possibilities, however briefly. Preliminary to that is the tricky question of the Atwood canon. What is included? Or, rather, what is excluded? I am excluding two works in which Atwood updates a classic, *The Penelopiad* and *Hag-Seed*, since as adaptations they are special projects outside the Atwood mainstream. The same is true for *The Heart Goes Last*, which began as a short piece written for a sci-fi website. Atwood, in response to users' requests, added to it, creating the short novel. Despite the appeal of its alternately ominous and hilarious predictions, including widespread organ harvesting and the development of sex robots resembling Elvis Presley or Marilyn Monroe, the book is another "side project." With those works excluded, we have fourteen novels, beginning with *The Edible Woman*.

The Rejected Candidates

The Edible Woman, Atwood's first, is reflective of its time and reads as dated half a century later. It is also narratologically weak, and its symbolism and shifts in narrative perspective can be confusing. *Surfacing* handles narratology better, but the unreliable narrator baffles some students. In addition, the novel's ending is both puzzling—due to a flood of symbolism (Christ; S. Grace, "In Search of Demeter"; Guedon; Murray, "For the Love of a Fish")—and not especially satisfying. Yet the novel is beautifully written and treats themes, such as gender-based oppression and environmental degradation, that will dominate Atwood's canon. With brevity also in its favor, *Surfacing* can work as a backup selection.

Lady Oracle is comic but rather diffuse and, like its predecessors, ends weakly. Students may not pick up on the way Atwood plays with the gothic tradition, a key dimension. Atwood's fourth, *Life before Man*, has long been most readers' and critics' least favorite. The characters live dreary lives and exhibit few positive traits, and not much happens in the plot (Beran; Greene). Also, Atwood's experimenting with form, bouncing among characters and times, seems without a clear rationale.

Bodily Harm offers action but features a central character that some have indicted for insensitivity to imperialist oppression of "silenced populations" (Marantz; see also Drichel; Tiffin). Others have cited Rennie's growth (Brydon; Pundir; Rubenstein), but the debate may detract from the novel's strong feminist message, one that is further developed in *The Handmaid's Tale*, Atwood's most famous novel decades after its publication thanks to the Hulu television adaptation and continuation. The book handles narratological matters well, offering a limited first-person narrator, a structure that moves forward alternating interestingly between day chapters featuring action and night chapters featuring reflection (Templin), and commentary on forms of gender-related oppression.

The Handmaid's Tale, then, may be many instructors' choice. The one limitation is that it is speculative fiction, and students reading it, with no familiarity with the novels that preceded it, may label Atwood a "sci-fi" writer without understanding that she is that and more. *Cat's Eye* surprised many who had pigeonholed Atwood. Both it and *The Robber Bride* return to twentieth-century Toronto (a setting used in *The Edible Woman*, *Lady Oracle*, and *Bodily Harm*). Both also focus less on how the patriarchy oppresses women than on how women oppress women (Tolan, "Sucking"; Zimmerman). The books offer a valuable counterpoint to *Bodily Harm* and *The Handmaid's Tale* but do represent a departure from Atwood's usual feminist ideology, apparent in most of her works although more prominent in some than in others.

Those anticipating futuristic fiction from Atwood were probably still more surprised by the extensively researched historical novel *Alias Grace* (see Atwood, *In Search of* Alias Grace). Fascinated by the infamous mid-nineteenth-century murderess Grace Marks (so much that she penned a CBC teleplay, *The Servant Girl*), Atwood offers us a fictitious version of Grace's account, introducing the troubled character of Dr. Simon Jordan as her investigator and having Grace fill in the crucial blanks in her recollection while being supposedly hypnotized by a quack whom she knows to be a quack (Brindle 91–117; Couturier-Storey and Storey; Darroch; L. Hall; Mannon; O'Neill; Rose; Siddall; Van Rys). Despite the narrative and historical riches that make this novel fascinating, the book is a departure from the rest of the Atwood canon, which typically uses a present or future scene

With *Oryx and Crake*, Atwood returns to speculative fiction, offering a book very different from *The Handmaid's Tale*. Against the backdrop of global warming, readers see what evil corporations—as well as a mad scientist—have done in what reads as the near future. Another view of the evil is presented in the parallel *Year of the Flood*, and *MaddAddam* goes beyond the apocalypse of these two books for the story of the world's few survivors. The three books are full of what Atwood sees as dangerous in present-day society, and they supplement (not supplant) greatly the feminist message that dominates most of her earlier work. The trilogy, however, does position Atwood as primarily a dystopian novelist. In addition, it is difficult to appreciate Atwood's message without reading all three books.

The Testaments poses a similar problem: it cannot be fully appreciated without having read *The Handmaid's Tale*. The book is very much a sequel, offering more information about the tyranny of Gilead, a surprise heroine in Aunt Lydia (T. Johnson), and an action-adventure story involving the Handmaid Offred's two daughters, but these elements fail to resonate if readers lack background. Further, the action-adventure story—not a common Atwood plot—is overly melodramatic and rather stereotypical.

The Blind Assassin

The novel not yet discussed is the one that I would argue best introduces students to Atwood's work. This Booker Prize–winning novel exhibits many traits of Atwood's fiction, discusses many of the issues she raises elsewhere, and offers students several avenues of engagement.

Narrative Perspective

From the beginning, Atwood has experimented with perspective. *The Edible Woman* moves from first person to third person, then back to first person, and *Surfacing* offers an unreliable first-person narrator who lies to others and to herself. Atwood, in general, seems to gravitate sometimes to third-person narration and sometimes to first, usually offering twists on each. In *The Blind Assassin*, the narrator is the octogenarian Iris Chase Griffen. She is writing the book we read, which is her history, slowly but surely, so her granddaughter Sabrina might eventually read it and know the truth. Iris is in failing health, and readers may wonder whether she recalls accurately what happened when she was a young woman (Filtness; Gilbert). Her account seems reliable but also motivated by revenge and perhaps colored by the desire for it (Bouson, "Commemoration"; Hyttinen; Ku; Ridout; Stein). What worries readers more than the account's reliability is whether Iris will complete it before passing away.

Iris, however, is not the only narrator. Interleaved with her story are invented newspaper clippings, excerpts from a novel (also called *The Blind Assassin*) understood to have been written by Laura, and tales in the voice of Iris's lover Alex Thomas, who tells sci-fi stories to her during their trysts in parks and rented rooms scattered around Toronto.

Genre

Although a memoir characterized by formal realism, *The Blind Assassin* is also a historical novel describing life in the 1930s in the fictitious factory town of Port Ticonderoga and the growing city of Toronto. The novel also contains speculative fiction. Alex spins a few examples, the most prominent being the story of Sakiel-Norn, with its carpet weavers turned blind assassins and its sacrificial virgins. The novel situates readers in the Ontario of 2000, when Iris is writing, but the novel is also historical and speculative. Being so generically diverse, the novel allows the instructor to point to the different genres Atwood's canon contains.

Structure

After publishing her first few novels, Atwood abandons linearity in favor of a pattern that has her looping back and forth among stories, finally completing them. Sometimes, nondiscursive elements, such as Elaine Risley's paintings in *Cat's Eye* (Howells, "*Cat's Eye*") and quilt patterns in *Alias Grace*, help the pieces of a story cohere (Delord; Michael; Murray, "Historical Figures"; Rogerson; Szalay; Wilson, "Quilting"). Sometimes, the looping relies on a strong narrative presence, such as Iris's.

In *The Blind Assassin*, Iris reports on her day-to-day reality, visiting a doughnut shop and commenting on the restroom graffiti, before revisiting moments from the past, revealing crucial information piecemeal. For example, readers are primed to believe that the young woman whose affair is described in the novel interleaved with Iris's memoir is Laura Chase. We do not know until close to the novel's end that the young woman was Iris. We also do not know that Iris wrote the scandalous novel that made Laura famous—and embarrassed Richard and his sister, Winifred Griffen Prior. We think for a long time that after Laura's suicide Iris simply published what her younger sister had written. We know from the beginning that Laura drove off a bridge, but we don't find out what prompted the suicide until much later. And even then, there is doubt. Discussing the structure of *The Blind Assassin* is an excellent introduction to

Atwood's technique of seeming to swirl through time, laying down pieces of a plot that come together by the end of a work.

Details

The Blind Assassin is also exemplary of Atwood's attention to detail, particularly when it comes to clothing (Kuhn) and places. Exact details are appreciated by readers: they assist in visualizing characters and events and convey a sense of reality. In *The Blind Assassin*, details such as clothing styles and geographic features, including Toronto locations, are correct for the times depicted. In this and several of Atwood's other novels, readers can put the characters onto a map and trace their routes around the city, as in *Life before Man* (Sheckels and Sweeney).

Atwood is especially precise about hotels and eateries. Establishments are named and located to send status signals legible to Torontonians but also to a broader readership. In *The Edible Woman*, Peter takes Marian out for drinks at the Park Plaza, a posh hotel up University Avenue Road north of Queen's Park (66); in *Life before Man*, Nate lunches with Lesje at the Varsity Restaurant, a greasy luncheonette on Bloor near the university (62); and in *The Robber Bride*, the three narrators lunch at a trendy place called Toxique on Queen Street West (26). We see this same suggestive specificity in *The Blind Assassin*: Iris is taken to lunch by the grooming Winifred at the Arcadian Court, "where the ladies lunched, up at the top of Simpsons department store, on Queen Street" (230); decades later, after driving an elderly Iris into Toronto, her friend's husband tries to take her to a barbecue place he remembers; since it has closed, he looks for one like it on or near King Street as it heads west (293–95). Where Winifred takes Iris tells us much about Winifred and Richard's habits and class pretensions, and where Walter takes Iris communicates his unassuming and working-class sensibilities.

Readers who know Toronto can follow the characters around the city, identifying not just places to eat but also structures, parks, and neighborhoods. They envision Toronto punctuated by ravines, for the city's ravines appear in book after book in Atwood's oeuvre (Cowdy; Porter-Ladousse). In *The Blind Assassin*, Laura drives off a bridge into one (1–3). In this work as well as other Atwood novels, a class could discuss how the ravines function in Toronto life and in the minds of the city's residents as represented by Atwood's characters, especially her female ones, for they time and again seem threatened by them.

Like these elements of landscape, assorted details in Atwood's novel perform a symbolic function. They are dimensions of plot, but they resonate beyond their literal use. Peter's camera in *The Edible Woman*, the "lynched" heron in *Surfacing*, and the Scrabble game in *The Handmaid's Tale* (Andriano) are examples. So, in *The Blind Assassin*, we have the photograph taken at a Chase Button Factory workers' picnic of Alex Smith flanked by the Chase sisters. Both sisters retain a copy, but each cuts the other sister out, except for her hand. This photograph is not exactly a symbol, but it is an item that resonates with meaning as the novel progresses (Dvorak; Reed).

The Blind Assassin, then, shows how Atwood writes, both large narratological matters such as perspective and structure and smaller ones. The book is also a good example of her style—colloquial but eloquent, moving at a quick pace, offering but not dwelling on details, full of wit—usually a dry wit. The novel, then, introduces well what one might label her "style," but it also introduces her concerns as a writer and as a citizen.

Message about Women

Although critics discerned an ideology in even Atwood's earliest novels, she downplayed the political dimensions of her work, which became very prominent in *Bodily Harm* and *The Handmaid's* Tale (see Hengen). Elsewhere I have tracked the early emergence of a feminist stance in Atwood's works (Sheckels, *Margaret Atwood and Social Justice*, *The Political in Margaret Atwood's Fiction*). *The Handmaid's Tale* is undoubtedly the strongest statement Atwood makes about women's plight, but consider Marian in *The Edible Woman* stalked by her fiancé, Peter, with his gun-like camera; the unnamed narrator in *Surfacing* seduced and compelled to have an abortion by an older art teacher; and Rennie Wilford in *Bodily Harm* threatened by rape in both the Toronto she leaves and the Caribbean island she visits.

At eighteen, *The Blind Assassin*'s narrator marries the thirty-five-year-old Richard Griffen, thinking that by doing so she is saving the family business. Instead, Iris finds the business soon shut down and her body subjected to marital rape and beatings. Richard, who has acquired not only Iris as wife but her younger sister Laura as ward, blackmails Laura, threatening to turn the communist labor organizer Alex Thomas in to authorities unless she surrenders her body. Richard's predatory interest in teenagers is well-known to his equally power-hungry sister Winifred, who plays a role in grooming Iris. And Alex's sci-fi serial features sacrificial virgins, reinforcing the role Iris and Laura both play in the novel's main plot. Exploring the oppression of women in *The Blind Assassin* permits the instructor to suggest how Atwood shows that oppression in other contexts, such as in *The Handmaid's Tale* and *The Testaments*.

Message about Those in Control

Another major Atwood concern is with those who control oppressive systems. In *Surfacing* and in *Bodily Harm*, it may be difficult to determine who is in control. In *The Handmaid's Tale*, however, it is clear that a patriarchal government has twisted the words of the Bible to deny women—all women—rights. Later in her career, Atwood shifts from blaming what government might become to blaming global corporations that seem to have taken over the task of governing. We see that in the three MaddAddam books and, comically, in *The Heart Goes Last.*

In *The Blind Assassin*, Richard Griffen aspires to a position in government, but he already has the power of his increasing wealth. Readers are introduced to Richard as the head of a manufacturing firm and watch as he takes over smaller businesses, like Chase and Sons, throwing workers who had been well taken care of out of jobs. In anticipation of World War II, imagined as a European conflict in which all parties (including Hitler's Germany) would have needs an enterprising Canadian business could meet, Richard secures German supply contracts. Whether his profiteering was legal or not is beside the point. As Atwood presents it, it is yet another example of how Richard and those like him pursue economic advantage regardless of who may be hurt. It is an easy transition from Richard's dealings to the corporations depicted in the MaddAddam trilogy, which control free expression in the compounds, where the privileged live; burgers, coffee, and sex in the pleeblands, where the less privileged reside; and pharmaceuticals globally.

Teaching Atwood

Choosing a single novel by Margaret Atwood to teach is a problem with two dimensions. The first has been the focus of this essay so far: picking a text that represents well all that Atwood does in her fiction. Doing so is difficult because Atwood's books are very different from one another: she is not an author who finds a successful formula and then repeats. She has said she thinks of characters or the core of a plot and then writes, the book becoming what it becomes—with a great deal of research along the way. Characters change as she writes, and a book's form emerges (Atwood, "Tightrope-Walking").

Given the variety that characterizes the Atwood canon, one probably wants, in picking a text, to avoid books that seem to be outliers. One might, then, arrive at the Booker Award–winning *The Blind Assassin* almost by process of elimination. However, one can arrive at the same choice if one asks first what is typical of Atwood and then what book exhibits these traits. *The Blind Assassin* is typical insofar as it plays with perspective; mixes genres; moves back and forth in time to piece together a narrative; attends to details, especially those concerning costuming and urban places; refers and refers again to items that, like symbols, resonate with growing significance throughout the text; and presents typical themes such as the oppression of women and the abuse of power by either government or business. So an instructor would be well positioned to depart occasionally from the text at hand to inform students of other Atwood works where they might encounter a particular theme or technique.

The other question concerns what one might call "teachability," asking what book would hold the attention of students as readers and discussants. There is no doubt that the speculative novels may have the edge here: students enjoy seeing what might happen in their world and pondering whether the events depicted could really occur. Conversely, historical fiction might seem to be at a disadvantage, as well as fiction that seems targeted to female readers. College students may be too quick to label historical fiction as boring, and some who label novels dealing with the oppression of women as "feminist" or "women's writing" are reluctant to engage with them. Atwood broadens her focus, thereby combating these unfortunate negative reactions. *The Blind Assassin*, although largely set back in time, does not read like a historical novel, and, although the story of the Chase sisters is central, it is not the only story of oppression in the book. Whether in Depression-era Ontario or on the planet of Sakiel-Norn in Alex Thomas's sci-fi serial, the economically disadvantaged and their would-be champions are oppressed, persecuted, and even enslaved. In addition, books have appeal if they raise current issues, and the relevance of Atwood's characters' plight today is clear. Have corporations lost power in the years following World War II? Are men like Richard Griffen, who lust after power and young girls, gone from the scene? Are the women who groom young girls for them? Are the rich no longer getting richer and the poor getting poorer? The issues in *The Blind Assassin* are not relics of the past; just follow the news. One last appeal is made by books that present a mystery. Atwood could have structured *The Blind Assassin* linearly. If she had, readers would know everything along the way, but Atwood's nonlinear structure keeps readers guessing. Who is Alex Thomas's lover? Will the sacrificial virgin and her rescuing blind weaver escape? Will Iris and her estranged granddaughter, Sabrina, be reconciled? Readers do not receive answers to all questions that arise, but there is enough suspense to hook readers until much is resolved.

I have argued that *The Blind Assassin* is the best choice if one must teach a single Atwood novel. Others might choose differently; what matters is not the choice I have made but what the choice does. It attempts to give students a sense of what, in general, Atwood does: what are her structures, her techniques, and her concerns. The goal, then, is to give students a work that, because it is representative, may motivate students to find other Atwood works.

Messages and Message-Bearers: Teaching Atwood's Fiction in the Creative Writing Workshop

Patrick Thomas Henry

In her essay "Flying Rabbits: Denizens of Distant Spaces," Margaret Atwood contends that texts broker a reader's passage into the terraformed expanses of an author's imagination. Through fiction, Atwood writes, "Something or someone moves from 'there' to 'here,' or we ourselves move from 'here' to 'there.' Portals, gateways, way stations, and vehicles abound, as in—come to think of it—ancient myths, with their cave entrances and chariots of fire" (23). As Atwood tells it, writers dispatch messages across these thresholds, assisted by the powerful technology of the text. In *Negotiating with the Dead: A Writer on Writing*, Atwood articulates this passage of information as a fluid relationship between writers, readers, and texts:

> Messengers always exist in a triangular situation, the one who sends the message, the message-bearer, . . . and the one who receives the message. Picture, therefore, a triangle, but not a complete triangle. . . . The writer and reader are two lateral corners, but there's no line joining them. Between them . . . is the written word. . . . This third point is the only point of contact between the other two. As I used to say to my writing students in the distant days when I had some, "Respect the page. It's all you've got." (125)

In the fiction workshop, this model challenges student writers to approach craft as an exchange between their rhetorical strategies, genre conventions and expectations, and the reader's capacity for interpretation. In other words, Atwood's messenger model compels student writers to couple their craft choices to the messages that their texts transmit to readers across the transom of space and time.

Atwood's messenger model shares a lineage with—but diverts from—a comparable theory with roots in the Iowa Writers Workshop. In his essay "The Writer's Workshop," Frank Conroy (who directed the Iowa Writers Workshop from 1987 to 2005) writes of the text as a "zone" where the writer's and the reader's energies converge (83–84). However, Conroy's model requires writers to winnow down their prose until they have "removed all excess language" and "distilled things to their essences" (85). As Eric Bennett suggests in the conclusion to his book *Workshops of Empire* (162–63), and as Mark McGurl's analysis of Raymond Carver's influence in *The Program Era* makes manifest (273–320), the Iowa model that produced Conroy's stern minimalism asserts a literary aesthetic that mirrors the ideology of a cis-het, white, male, working-class, and

American readership. In *Craft in the Real World*, Matthew Salesses contends that perspectives like Conroy's mistake craft—"a set of [readers'] expectations," as Salesses defines it (16)—for a set of immutable rules.

Atwood tacitly rejects Conroy's formulation in that her messenger model invites writers to manipulate readers' expectations and—if needed—trick them. Atwood therefore anticipates Salesses's belief that craft is a tool "to engage with how we know each other" (Salesses 30). To this end, Atwood cites the poet Gwendolyn MacEwan, who said that "poets are magicians without quick wrists" (qtd. in *Negotiating* 111). Extrapolating from MacEwan, Atwood concludes that writers conjure "illusions that can convince people of their truth" (111, 113). When Atwood tells writers to "respect the page," she means that our "illusions" are the only means of communicating with readers. Not unlike the Grail knight at the end of *Indiana Jones and the Last Crusade* (1:49:50–1:51:16), then, Atwood exhorts writers to make their choices on the page wisely—and patiently.

Young writers often feel that they must obey the "rules" of craft instead of boldly following their judgment. Atwood's messenger model is especially powerful in the creative writing workshop because it prompts students to reject this mindset and center their role in transmitting messages through fiction. Teaching Atwood's fiction and her messenger model activates a process-based pedagogy for undergraduate and graduate students alike, which empowers student writers to stake their own identity as creators and cultivate their own writing strategies.

The Message-Sender: Atwood's Public Persona

A process-based approach to creative writing pedagogy centers the student writer—"the one who sends the message," to lift Atwood's phrase. I therefore begin lessons on Atwood's fiction by introducing students to Atwood as message sender. Atwood brands herself as a generalist with a penchant for tornadic thoughts who remains certain of her creative and critical agenda. In an early example of this self-presentation she writes, "I am not a professional academic, and my collecting and categorizing of monsters must be ascribed to an amateur, perverse and private eccentricity, like that of, say, a Victorian collector of ferns" ("Canadian Monsters" 229). She performs a similar sleight of hand in *Strange Things* by elevating her knowledge of Canada's folklore to an equal footing with the literary traditions known to a British audience steeped in "everything about Beowulf and Virginia Woolf and even Thomas Wolf" (2). Atwood even uses her occasionally folksy, down-to-earth persona to contend that fictional narratives are couriers of truths and to pan the manipulative rhetoric of politicians who "concoct plausible whoppers" (*In Search* 1). Fiction, she insinuates in this lecture, produces a higher-caliber truth.

In these instances and others, Atwood's self-appraisal resonates with Elaine Showalter's description of a teaching persona: "an exaggeration or an evasion of our private self," one that embodies a "literary theory . . . consistent with [the individual's] teaching theory and practice" (38, 39). Atwood's public persona sprouts from precisely the kind of sincerity that Showalter points to. Specifically, Atwood's public persona extends from her lived experience, one that straddles the divides between academia and popular culture, between Canada and the United States, and between rural and urban settings—to name only a few. In *The Red Shoes*, Rosemary Sullivan gestures to Atwood's graduate-student years at Radcliffe and Harvard as part of this origin story; Atwood had to resist both Ivy League misogyny and her displacement as a Canadian in the United States (118–25). First-generation students, women students, and queer students particularly identify with Atwood's assessment of the power dynamics at play in academia, while many students from rural areas (including the northern plains of North Dakota, Minnesota, and Manitoba) recognize themselves in the urban-rural or Canadian-American divides in Atwood's biography.

Prior to classes on Atwood's fiction, I prepare a handout of excerpts from the lectures and essays collected in books like *In Other Worlds*, *Negotiating with the Dead*, and *Strange Things*, which document several instances in which Atwood positions herself as a writer. This enables us to discuss Atwood's authorial persona as a message-sender. To complement this, I often ask students to draft an artist statement that articulates their own relationship with the institutions and environments in which they're writing. For advanced undergraduates and graduate students interested in teaching, this task facilitates a dialogue about their teaching persona. In either case, this artist statement activity empowers students to claim agency over their creative and academic experience in higher education.

The Messenger Model and Plot: Teaching "Happy Endings"

Foregrounding the author's role as the message-sender invites student writers to seek out strategies for leveraging rudimentary elements of fiction, like structure and plot. Such strategies are in evidence particularly in Atwood's short fiction, which engages in wordplay, subterfuge, and misdirection. Kathryn VanSpanckeren has observed that many of Atwood's short poems, microfictions, and flash fictions operate as "trickster texts," short pieces that "are almost wholly a trick—usually a trap—and . . . primarily concern the communication process" (77). In the introductory undergraduate workshop, I facilitate a discussion of craft as authorial strategy by assigning one of these "trickster texts"—the widely anthologized "Happy Endings"—alongside the fifth chapter of *Negotiating with the Dead*, which opens with Atwood's discussion of the messenger model. "Happy Endings" serves our purposes especially well because it foregrounds plot, a bugbear even for seasoned writers. As Alexander Chee has opined, "[P]lot was disdained if it was ever discussed" in many workshops, possibly to avoid the "prescriptive" implications of Freytag's pyramid (204).

A class on Atwood's "Happy Endings" provides an opportunity to redress this frequent oversight while outfitting students with creative strategies. "Happy Endings" begins with a tercet that seems equal parts riddle and provocation: "John and Mary meet. / What happens next? / If you want a happy ending, try A" (50). This authorial directive broadcasts the story, its structure, and its "trick" to the reader: as a work of metafiction, the story demands that the reader participate in the act of selecting the plot and its resolution. At this stage in a class discussion, I'll draw the inverted *V* of Atwood's messenger model on the classroom whiteboard and label the crucial nodes—writer, text, and reader.

In small groups (for a longer class session) or as a class (for a shorter time slot), we annotate this diagram in response to several questions. First, how does the model allow us, the readers, to draw conclusions about the writer and their craft choices in "Happy Endings"? How do plot and structure function in this story? How might we describe this story and its sequences of events? Lastly, what expectations do we bring to this story? Through this activity, student writers implement and respond to their understanding of Atwood's authorial persona. Frequently, students remark that "Happy Endings" rejects the emphasis that the short story, as an academically studied and replicated form, imposes on characterization and narrative strategy. Building on this premise, students often contend that this formal move extends something they discovered in Atwood's biography—namely, Atwood's discontent with the rituals and prestige-jockeying of academe. This theme calls to mind the conference proceedings that comprise the "Historical Notes" in *The Handmaid's Tale* (297–311).[1] As a result, students can better understand the aesthetic and intellectual aims of Atwood's use of metafiction, whether that is in *Good Bones and Simple Murders*, *The Handmaid's Tale*, or in the blend of pulp novel, memoir, and historical fiction that constitutes *The Blind Assassin*.

Drawing further on *Negotiating with the Dead*, the student writers turn their attention to their complicity as readers and the story's form. Most students quickly recognize the story's iterative structure and its built-in retellings as a cousin to the similar narrative form utilized in gamebook series like Choose Your Own Adventure or Give Yourself Goosebumps. However, "Happy Endings" eschews the Choose Your Own Adventure matrix, which simply outsources the implementation of a linear plotline (complete with rising action, conflict, and resolution) to the reader's choices. Instead, the story contains six narrative summaries, each labeled with a letter from A to F. Like an anthology series in miniature, each section glosses a love story with a rotating cast of characters—John, Mary, James, Fred, and Madge—while crackling with Atwood's zest for humor. As Atwood states at the story's conclusion, each iteration of the John-and-Mary story ends with the same gesture—"*John and Mary die. John and Mary die. John and Mary die*" (56). This occurs regardless of the plot points and characters sampled in the stories—to name a few, an uneventful adulthood, an affair, a James Dean clone with a motorcycle and "some top-grade California hybrid," a tidal wave that ravages real estate values, or a counterbourgeois scenario where John is a "revolutionary" and Mary "a counterespionage agent" (54, 55).

"Happy Endings" dismisses plot as "just one thing after another, a what and a what and a what," before exhorting writers and readers alike to "try How and Why" (56). This challenge alerts students to Atwood's ultimate strategy in this work of metafiction. Rather than spin us a looping record about John and Mary and their ill-fated love, Atwood crafts a story about John and Mary's story. The story's frequent acts of redirection veer student writers to the discovery that plot and structure must center not the sequence of events but the relationships between characters. This is where authorial choice comes into play: the writer chooses which details and events deserve emphasis and why. As writers, then, students must ask not only what comes next but how they can most effectively sequence a story's events, why they are doing so, and what reaction they hope to provoke in the reader.

If class time permits, I incorporate one additional exercise, inspired by Jane Alison's craft book *Meander, Spiral, Explode: Design and Pattern in Narrative.* Even though we initially experience a story word by word, Alison contends, "Other movement takes place inside the content of the story: what happens, whether things happen chronologically or are tangled and must be unraveled, whether you move less through events than ideas, and so on" (27). To model this, our additional activity scrambles the synopses in "Happy Endings" so that students can tinker with other modes of movement that generate new tensions in the John and Mary stories. Before class, I select one of the blocks in "Happy Endings" and print each discrete event on a slip of paper. To introduce this activity, I present students with a claim that Atwood herself made in a conversation with Geoff Hancock: that in stories like "Happy Endings" she was concerned primarily with "having fun" and creating "a certain vibration" for the reader ("Tightrope-Walking" 211). Students usually perceive this as permission to have their own fun with Atwood's story. To conduct this activity, I use a randomized group generator to divide the class into small groups. Each group then receives an envelope or packet of preselected slips. I instruct the students to either shake the envelope or spill the slips face down onto the table and shuffle them. The students then draw one random snippet at a time, thereby creating a new structure for a story. Each group then conducts a thought experiment based on their randomized sequence. How might this new order shape the reader's experience? Would the writer be able to construct this story in a linear fashion, or would they need to incorporate flashbacks, flash-forwards, and section breaks? What opportunities and obstacles would this organization create for the writer?

This textual analysis and critical speculation, though, must develop toward a writing activity—especially in a workshop class. As C. Connor Syrewicz has argued, "[T]ext-centered instructors often hinder the efficacy of their instruction . . . by failing to address how this knowledge should be *used* as their students are writing" (5). As an antidote to this, Syrewicz suggests incorporating writing activities that provide students with precise (yet elastic) ways of applying creative strategies and tapping into their own store of "textual knowledge in particular ways throughout the writing process" (Syrewicz 6). In the context of a craft lesson on "Happy Endings," a flexible writing task would grant students choice and agency over the "how" and "why" of plot. To that end, I give students the following prompts:

> Select one of the John and Mary scenarios from "Happy Endings" and write a story that dramatizes that narrative summary.
>
> Think of your favorite genre of story. Brainstorm a list of familiar plot events from that genre. Then write your own riff on "Happy Endings" in which a narrator presents and comments on a sequence of narrative summaries.

After five to ten minutes of in-class writing, students pair off, share their works-in-progress, and discuss the choices they made on the page. In doing so, they must draw on Atwood's messenger model to explicate their formal choices and the desired effect in the reader. Rather than reinscribing plotting as cookie-cutter, mechanical labor, this exercise situates plot as a tool not unlike an adjustable crescent wrench—something student writers can ratchet or loosen as needed.

Messengers and Narrative Strategies: Atwood's Historical Fiction and Creative Research

Atwood's messenger model remains informative and empowering beyond the introductory and intermediate levels. For advanced undergraduate and graduate students alike, the messenger model scaffolds discussions of advanced narrative strategies that center a specific character's experiences, sensibility, and worldview. As Christopher Castellani notes in *The Art of Perspective*, point of view troubles many student writers, who fail to "understand how certain craft choices contribute to or diminish" the story's role as a communication medium (17). As Castellani observes, an engaging narrative strategy must represent the story's central characters: "It's the unique philosophy behind the construction of a work of fiction that applies to that work alone," Castellani writes, adding, "It's the type of narrator, limited by age and education and experience, speaking from a particular point in time" (17). This work is especially crucial for writers who wish to cross the threshold into some of the other worlds that Atwood has identified in essays like "Flying Rabbits"—the depths of space, alternate timelines, or history.

Here, the messenger model reinforces the ties between writer (as message-sender) and text (as message-bearer), by tasking advanced student writers with conducting creative research, explicating and refining their conceptual frameworks, and synthesizing research findings through their narrators. For the sake of this discussion, I will select only one of these fabulous and distant fictional realms identified by Atwood in her essays, in order to suggest some ways that instructors might facilitate student writers' discoveries of effective narrative strategies—Atwood's forays into historical fiction, which include *Alias Grace* and *The Blind Assassin*. Atwood's novels, essays, and talks highlight research as central to constructing a plausible iteration of the historical setting and the consciousness of the text's central characters. Teaching Atwood's *Alias Grace* alongside her lecture *In Search of* Alias Grace*: On Writing Canadian Historical Fiction* directs advanced undergraduate and graduate students to approach research as a creative activity.

The role of research is a touchy subject for many creative writers, but recent pivots in creative writing studies have demonstrated that archival work sparks the imaginative capacity of student writers, generates opportunities for self-reflection and metacognition, and reinforces nonlinear and process-based pedagogies. Dianne Donnelly has remarked that this combination of practice, discovery, and engagement mirrors the conceptual and theoretical work in other research disciplines (120–21). Brandi Reissenweber draws on neuroscience to demonstrate that research allows elements of story worlds to "incubate" and "branch out further, and dredge up more—and perhaps more disparate—possibilities for connection" (5). Reissenweber refers here to a neural networking of concepts, images, details, and factoids, but her analysis also suggests that this nonlinear process allows writers to absorb elements of style or narrative structure. A student writer saturated in Atwood's trickster texts may thereby channel their influence, intentionally or otherwise. The historical fiction writer Andrea Barrett concurs, on the generative potential of research: "As long as our research feeds what we're actually writing and is transformed by embodying it in story and scene, we may find a home for things that at first seem disparate, but actually aren't" (47).

Atwood infuses *Alias Grace* with many such "disparate" items through her judicious use of the historical record and its gaps. The novel's subject is the gruesome murder of the wealthy Thomas Kinnear and his housekeeper, Nancy Montgomery, in 1840s Ontario—a historic event that resonates with true crime, mystery, and police procedurals. *Alias Grace* troubles the popular theory that Kinnear's servant Grace Marks, coerced by her possible lover James McDermott, was an accessory to the murders of Kinnear and Montgomery. In her lecture on the novel, Atwood remarks that she returned from delving into the archive's murky depths with a discovery that the past is hardly objective. Period newspapers lionized or vilified Grace in line with their political agendas and attitudes toward the wealthy and the laboring classes (*In Search* 33–34). Even Atwood's initial inspiration to write on Grace Marks's alleged role in the murder, Susanna Moodie's 1853 memoir *Life in the Clearings*, contains faults: Moodie wrote from memory about a singular interview with Marks in a Toronto asylum, and this account brims with Moodie's own biased presumption that Canada's rural outposts were a savage wilderness, too far beyond the civilizing reach of the metropole (*Alias Grace* 464–65, *In Search* 33, *Strange Things* 96–97).[2] Because of these incongruities, Atwood concludes that the archive set some parameters for *Alias Grace*: "when there was a solid fact, I could not alter it . . ., but in the parts left unfilled—I was free to invent" (*In Search* 35).

Atwood's attitude on the archive resonates with the novelist Thomas Mallon's claim that historical fiction "is a work of inference, speculation, and outright invention" (357). For Atwood and Mallon alike, character and point of view control the reader's access to information and fabricate a simulacrum of a historical era. A. S. Byatt labels this technique "ventriloquism," as a writer imitates "vocabulary and habit of mind" to effect a linguistic resurrection of a character and an era (43). Here, again, history functions as both regulator and liberator: a writer practicing this maneuver will have to evade anachronisms and follow the historical record, but they otherwise have carte blanche for the character's interior life, their reactions, and their agendas.

In *Alias Grace*, Atwood effectively ventriloquizes Grace Marks, whose true identity was lost in the political jockeying of Canadian newspapers and the self-serving account in Susanna Moodie's memoir. In her afterword to *Alias Grace*, Atwood writes, "The true character of the historical Grace Marks remains an enigma" (465). Although Grace herself may be an enigma, she still existed in 1840s Ontario, meaning that in order to render Grace on the page Atwood had to channel the mannerisms and the rhetoric of her sources. Moreover, she had to ensure that Grace's sensibility mirrored readers' expectations of a young, nineteenth-century household servant. An instance halfway through the novel speaks to Atwood's deftness with ventriloquism. In one of her confessions to the psychiatrist Simon Jordan, Grace recounts the course of her duties: "I reached the privy and emptied the slop pail, and so forth" (216). When Simon presses Grace on the exact meaning of "so forth," she remains stoic and says nothing. Her narration takes over: "I look at him. Really if he does not know what you do in a privy there is no hope for him" (216). It is coy and sarcastic—Atwood at her most searing—but also chimes with the cadences of nineteenth-century diction. While the reader is treated to Grace's narration of using the privy, down to the "old copy of the Godey's Ladies' Book" used as toilet paper, none of this information gets conveyed to the psychiatrist (216). Atwood balances Grace's nineteenth-century propriety and the modern reader's craving for access to her psyche.

A robust reading list on historical fiction and craft stages heightened scrutiny of authorial strategies, like Atwood's construction of Grace Marks through and against the archive, for advanced undergraduate and graduate students. A workshop course on historical fiction might include Atwood's fiction, essays, and talks; novels by contemporaries like Mallon, Byatt, and Toni Morrison; and critical concepts like Byatt's ventriloquism and Castellani's analysis of narrative strategy.

However, Syrewicz's warning about text-based instruction remains true at the advanced level: students best synthesize these lessons through process-based activities. As with the undergraduate workshop, I provide students with a combination of text- and process-based assignments, which drive them to conduct research, ruminate on their findings, and incorporate those discoveries into works of fiction. Early in the semester, students complete several in-class writing prompts and brainstorming exercises modeled after Kelly Link's advice to use list-making and data-gathering as tools to stimulate the imagination. Throughout the semester, students will update these lists as their creative obsessions and potential research topics evolve, conducting ongoing research in library sources, digital collections of period-specific artifacts, and (in some instances) special collections holdings at our university library. I encourage students to track their creative archive using multimedia tools: voice memos, commonplace books, *Pinterest* boards, *Google Jamboards*, and so on. Students further analyze their archives through in-class presentations and craft essays in which they articulate the intersections of their research methods and their creative practice. In effect, these assignments scaffold research methods, "incubation" (as Reissenweber puts it), and metacognitive self-analyses into the creative process.

Students then apply these findings through Atwood's dictum from *Negotiating with the Dead*: "respect the page." Here, "respecting the page" means developing a narrative strategy that channels their research through, to borrow Byatt's term, literary ventriloquism. That is, students filter their research findings through point of view, narration, and characterization. By thinking of fiction as a medium that communicates narrative, historical data, sensory information, and more, students must craft their stories in line with any rules established through their archival research process—like Atwood's own realization that she could not alter documented historical events. (Obviously, students writing speculative history will have license to bend that expectation.) With these guidelines in place, students will spend the semester drafting a single piece of writing, with frequent opportunities to initiate dialogue with their readers through in-class workshops and conferences with me. In each of these forums, I foreground Atwood's messenger model by allowing the author to voice their intentions and actively engage with readers' comments, questions, and suggestions.

Here I have addressed strategies for teaching only a few of Atwood's stories through the messenger model. The approaches above are easily customized: one could substitute any of Atwood's rule-bending stories in *Good Bones and Simple Murders* or the genre-twisting tales in *Stone Mattress* for the introductory-level workshop, whereas an instructor could tether *The Handmaid's Tale* or *The Blind Assassin* to cultural studies or historical research projects at the advanced level. The messenger model outlined in *Negotiating with the Dead* brings vitality to the student writers' creations, because they come to view their writing as a living entity, one engaged in transmitting emotional depths and uncanny experiences to the reading audience. Atwood's work empowers students to experiment with unconventional narrative strategies—all while telegraphing their own vision to their audience.

NOTES

1. This essay cites the 1998 Anchor edition of *The Handmaid's Tale*.
2. This essay cites the McClelland and Stewart edition of *Alias Grace*.

INTERTEXTUAL ANALYSIS AND ADAPTATION THEORY

The Value of Atwood's Adaptations for Twenty-First-Century Students

Melissa M. Caldwell

Adaptations are, by their very nature, acts of interpretation (Cutchins et al., Introduction xiii). Literary adaptations engage students in new ways to explore literary history, textual meanings, and the importance of creative reimagining. Margaret Atwood's adaptive novels offer a rich reading experience for twenty-first-century students at almost every level. Guided readings of *The Penelopiad* and *Hag-Seed* allow students to observe Atwood as both a critical reader and an inventive writer. When used with intent beyond simply reading an updated version of a well-known text in the Western canon, these novels can lead not only to a fresh interpretation of literature and a deeper understanding of literary history but also to a transfer of knowledge that encourages students to make connections between literature, their own voice as interpreters and writers, and the world in which they live.

Writing of novel-to-film adaptations, Thomas Leitch discusses the benefits of teaching adaptation. For him, adaptation answers many of the questions being asked in English departments today about the parameters and goals of the major and what skills we instructors want our students to be equipped with when they leave our classes. He argues that "[t]he starkest challenge facing college English teachers is helping their students move from a passive literacy—being uncritical consumers of the texts they face—to active literacy—being able not only to follow texts word by word and point by point but to engage them critically by producing powerful texts themselves" (9–10). In his view, student projects focused on writing adaptations are transformative in creating active readers, ones more likely to question and engage than to passively accept a text (10). Though Leitch is interested in film adaptation, I believe that teaching Atwood's adaptations can yield similar outcomes, for in these texts Atwood demonstrates just what active literacy is. When we ask students to do what Atwood does by reading a text critically and imagining another text that can exist in dialogue with it, one inscribed with their own ideas, values, and questions, we are teaching them active literacy, for there is no better way to help students understand literature and literary history than by asking them to make a space for themselves in that very history.

Many scholars have noted the importance of intertextuality for a study of Atwood's work, particularly her fairy-tale and mythic intertexts (Wilson, *Margaret Atwood's Fairy-Tale Sexual Politics* 3–34). As adaptations, *The Penelopiad* and *Hag-Seed* demonstrate a particular kind of intertextuality, one in which Atwood forces the reader to confront the narratives that have come to define Western literature and to see the limits of these narratives when we re-view them (and review them) from a different perspective. By focusing on Atwood's adaptive strategies, instructors can help students understand dynamic examples of intertextuality and empower them with strategies they can use to create their own adaptations. By recognizing their own place as adaptors, students must confront and work through several key questions of literary analysis: What value does intertextuality have for modern readers? Does the process of adaptation ultimately reinforce dominant narratives or undermine them? Does the process keep the reader and writer in separate intellectual spaces, or is adaptation liberating for reader and writer alike? Is the purpose of adaptation simply to modernize older texts, or does the creator of a twenty-first-century adaptation have an ethical responsibility to promote larger conversations about gender, race, class, sexuality, or other pressing social questions? Is it possible to do both at the same time?

The Penelopiad is Atwood's first full-fledged adaptation, though Atwood's interest in retelling mythology from marginalized or elided points of view is on full display in her early poetry collections *You Are Happy* and *Interlunar* in her Circe and Eurydice poems (Wilson, "Mythological Intertexts" 221), whereas works such as *The Robber Bride* were inspired by *The Iliad* (Suzuki 267). *The Penelopiad* retells the story of Homer's *Odyssey* by recounting the events of the text from the viewpoints of Penelope and the twelve maids that Odysseus slaughters in book 22. But the novel also draws from other sources and imagines events not included in *The Odyssey*, such as Penelope's childhood, her marriage to Odysseus, her pregnancy, and her relationship with the other women of her household. It is a short novel, but in order to encompass all these perspectives, Atwood strategically includes within its pages poetry and several other genres, which she uses to "parodically disrup[t] the hierarchy between 'high' and 'low' literary genres" (Staels, "*Penelopiad*" 100).

In *Hag-Seed*, an adaptation of William Shakespeare's play *The Tempest*, Atwood adapts the story by setting the revenge tragedy in present-day Canada. Here, too, Atwood makes several adjustments to her antecedent text. In addition to killing off Miranda before the story even begins, she literalizes what is largely only a metaphor in the play. Prospero becomes Felix Phillips, the ousted director of the Makeshiweg Festival determined to regain his former glory and take revenge on Anthony (Tony) Price, who has seen to Felix's removal and his own installation as festival director. But the adaptation does not end there, as the reader watches Felix use *The Tempest*—that is to say, adapt *The Tempest*—as a means to his revenge.

Despite their differences, *The Penelopiad* and *Hag-Seed* use adaptation for similar ends—that is, to destabilize the reader's notion of an original text and to lead the reader to recognize a central paradox of storytelling: the same story may be told many times, and yet it will occasion entirely different experiences and interpretations depending on how the story is told and who tells it. Atwood's adaptations create the conditions for a multidirectional dialogue not only among texts but also between texts and readers. A study of Atwood's adaptations can allow students to undertake—with each other, with the teacher, with Atwood, and with literary history itself—the process of what Ayanna Thompson and Laura Turchi call "collaborative meaning making" (49). Such collaboration fosters stronger, more confident readers of literature, who can understand both the text itself and how to think creatively and analytically beyond the text to make another's stories a part of their own world. In what follows, I briefly outline how Atwood's novels offer opportunities for students to understand adaptation as product and adaptation as process. These two concepts lay the groundwork for students to undertake their own adaptations. In a final section, I discuss how students can develop from readers of adaptation into writers of adaptation.

Adaptation as Product

When we think about intertextuality and adaptation, we are really thinking about adaptation as both a product and a process (Hutcheon, *Theory of Adaptation* [2006] 15). As Linda Hutcheon has noted, adaptations should be studied as adaptations rather than as derivative texts that can be evaluated only on their fidelity to the source text (6). Hutcheon's critique of "normative and source-oriented approaches" to adaptation is essential in moving students away from an evaluative reading to an analytical reading of adaptation (8). Surprisingly, in my experience teaching both Shakespeare and courses focused on adaptations at the undergraduate and graduate level, students often have a deeply entrenched bias toward the original text and are quick to judge an adaptation as inferior to the original rather than as an extension, remediation, or complement of it. Unless students can move beyond comparison to engage deeply with an adaptation, they will fail to see the adaptation as a work of art or to understand the act of adaptation as an art form.

Any study of adaptation must begin by exploring fundamental questions about the relationship between an adaptation and its source text or texts; the difference between the forms of intertextuality such as adaptation, appropriation, and allusion; and the role of audience, medium, and genre in the work of adaptation. To that end, it is important at the outset to interrogate terminology, and I typically devote at least the first two weeks of class to the task of defining adaptation as a literary genre. Since not even critics can agree on this question, it is a discussion likely to produce a multitude of valid responses. In her list of the "lexicon of adaptation," Julie Sanders includes "version, variation, interpretation, continuation, transformation, imitation, pastiche, parody, forgery, travesty, transposition, revaluation, revision, rewriting, echo," all of which she notes "can possess starkly different, even opposing, aims and intentions" (*Adaptation* 22). Using Hutcheon and Sanders as a foundation, students are able to turn to their knowledge of fan fiction, memes, video games, comics, *TikTok* videos, and other contemporary forms of intertextuality to enrich this discussion. My goal in these opening weeks of class is to get students to identify and rethink their own assumptions about creativity and originality. Unless students accept the idea that "literature . . . is always understood as relative, rather than absolute" (Cutchins, "Bakhtin" 72), they are unlikely to be able to approach the possibilities that adaptation affords.

Adaptations have a wide variety of rhetorical aims and outcomes, and contemplating Atwood's reasons for choosing her source texts is key to understanding her adaptations. Atwood makes clear that *The Penelopiad* is meant to be a critique. The degree to which students can understand this text as critique will hinge in some part on their knowledge of *The Odyssey*; however, even general knowledge of *The Odyssey* should equip students to understand the sociopolitical nature of Atwood's commentary. Atwood's novel is a "necessary addition" to Homer in that it lays bare the gaps in narrative and perspective that have been elided for centuries (Haynes 285). As a ghost in the underworld, Atwood's Penelope informs the reader about her own textual history, which in turn validates the importance of adaptations. In Hades, "everyone arrives with a sack, like the sacks used to keep the winds in, but each of these sacks is full of words—words you've spoken, words you've heard, words that have been said about you. Some sacks are small, others large; my own is of a reasonable size, though a lot of words in it concern my eminent husband" (Atwood, *Penelopiad* 1–2).[1] Atwood draws our attention to the narratives that have been told *about* Penelope, which stand in stark contrast to the narrative *by* Penelope. Up until this point, Penelope has been a byproduct of the narratives of Odysseus's heroism. Empowered only in death (40), she now finds her voice: "It's my turn to do a little story-making. I owe it to myself. I've had to work myself up to it: it's a low art, tale-telling" (3–4). "The difficulty," she says "is that I have no mouth through which I can speak. I can't make myself understood, not in your world . . . and most of the time I have no listeners, not on your side of the river" (4). Penelope is only given agency—a mouth through which to speak—if an author such as Atwood decides to return to her story and retell it. Even still, although her time as a storyteller has finally come, the question remains as to whether we are ready to hear the tale she has to tell.

In her brief introduction to the text, Atwood emphasizes the uncertainty of mythology and the opportunity it affords the writer, both because multiple versions of most myths have survived at least in some form and because of the oral nature of myth. Atwood's narrative strategy exploits both this multiplicity and orality, as the form of her narrative undercuts the idea of a single story.

Penelope may have a voice, but hers is not the only or even the dominant one. Atwood gives the telling of the story both to Penelope and to the twelve maids. If Penelope arrives with a sack of words written about her—or at least about her husband—the maids likely have no sacks at all. They are shades, both in the sense that they are ghosts and in the sense that they lurk in narrative shadows. They call out to Odysseus, "Yoo hoo! Mr Nobody! Mr Nameless! Mr Master of Illusion! . . . We're here too, the ones without names. The other ones without names. The ones with shame stuck onto us by others" (191). Atwood uses intertextuality here for satiric ends: the well-known heroic episode of Odysseus playing at being "nobody" from his position of power to get away from the Cyclops stands in stark contrast to the reality of the maids, who have been rendered into nonexistence by the gaping narrative lacunae of epic poetry.

It is less likely that, even at the college level, students will have any familiarity with *The Tempest*. This perhaps does not matter since the novel is less a critique of a text, not to say an entire literary tradition, than a reimagining of that text in a new time and place. Nevertheless, Atwood's intertextuality is highly conspicuous here too. The title of the novel is, of course, a reference to Caliban, Shakespeare's antagonist, who by the end of the novel will "escape the play" itself (279). The novel is broken into five acts, each with a title and chapter headings that are direct quotations of the play. Atwood seeks an "equivalence" for each character and setting in the antecedent text, going so far as to create a human stand-in for the "auspicious star" that first brings Prospero's enemies near the island of his exile in the play (Atwood qtd. in Bethune). But perhaps what is most striking about this novel is the way in which it foregrounds the process of adaptation itself. As we watch Felix not only embody Prospero but also direct his own version of *The Tempest*, Atwood builds an adaptation that is at once in conversation with Shakespeare and itself. As readers, we cannot escape the continual reminders that we are reading an adaptation.

Having varying knowledge of antecedent texts will undoubtedly produce different reading experiences, a fact that should be made visible to students. By becoming aware of how their background knowledge produces these varied outcomes in the minds of readers, students begin to understand the epistemology of adaptation. On the one hand, knowing both texts is precisely the point, as studying adaptations requires an "essential and persistent double-mindedness" because "students must hold at least two texts in their mind at once" (Cutchins, "Why Adaptations Matter" 88). Since one indicator of adaptation is its intentionality, it is reasonable to conclude that the reader must recognize that intentionality and understand what it means to the work in order to read a text as an adaptation. On the other hand, it is also possible to upend the notion of original text and adaptation by beginning with the adaptation as the primary text, which is likely more in keeping with many students' experiences with Atwood's adaptations (Jeffers 124). Doing so can have the advantage of calling into question the very idea of "what is 'shared' or indeed even familiar," which in any case is constantly being rewritten in our electronic age

(Sanders, *Adaptation* 125). But regardless of whether or not students are familiar with an antecedent text, studying adaptation as adaptation allows students to perceive literary history not as a linear process but as a network or a web of meaning (Chapple 56; Cutchins, "Bakhtin" 44). When they understand that it is also a process of reinvention, they can find a way into that network themselves.

Adaptation as Process

The highlighting of the adaptive process in *The Penelopiad* and *Hag-Seed* is a unique and particularly useful feature of Atwood's adaptations, which create intertexts that showcase the "hydra's head" of the adaptive process (Jeffers 123). This literary autogenesis has the benefit of undermining the notion of an authoritative text or of a text as an absolute thing (Cutchins, "Why Adaptations Matter" 92–93). Atwood's treatment of the adaptive process ranges from tragedy to comedy and even parody, yet adaptors in Atwood tend to have something in common: they are among the most vulnerable and oppressed characters. They reveal how anyone has the authority to be an adaptor.

In *The Penelopiad*, the proliferation of the adaptive process occurs through the voices of the maids and the many genres in which they speak. Although *The Penelopiad* clearly critiques patriarchal narrative structures, Penelope does not come out altogether unscathed (Suzuki 273). Alongside Atwood's critique of a heroism that is founded on the exploitation and powerlessness of women is the suggestion that perhaps Penelope does not have the story right either. As I have argued elsewhere, Atwood uses the maids to create a multivocalism that produces a counternarrative against which we are asked to read Penelope's narrative (Caldwell 131). Although the maids take aim at Odysseus at the end of the story, the main focus of their critique throughout the text is Penelope herself. They create generic dissonance, interrupting Penelope's linear narrative with ballads, shanties, chorus lines, dramas, an anthropology lecture, and a trial. Acting as a Greek chorus that refines—and perhaps even corrects—Homer's narrative as well as Penelope's, the maids highlight the need for multiple narratives—that is, the need for adaptation: "As we approach the climax, grim and gory, / Let us just say: There is another story. / Or several" (147).

In *Hag-Seed*, Atwood also foregrounds the process of adaptation through Felix, who both excels and fails at adaptation. From a *Pericles* "staged with spaceships and extraterrestrials," complete with "the main goddess Artemis with the head of a praying mantis," to a *Winter's Tale* with a vampiric Hermione, Felix's adaptive methods have garnered him a reputation for eccentricity (13).[2] After he is ousted from his position, Felix takes a job as a teacher at the Fletcher Correctional Institute, where he begins a class in which the students stage one of Shakespeare's plays each year. With the Ponzi schemer SnakeEye as Antonio, the ingenious hacker 8Handz as Ariel, and the con artist Wonder Boy as Ferdinand, Felix's casting for *The Tempest* allows us to imagine further contemporary analogues for Shakespeare's characters, suggesting both the universality and the limitations of the antecedent text. Felix defends his project to naysayers by arguing that for Shakespeare's actors, "the text wasn't a sacred cow" (52–53). For him, Shakespeare's plays are an unlimited resource for adaptation.

As we readers watch Felix direct a new *Tempest* with the Fletcher Correctional Players, Atwood deepens our understanding of the transformative and liberating possibilities of the adaptive process, for as Felix adapts this play to "suit a new environment" (Elliott 34), adaptation begets adaptation. The creative, transactional space that emerges when Felix works with his new group of actors shows us that "a *work* is the sum of its versions; *creativity* extends beyond the solitary writer, and *writing* is a cultural event transcending media" (Bryant 47). We witness the unfolding of such a "cultural event" as Felix and the players evolve their own collaborative version of *The Tempest*. Felix encourages his players to take part in the adaptive process with a class assignment that divides them into groups and gives each group the task of modernizing the lines of the play. Nevertheless, even Felix does not fully expect what happens next: the players begin to improvise, creating a rap for Caliban and Antonio (160), choreography, and other inventions. At first, Felix feels threatened by his loss of control over his adaptation. But when SnakeEye performs his rap for "evil bro Antonio," even Felix has to admit "it has something" (163). The text ends after the performance, with each group imagining a new ending for one of Shakespeare's characters that goes beyond the play itself. The creative power of adaptation and the performance of adaptation create a space for agency even within the strictures of a prison (Jayendran 20–21) or, I would suggest, those of a classroom.

Turning Readers into Writers

Students can develop a rich understanding of adaptation as a product and a process by studying Atwood's adaptive techniques in *The Penelopiad* or *Hag-Seed*. Penelope, the maids, Felix, and the Fletcher Correctional Players all provide models of adaptors. Atwood's texts can be taught in a wide variety of courses—including composition, literature, and creative writing—at the high school and college level that seek to help students understand intertextuality and adaptation as a literary practice. These novels exemplify active literacy as we readers observe Atwood's adaptive process and as we observe characters who themselves are empowered by that process. Atwood's novels also make clear that adaptation can be a liberating and democratizing force whereby all are invited to participate and make their own contributions to literary history. And so, by asking students to undertake their own adaptations, we are asking them to be both astute readers and writers and also critics undertaking the political act of adaptation (Sanders 123). Adaptation invites students to be "'revising readers' who enact their interpretations, not through criticism, but by altering the material text itself" (Bryant 50). In "transform[ing] a text for new or different audiences, and address[ing] new conditions and problems in a culture" (48), students are given the opportunity to make connections between a text and contemporary society. Teaching adaptation can also offer important benefits when working with students from diverse cultural backgrounds and traditions, since adaptation allows students to "reshape classic texts to their own local culture using whatever language . . . they prefer. . . . [B]y this means, they can understand how the act of adaptation offers a research-based space for experiment and creativity" (Sahin and Raw 73).

Adaptation redresses student passivity by authorizing student agency. There are many possibilities for creating assignments around either of Atwood's adaptations. In my own upper-division undergraduate and graduate classes on literary adaptations, I allow students to choose an adaptation project most suited to their own academic goals. Students of literature may choose to conduct their own investigations on the figure of Penelope and her legacy as one of the most popular exempla for an ideal wife noted for her patience, her unwavering loyalty, and her chastity; they might compare Atwood's adaptations to other adaptations of the same text or examine the publishing history and reception of the pre-texts and think about how Atwood's texts fit into that history; or they might develop lesson plans around teaching parts of these adaptations to their future students. But in my view, the best use of adaptations in the classroom is to use them to beget further adaptation.

By the end of the third week of the class, students are required to identify an "original" text that they wish to engage with by creating an adaptation. Using the theoretical underpinnings of class discussions of adaptation, intertextuality, and creativity, the assignment requires students to think critically about a text and decide upon a meaningful way to adapt it. A crucial part of this creative project is the five-hundred-word critical preface in which students must articulate a rationale for their choices (of character, point of view, setting, genre, medium, and so on), a purpose, and an audience for their adaptation. Atwood has inspired students in my courses to explore the effect of retelling a story in a different genre or from a particular perspective. Some students have opted to use experimental forms or multimedia formats; others have explored the stories by adopting alternative points of view such as that of a nonhuman or inanimate object or by choosing to be a "mouth through which" the voice of a previously neglected or negated character or perspective emerges (Atwood, *Penelopiad* 4); still others have chosen to update a work's setting or to expand its characterization to include characters who possess a more diverse range of racial, ethnic, gender, and sexual identities. The critical preface encourages students to think critically about the purposes and goals of their retellings.

Once students have committed to their focus, I establish small (usually four-to-five-person) adaptation work groups. Through weekly tasks and check-ins, these groups offer a collaborative space and serve as sounding boards, critics, and editors who help individual students shape their projects. In these groups, students must wrestle with aspects of the adaptive process that Atwood herself surely confronted—considering, for example, whether it is possible or even desirable to "remain true" to the antecedent text and how to make an adaptation meaningful to an audience that may not have read the antecedent text. As adaptors themselves, students experience the realities of adaptation and literary production more largely: "as soon as words are uttered, they enter into a negotiation or dialogue both with listeners and with other words" (Cutchins, "Bakhtin" 73). These work groups help students understand that the adaptive project is, by its very nature, dialogic and that as adaptors, they can orchestrate but perhaps not fully control that dialogue. By creating their own adaptations—that is, learning by doing, both individually and in groups—students perform acts of literary interpretation, rhetorical invention, and, crucially, meaning-making. When invited "to make and defend their own decisions about cutting, transforming, adding, and rewriting instead of commenting on" prior texts (Leitch 14), students become not observers but collaborators in the project of literature. They understand literature and their place in it more deeply.

Taken together, *The Penelopiad* and *Hag-Seed* do not only critique the texts that inspired them and destabilize accepted narrative; they ask us to reevaluate historicism itself, an evaluation that students of literature must also undertake for themselves. To take an example from *The Penelopiad*, one of the final incursions of the maids is the trial of Odysseus. The trial judge appeals to Homer's *Odyssey* as "a book we must needs consult, as it is the main authority on the subject" of the maids' rape and killing (179). Odysseus's attorney claims he cannot possibly offer any judgment on Odysseus, who lived four thousand years before his time (180). In the end, the judge comes to a decision based both on a historicist argument and a defense of epic heroism itself: "[Odysseus's] times were not our times. Standards of behaviour were different then. It would be unfortunate if this regrettable but minor incident were allowed to stand as a blot on an otherwise exceedingly distinguished career. Also I do not wish to be guilty of anachronism. Therefore I must dismiss the case" (182). And so Atwood leaves us hanging with an important question about the nature of literature itself. Holding on to our notions of an "original" text keeps patriarchal literary structures and canons in place, negating or at the very least lessening the value of any texts produced outside them, perhaps especially texts that do not follow the logic of heroic narrative. But Atwood also asks us to confront another important question that sits at the heart of how we value adaptation: At what cost do we defend these narratives? As the seeming order of the courtroom falls into disarray, the judge cries out, "What's going on? Order! Order! This is a twenty-first-century court of justice" (184). Adaptation offers students a seat in the courtroom, as it were, to make their own judgments with their own voices.

NOTES

1. This essay cites the Canongate edition of *The Penelopiad*.
2. This essay cites the Hogarth edition of *Hag-Seed*.

Teaching *The Handmaid's Tale* in Adaptation

Katherine V. Snyder

In this essay, I describe an adaptation studies approach to teaching *The Handmaid's Tale*, as developed in a fall 2019 lower-division English course for non-majors. Even before the popular and critical success of the Hulu TV series, Margaret Atwood's dystopian masterpiece had been adapted widely: as a film, radio drama, stage play, ballet, and opera, not to mention having been translated into more than forty languages. But the cultural impact of the Hulu series, which precipitated additional adaptations, including a graphic novel and a sequel, cannot be overstated. Its first season, developed when a Hillary Clinton presidency seemed likely, premiered soon after the January 2017 Women's March and just before the consolidation of the Me Too movement in October of that year. During this period, the Handmaid's red cloak and white bonnet became a highly visible feminist symbol, worn by activists across the world to protest violations of women's sexual, reproductive, and other rights.

The synergy of *Handmaid*'s political currency and the proliferation of adaptations provided a pedagogical opportunity on several fronts. First, it gave my students the opportunity to consider Atwood's landmark novel in a particularly potent historical and cultural context: our own. It provided, moreover, a framework for examining the continuities between our present and the moment, thirty-four years earlier, when Atwood had published her novel. As importantly, it afforded a unique window onto critical ideas about literary meaning and the complex interpretive and creative potential of adaptation itself. And, significantly, it did so at a moment when adaptation across media had become a new norm in popular culture. The many adaptations and other reuses of Atwood's novel vividly substantiated for my students the idea that literary texts must not be reified as mere artifacts of their moment of production or their author's intentions. Rather, the proliferative afterlives of these texts are what makes them most alive.

The main adaptations that we studied were the movie, the radio play, season 1 of the Hulu television series, the graphic novel, and the novel's sequel, *The Testaments*, which was published halfway through the semester. Other adaptations were excerpted in class: we viewed video clips of live opera and ballet performances,[1] and we listened to the dramatized Q and A written by Atwood for the novel's 2012 special edition audiobook, which imagines how the audience at the Twelfth Symposium might have responded to Professor Pieixoto's "Any questions?" and how he could have responded in turn. We sampled a welter of popular *Handmaid* reuses and parodies: costumes worn by protesters and Halloween revelers, crocheted *amigurumi* (dolls) of *Handmaid*'s characters, *Handmaid* fan art and fan fiction, a *Mad Magazine* comic entitled "The Manmaid's Tale," and a New Zealand comedy sketch entitled "The Handyman's Tale," in addition to many others.

The assigned work, like the assigned texts, required students to perform a variety of interpretive, creative, and reflective practices. Low-stakes assignments graded for completion included weekly online discussion posts in preparation for class meetings, written responses to live events promoting the release of *The Testaments*, and a collaborative annotated bibliography of reviews, think pieces, and interviews that attended the Hulu series and the book launch of the sequel. Graded work included two argument-based essays analyzing *Handmaid* adaptations, a final written reflection on the adaptability of Atwood's novel, and a creative engagement with *Handmaid* and its adaptations.

Judging the Book by Its Covers

On the first day of class, I gave the students a taste of our subject matter by projecting several striking book covers selected from among the many editions, published in various languages, of Atwood's novel. I asked them, What do you think this book will be about? How does the cover shape our expectations? Would any of these covers especially tempt you to buy the book? (I encouraged those already familiar with the book or any of its adaptations to "blank" their mental screens to simulate a first encounter.) This exercise bears a family resemblance to a pre-reading technique aimed at promoting reading comprehension through contextual cues in primary or secondary education. But my goal here was more meta: to introduce the idea that reception, including marketing and consumption, can be understood as part of a text's meaning. The exercise formed the basis for the students' first essay, in which they were to analyze how one cover of their choice highlighted a particular aspect of the novel. They might consider, I suggested, how their chosen design underscored the bonds among the handmaids, the prohibition on certain kinds of speech in Gilead, or the fragmentation of Offred's sense of self.

Setting the Stage

This assignment came on the heels of our course's first unit, in which we read the novel in tandem with the first two chapters of Linda Hutcheon's magisterial *A Theory of Adaptation* (2012). Because this was a lower-division course, our discussion of the novel was focused on basic points of plot, character, theme, and narrative form, elements that we would consider in context of the adaptations to follow. For example, I developed an in-class activity, a game called "Aunt Lydia Says," intended to help my students develop their understanding of how tone and voice can produce a sense of character. We first analyzed several examples of the bossy, moralizing, jingoistic adages frequently uttered by Aunt Lydia in Atwood's novel; then I directed students to invent their own Lydia-esque aphorisms based on these models. Finally, I read aloud their inventions together with some of Aunt Lydia's actual sayings, and the class voted on which ones were original to the novel. This last step required them to use the formal and thematic elements they had discerned in the text as clues. The activity had the further benefit of providing a basis for considering Aunt Lydia's development as a character in the adaptations to come.

Our engagement with those adaptations would be informed by Hutcheon's key points, including her characterization of adaptation as "repetition without replication" (7), as "process and product" (9), and as a textual engagement requiring both interpretation and creation. When discussing Hutcheon's concepts, we asked, What exactly is transformed or left intact when a text is adapted? What counts as an adaptation . . . and what doesn't?

Hutcheon influentially debunks the twin shibboleths of adaptation studies: "fidelity discourse," or assignment of value solely based on faithfulness to the original, and "medium specificity," the assumption that certain media are uniquely suited to "showing" whereas others are the proper terrain of "telling." As an alternative to medium specificity, she proposes that attending to the modes of engagement themselves—showing, telling, and a third mode she calls "interacting"—can provide a more productive framework for considering adaptations in all media. Hutcheon acknowledges that mode itself has been subject to specificity claims that are not so different from those made about media: claims that telling is better than showing at rendering the complexities of point of view, interiority, and temporality as well as the nuances of ambiguity, irony, symbol, metaphor, silence, and absence. She nonetheless acknowledges that, although "no one mode is inherently good at doing one thing and not another, . . . each has at its disposal different means of expression . . . and so can aim at and achieve certain things better than others" (24).

Having come of age in the rich media environment of the twenty-first century, my students were not predisposed to accept the primacy of telling over showing or writing over televisual media. But the very premise of the course—taught in an English department and giving top billing to a single literary text—nonetheless suggested our shared susceptibility to treating our printed source text as the authoritative original. To resist the temptation to deprecate adaptations as inauthentic or derivative, we needed to keep in mind Hutcheon's insights that the pleasures of adaptation depend upon the combination of familiarity and novelty and that adaptations are necessarily palimpsestic.

The Movie

Hutcheon's challenge to fidelity discourse was sorely tested by our, and the novel's, first adaptation: the often disparaged 1990 movie. The movie's most radical revisions to Atwood's plot include scenes in which Kate (the movie's name for Offred) slits the Commander's throat, is then unambiguously rescued by Nick and members of the Mayday resistance, and, in a final vignette replacing the novel's "Historical Notes," waits pregnant in the mountains for Nick to return, dreaming of reunion with her daughter. Rather than excoriating the film for its lack of fidelity, we asked what its transformations might have accomplished. It was important for us to recognize that these changes are in line with Volker Schlöndorff's reported intention of making a Hollywood thriller. That is, the movie's departures from Atwood's *Handmaid* are directorial choices, not something imposed by medium specificity—in this case, the supposed inability of film to "tell" with sufficient subtlety to communicate characters' subjectivity interiority and relationships. In fact, as we discovered, a crucial choice within the affordances of film reinforced the tilt from psychological narrative to action thriller. This was the decision, made late in the editing of the film, to eliminate Offred's voice-over interior monologue, which had already been recorded by the actor Natasha Richardson, from all but that final sentimental vignette.

The Radio Play

As a vehicle for interior reflection, voice-over is an obvious choice for radio drama. And the late revelation in the "Historical Notes"—the disclosure that what we've been reading is a transcription of an audio recording—makes radio a particularly apt medium for adapting Atwood's novel. The 2000 BBC Radio 4 adaptation of *Handmaid*, which combines elements of documentary style (exterior scenes were recorded outside the studio) with multilayered sound editing, uses voice-over to indicate interior reflection in at least two different registers. For one, the radio production adds a tinny resonance to some segments of Offred's voice-over, obliquely foreshadowing the belated disclosure of the fictional conceit of the taped and transcribed narrative. By contrast, where the voice-over is unmarked by this deliberately lo-fi sound effect, it seems that we are hearing not the taped recording of narrated memory of Offred's past in Gilead but her inner thoughts as they occur during her experiences there.

The selective use of this sound effect communicates complex shifts in both temporality and perspective—namely, the movement of the narrative between the remembered past and the enacted present as well as listeners' vertiginous shifts in perspective when we discover that we are both farther from and closer to the story than we had realized. That is, we are separated from the story by hitherto unrecognized degrees of technological and editorial separation but are brought closer by our unsuspected alignment with the members of Professor Pieixoto's audience. The radio play's distinctive aural rendering of these shifts applies its special affordances to replay without replicating Atwood's narrative.

The Television Series

Occupying the three middle weeks of the semester, the Hulu series marked the culmination of our performance-based adaptations. By fall 2019, there were already three seasons and thirty-six episodes, but we watched only the first season, which cleaves more closely than later ones to the novel's time frame while still offering considerable developments in plot and world-building. Among these many changes, what most fully engaged my students was the series' development of the character of Offred as a figure of feminist resistance and fury, one who joins in suffering and solidarity with other oppressed women in Gilead, both Handmaids and more powerful figures like Serena Joy and Aunt Lydia.

This narrative arc is consistent with the expansion of the roles of the Handmaids Ofwarren and Ofglen, both of whom are subjected in the series to punitive mutilation against which they violently rebel in protest. The seriality of television, with its multiplication of narrative arcs at the scales of the episode, the season, and the series as a whole, well suits it to the melodramatic cycle of suffering and revenge, the repeated rise and fall of the main character and her allies as they battle their oppressors and seek freedom. We wrestled with the potentially retrograde aspects of this melodrama—the Hulu series has been accused of being "torture porn"—as well as with other critiques, especially the series' failure to address racial oppression, despite its commitment to colorblind casting.[2]

While attending to these broader thematic and contextual issues, we focused on how the show's meanings were shaped by the affordances of television drama as a genre and television as a medium. The conventional division of episodes into "A" and "B" (and sometimes "C") stories allowed the show makers to contrast character arcs and plot lines. Stories A and B within a single episode might juxtapose two characters, often Offred and one of the other main characters; or A and B might use flashbacks to contrast a character's present with their past. The use of shallow focus and close-ups that zoom in on Elisabeth Moss's face glowering beneath the claustrophobic white "wings" of her Handmaid's bonnet, often in combination with voice-over of her interior monologue, are signature formal devices, as are overhead tracking shots that miniaturize clusters of Handmaids against comparatively vast backgrounds and slow-motion shots of Handmaid groups that gradually move into the foreground to suggest accumulating resistance. Another signature device is the series' inventive and often ironic practice of running a different popular song, rather than a repeating score, over the closing credits of each episode. Among the most startling of these choices are Lesley Gore's defiant "You Don't Own Me," which closes out episode 1, and Simple Minds' "Don't You (Forget about Me)" at the end of episode 2. Learning to recognize the conventions of televisual genres and the audiovisual techniques employed by the show's creators enabled my students to analyze the innovative work of this adaptation.

The Graphic Novel

One might anticipate that the shift from performance-based and technologically mediated adaptations like film, radio, and television to the graphic novel would require a drastic shift in formal vocabulary and hence a steep learning curve for students. But this word-and-image hybrid medium actually has a good deal in common with televisual media, and even with radio, in its layering of elements that both tell and show. Of course, comics have their own unique narrative and formal conventions: the panel, splash, bleed, and gutter; graphic weight; and other elements of drawing style and lettering. And they have their own genre history—of particular relevance here is the recent acceptance of comics as appropriate for relaying traumatic historical and biographical testimony, which has been called "the *Maus* effect" (Harvey). Even though many college students are already familiar with this medium given its popular and critical ascendance and its increased use in high school classrooms since the mid-1990s, there is no question that a more developed awareness of the techniques and background of the graphic novel enabled students to produce more nuanced analyses.

Renée Nault's stunning 2019 graphic novel adaptation of *Handmaid* makes full use of the affordances of the medium to represent the world of Gilead and relay Offred's story. Her painterly style and dynamic use of the space of the page powerfully bring to life the novel's visual imagery, including its attention to color and hue, shape and space, luster and reflection. The striking visuals are complemented by Nault's canny selection of textual excerpts, which at once compress and unfold Atwood's narrative while capturing the complexity of Offred's interior reflections and her interactions with other characters.

The nuances of meaning in this hybrid medium do not depend, however, on the distinction between showing and telling. One striking example of the telling power of images and the showing power of words is a two-page spread in which Offred describes the evolution of media formats—computer disks replacing books, plastic replacing paper money—to exemplify the separation of one era from the next (ch. 10). The mementos in her mother's scrapbook displayed on the left side of the spread—dollar bills and coins, stamps and movie ticket stubs, family photos and picture postcards—give way on the right side to newspaper clippings reporting "President Assassinated" and "Army Declares State of Emergency." Inset on the bottom right corner of this page is an impassive—intimidated? officious?—male television newscaster; overlapping the TV screen, a jagged text box announces, "Keep calm. Everything is under control," in a blandly sinister, low-resolution font.

The image of textual layers here evokes the complex layering of nostalgia, traumatic memory, and testimony in Atwood's novel while adding yet another layer in the form of the adaptation itself: the two-page spread of Offred's mother's scrapbook corresponds to the two-page spread of the graphic novel itself. This correspondence, though, is inexact—while roughly lined up with each other, the gutter of the scrapbook runs at an angle to the gutter of the graphic novel in which it is portrayed. The adaptation is thus both a representation of the source text in another medium and a re-creation, a revision from another angle.

Adaptation and Its Others

After discussing the graphic novel, we turned our attention to some types of textual transformations—parodies and pastiches, spin-offs and tie-ins, fan art and fan fiction, prequels and sequels—that aren't always accepted as full-fledged adaptations. In the first edition of *A Theory of Adaptation*, for example, Hutcheon was leery of making room for all these textual reuses under the umbrella of adaptation. But the 2012 second edition of her book assumes a somewhat more catholic stance, as reflected in Hutcheon's new preface and an added epilogue by the media scholar Siobhan O'Flynn, both of which we read at this point in the semester. Their new theoretical and critical work responds to the dramatic developments in media technology, commercial franchising, and fan culture that had transpired in the six years between the first and second editions, developments that have only accelerated since 2012. Hutcheon and O'Flynn also take a page from corresponding advances in the scholarly fields of adaptation studies and transmedia studies, especially Henry Jenkins's influential work on "convergence culture," which describes the interplay between old and new media (*Convergence Culture*), and on "participatory culture," which acknowledges new modes and forms of interaction in our digital era (Jenkins et al.). O'Flynn's theorization of "transmedia adaptation," like Jenkins's "transmedia storytelling," highlights the world-building effected by these diverse types of adaptative reuses.

It may seem odd to categorize a sequel like *The Testaments* as a transmedia adaptation, given that it shares the print medium of its predecessor. But consider that many of Atwood's choices for her sequel were informed by the Hulu adaptation of *Handmaid*. Notably, she based the sequel's three narrator-protagonists—Aunt Lydia, Agnes, and Daisy—on characters as portrayed in or invented for the TV adaption. Hulu has, in turn, optioned *The Testaments* for a spin-off series. This multidirectional, multimodal network of production and consumption epitomizes the world-building that is a key feature of transmedia storytelling. *The Testaments* extends and deepens the Gileadverse by fleshing out familiar characters and introducing new ones, mapping spaces both within and beyond the Gilead we know from the novel and the TV series. *The Testaments* also broadens the timeline, detailing events leading to the fall of Gilead fifteen years after Offred's captivity as well as the deeper future reflected in the Thirteenth Symposium on Gileadean Studies, set one year after the Twelfth Symposium in Atwood's original "Historical Notes."

Our reading of *The Testaments* took place against the background of a media blitz staged for the book's launch in fall 2019. This elaborate multimedia and multiplatform campaign included midnight release parties at bookstores across

North America and the United Kingdom, followed by an extended book tour. One spectacular event was a simulcast in more than a thousand movie theaters worldwide on the day of the launch. Staged at London's National Theatre, it featured a procession of costumed characters, an interview with Atwood, and readings by actors, including Ann Dowd (Hulu's Aunt Lydia), of passages from the novel. As a class, we viewed the simulcast and compiled a collaborative, annotated bibliography of reviews, think pieces, and interviews that attended the book launch and the ongoing Hulu series.

In these events, we noted the sometimes compatible, sometimes competing impetuses of promotional marketing and community building. Such tensions are equally in play for *Handmaid* fans who encounter a panoply of licensed and unlicensed tie-in merchandise. How might we understand, for example, the marketing on *Etsy* of patterns for decorative cross-stitch samplers featuring mottoes such as "Nolite te bastardes carborundorum" and "Praise be, bitches"? Should we see the creator-sellers of these products as cynically, or cluelessly, capitalizing on seemingly defiant feminist statements? Or might the sale and purchase, as well as the completion and household display of these samplers, be better understood as gestures of community with the show's other fans, as expressions of identification with its heroine, or even as self-aware commentary on uneven gendered divisions of labor in our own world? So, too, the robust crop of *Handmaid* parodies that my students and I puzzled over. What is the substance of satire, we asked, in the *Saturday Night Live* parody "Handmaid's Tale in the City"? And how does this takeoff compare to "*Handmaid's Tale*: The Musical"—excerpts of an original show that was performed at a Kennedy Center comedy festival? Or to a running Handmaid gag in season 10 of *RuPaul's Drag Race*? Or an Australian hip-hop music video parody featuring rapping, dancing Handmaids ("Handmaid's Tale [Fancy Parody]")? Or the brief comic video monologue "If 'The Handmaid's Tale' Was Scottish," which was praised by Atwood herself (Storrie, "If" and "Ashley Storrie")?

Adaptation in Creative and Interpretive Practice

The ethos of participatory culture and the potential of transmedia storytelling informed our final assignment, a creative project in which students created their own adaptations, spin-offs, or other artistic engagements with our course material using the genre, medium, and platform of their choice. Suggested options for these projects included written mash-ups, parodies, or invented episodes; book covers, posters, or video trailers; alternative song choices for the TV show's credits; graphic novel spreads; tabletop games or video game mock-ups; or other types of interactive adaptation. Students experimented with all these possibilities and generated many others.

Among my favorites for their aesthetic finesse or interpretive subtlety were detailed liner notes for alternative songs for the credits at the end of each

Hulu episode; three students' rewritings of novel episodes from the perspective of other characters: "The Wife's Tale," "The Chauffeur's Tale," and "The Commander's Tale"; and a remarkably accomplished set of graphic novel spreads featuring scenes leading up to Offred's nighttime visit to the Commander's office, with the signatures of the student cocreators spelled out on a Scrabble board.

Other projects I appreciated for their innovative use of interactive modes. Among these was another alternative narrator project in the form of a *Twitter* account, @realCommanderJudd, repurposing tweets by Donald Trump ("KEEP GILEAD GREAT!"); a complex text-to-speech computer program based on the radio adaptation of chapter 10 of the novel; and an interactive *Google Map* of Cambridge, Massachusetts, entitled "Following Her Footsteps," with linked captions discussing Offred's movement through Gilead. Two delightful interactive projects were games: a Cards against Humanity spoof and "The Game of Life: Gilead Edition."

Importantly, each student was required to submit with their creative project an artist's statement, which served double duty as a metacognitive reflection for the student and a gloss for the benefit of the professor, helping both of us understand the aesthetic and interpretive goals of the project. But I was not the sole audience for these innovative additions to the *Handmaid* universe. The course culminated with a creative project showcase in which each student presented their work to the entire class, with commentary on their methods and aims as adaptors. It was a fittingly celebratory acknowledgment of the communal potential of participatory culture and a shared recognition of the pleasure and power of Atwood's *The Handmaid's Tale* and its adaptations.

The pedagogical approach that I have described in this essay is itself adaptable to classroom study of almost any adapted text, literary or otherwise. Even texts without any existing commercial or grassroots adaptations can be made available for adaptation by students themselves, a valuable activity that can serve as scaffolding for subsequent work in a course or, as in my class, an end-of-semester creative capstone.

More broadly, it is worth asking what adaptation can teach us about teaching itself. The diverse kinds of textual engagement that adaptations enact—such as repetition without replication, revisiting while remaking, and celebration and critique—might well serve as instructive models for our classroom practice. While I would not go so far as to claim that teaching is a form of adaptation, the creative and interpretive interventions that we make as teachers, like adaptations themselves, are part of what makes texts continue to matter. The explorations that we undertake in the classroom, also like adaptations, provide windows onto the texts we study and even doors that we walk through in order to enter these texts more fully. By taking adaptations as seriously and playfully as we do their originals, we can more fully inhabit the worlds of their sources while venturing into territory that is at once recognizable and new.

NOTES

1. Although the videos shown in class are no longer available, excerpts from the opera by Poul Ruders and the ballet by Lila York are available on *YouTube* ("*Handmaid's Tale*—Excerpts"; "*Handmaid's Tale* au Ballet royal de Winnipeg").

2. These issues have been extensively addressed in the popular press; for more scholarly critiques, see The Handmaid's Tale: *Teaching Dystopia, Feminism, and Resistance across Disciplines and Borders* (Ritzenhoff and Goldie) and *Adapting Margaret Atwood:* The Handmaid's Tale *and Beyond* (Wells-Lassagne and McMahon).

Atwood's Canadian Shakespeare: Allusions and Intertextuality in *Cat's Eye* and *Hag-Seed*

Heidi Tiedemann Darroch

Margaret Atwood's works draw on a formidable array of literary references, ranging from the Bible and classical literature to contemporary gothic romance and advertising slogans. As Coral Ann Howells has observed, "Atwood's fictions are criss-crossed with allusions to other texts, signaling her literary inheritance while at the same time marking significant differences from her predecessors" (*Margaret Atwood* 9). But, as Atwood notes, the use of allusion is fraught for contemporary writers in the wake of challenges to the literary canon: "now that there is no longer a body of work with which we are all supposed to be more or less familiar, how can you count on anyone *getting it*?" ("Comments" 382). Atwood has made her use of literary sources accessible to a range of readers by incorporating familiar Western literary texts, from the Bible and Shakespeare to tales collected by the Brothers Grimm. In a classroom context, exploring Atwood's Shakespearean allusions and intertexts helps construct shared common ground and enable assessment of the author's deeply thoughtful but irreverent relationship to canonical texts. Focusing on Atwood's conversation with the canon also offers student readers ways to identify the author's enduring concerns as a Canadian woman writer for whom "writing back" (Ashcroft et al. 97) is an active strategy of refashioning literary authority.

Atwood draws on direct citation, indirect allusion, and ironic and parodic revisioning to critically dissect or reinvent literary characters, plots, and tropes in fresh and surprising ways. Most frequently, Atwood has sprinkled her prose, and occasionally her poetry, as in "King Lear in Respite Care" (*Morning* 85–87), with references to Shakespeare's dramas, typically incorporating ironic distance from the original to deflate or undercut its seriousness. Atwood often signals her intentions explicitly, as she does by identifying Lear in her poem's title; in her short humorous piece "Gertrude Talks Back," she incorporates a lengthy quotation from one of Hamlet's soliloquies, whereupon Gertrude picks apart its language and claims (*Good Bones* 15–18). Atwood thus invites readers, even those who may have only limited knowledge of the particular Shakespeare text that she is referencing, into her work.

In her novels' more extended takes on Shakespeare, Atwood links postmodern irony to feminist historical revisionism as she explores what Shakespeare can and should mean for Canadian literature, a national literature that Atwood has helped define and extend over more than five decades. Helping students read Atwood through her Shakespearean engagements enables them to assess the various labels—feminist, cultural nationalist, postmodernist—that have been ascribed to the author and also permits them to consider how Atwood situates her writing at a critical remove from British influences.

Atwood expands the tradition of postcolonial and feminist rewritings of Shakespeare, demonstrating that with a shift in national context, gender, power, and language must be reconsidered. A first task for students is to identify the Shakespearean intertexts; then they can be prompted to consider how Atwood's revisioning creates a dialogue with key elements of the original text. In *Cat's Eye*, the protagonist, Elaine Risley, has a protracted but fraught friendship with Cordelia, who is herself a Shakespearean heroine manqué; the tragedies of both *Macbeth* and *King Lear* are developed as significant intertexts. In *Hag-Seed*, a Shakespearean companion work from later in Atwood's career, Felix Phillips, an ousted theater festival director, schemes revenge against his enemies in a plot that reflects key elements of *The Tempest* and culminates in a prison production of the same play. As Howells and others have noted, Atwood rarely merely quotes or refers to her sources, more typically incorporating them by means of ironic juxtaposition of the original source material and her own fresh reimagining or through a parodic "repetition with ironic critical difference" (Hutcheon, *Theory of Parody* xii). To help students identify the ways in which Atwood diverges from her source material, key scenes can be drawn from filmed Shakespeare productions, including those from Ontario's Stratford Festival. Comparative analysis could pair Atwood's *Cat's Eye* with scenes from *Macbeth* and *King Lear* and *Hag-Seed* with *The Tempest* to consider constructions of political power, inheritance, and sovereignty vital to late-twentieth-century Canadian postcolonial debates about Indigenous nations and the status of women.

A recent book on adaptations of Shakespeare by women authors observes that "Shakespeare appears in multiple guises in Atwood's work" (Carney 57), with varying degrees of subtlety. Classroom study of the novels in which the Shakespearean intertexts are both most prominent and most overt, *Cat's Eye* and *Hag-Seed*, offers student readers an accessible entry point to Atwood's extensive use of irony and a broader understanding of Atwood's relationship to her own national literature—one suggesting that, for Canadian writers, Shakespeare's canonical authority is double-edged. Shakespeare offers a cultural touchstone for English-language writers, but his writing is also part of a fraught colonial legacy that requires reassessment and revision.

In invoking Shakespeare, Atwood can anticipate that most readers, including her domestic audience, will recognize the intertexts and allusions. While Shakespeare is, of course, globally prominent, Dana M. Colarusso points out that since the inception of formal education in Canada, Shakespeare has been central to the curriculum; only two provinces formally mandate the study of the playwright, but "emphasis on Shakespeare units, sometimes in every year of high school, continue to feature in many English programs" (216). In fact, "Shakespearean education has had an uninterrupted role in linking a bilingual, (now) multicultural Canada to its British roots" (219). Beyond the pedagogical realm, Ric Knowles argues that Shakespeare helped "to constitute Canada as a Nation state, while Canada in turn constituted Shakespeare as its national bard, its sign of high cultural maturity and value, and its great Canadian Playwright" (13). Irena Makaryk concurs, noting that Shakespeare has been used "as a bulwark against other 'undesirable' traditions or cultures" and "as an ally of solid British values" as well as a "tool of anglicization" (5). For Atwood, this inheritance is complicated: while a reliance on Shakespeare may help differentiate Canadian literature from the bordering US literature, it also sustains a relationship of dependence of a peripheral former colony on the imperial center.

In most instances, Atwood employs Shakespeare as part of a feminist revisioning project with nationalist elements, subjecting the original text to critical scrutiny and considering how Shakespeare can be useful to a Canadian woman writer in the late twentieth and early twenty-first centuries. To achieve this, she uses strategies frequently associated with postmodern writing, notably parody and irony. As Linda Hutcheon has observed, "Parody—often called ironic quotation, pastiche, appropriation, or intertextuality—is usually considered central to postmodernism, both by its detractors and its defenders" (*Politics* 93). While not all of Atwood's fiction uses characteristic postmodern elements such as self-reflexivity and self-referentiality, playfulness with language and form, or historiographic metafiction, engagement with postmodernism is evident throughout her career. And Atwood's use of postmodern techniques is also explicitly linked to her engagement with issues of gender and nationalism (Djwa 170).

This is particularly apparent in Atwood's extensive use of Shakespeare in her 1988 novel *Cat's Eye*, which is about female friendship, memory, and art-making. Atwood incorporates multiple additional intertexts, including an array of scientific texts, as she considers how the past continues to exert influence on the present. One of the novel's epigraphs is drawn from Stephen W. Hawking's *A Brief History of Time*: "Why do we remember the past, and not the future?" The narrator thinks of "time as having a shape, something you could see, like a series of liquid transparencies, one laid on top of another. . . . Nothing goes away" (3). Given this thematic preoccupation with time and history, the use of allusion becomes especially significant. Elaine Risley, a midlife, mid-career painter, has returned to Toronto, where she grew up, for the first retrospective of her work, held, to Elaine's dismay, at a small feminist art gallery rather than at the provincial gallery. "Their bias," Elaine reflects, "is towards dead, foreign men" (16). As this example suggests, the novel is preoccupied with issues of cultural authority and significance as they relate to gender and nation. Atwood is attentive to the sexism facing Canadian women in the arts who, before feminist efforts to reenvision the canon, had been marginalized.

Elaine's own work is inspired by figures and images from her childhood, including the families and homes of the three friends who bullied her relentlessly in elementary school. One of these friends is Cordelia, the youngest of three daughters, like her namesake. But while *King Lear* is the most obvious intertext, given Cordelia's name, in some ways *Macbeth* is the more significant Shakespeare source for the novel. Even before the play is cited explicitly, Atwood alludes to it in the name of their secondary school, Burnham High School, which conjures up *Macbeth*'s Birnam Wood. The principal, a "Scot by affiliation" (231), has endowed the school with his own clan's plaid, crest, and motto. *Macbeth* is also referred to when the adult Elaine notices in a department store that the plaid dresses of her childhood have made a comeback; she envisions small girls with "slippery deceitful smiles" who are "tartaned up like Lady Macbeth" (128). The play has a particular resonance for Elaine in midlife, as she is considering her two marriages, her daughters, and her painting, and she recalls the lines that she was required to memorize in school: "*My way of life*, new line, *Is fall'n into the sere, the yellow leaf*" (128). The quotation points to Elaine's identification with Macbeth's far more dramatic midlife identity crisis while also calling attention to her painterly interest in the way the lines of the text appeared on the page, which she recalls perfectly.

Although Shakespearean figures do not appear in Elaine's visual art directly, one painting is intriguingly titled *Three Witches* and features three sofas, a possible reference to the torment that Cordelia and her other two friends meted out to Elaine. *Macbeth* is also the second play that Cordelia, an aspiring actress, appears in while still in high school. A touring production relies on local students to fill out the cast, and Cordelia plays two minor parts and assists with props. Disastrously, she replaces a rotting cabbage used to represent Macbeth's head with a fresh one, so that "when Macduff comes in at the end and tosses down the cabbage in the tea-towel, it doesn't hit once and lie still. It bounces, bumpity-bump, right across the stage like a rubber ball, and falls off the edge . . . the curtain comes down on laughter" (276). Cordelia is humiliated by her error, but the image of this pseudo-head is also closely aligned to other depictions of dismemberment and beheading in the novel, which include a game involving Mary, Queen of Scots, and the work of Elaine's first husband, Jon, who designs bloody prosthetics for slasher films. Both *Macbeth* and *King Lear*, of course, also include a range of similar bloody imagery, such as the gouging out of Gloucester's eyes.

Cordelia also spends two seasons at the Stratford Festival playing minor, usually nonspeaking roles, a nod to Shakespeare's Cordelia, who first utters "Nothing" when called on by her peremptory father to describe the depth of her love for him (*King Lear* 1.1.80). In *Measure for Measure*, Cordelia's character, a nun, has only one line, which she confesses to Elaine that she repeatedly muddles, while in a production of *The Tempest*, Cordelia is indistinguishable from the other attendants to Prospero who are similarly attired. Notably, Cordelia's hope is to appear as the First Witch in *Macbeth*, and she cites no less an authority than the festival artistic director, Tyrone Guthrie, recruited from Britain to grant the festival cultural stature, as a supporter (339). Instead, however, Cordelia's brief theater career sputters to a halt and she descends into despair. The last time Elaine sees Cordelia is shortly after her suicide attempt, when she is living at a convalescent home and begs Elaine to help her escape, a one-time tormentor relegated to dependency on her former target.

As Cordelia's Stratford experience suggests, the performance of Shakespeare was, until well into the 1970s, dominated by English expatriates and visitors in key positions, a phenomenon evident both in touring productions and in the founding of the now world-renowned Stratford Festival in 1952. Atwood identifies the touring company with which Cordelia performs during high school as the Earle Grey players, a real-life Toronto theatre troupe led by an English actor who asserted that "the only way to present Shakespeare's plays is as Shakespeare would have presented them," eschewing twentieth-century "psychological or Freudian" interpretations or costumes dating from after the seventeenth century (K. Johnson).

This preoccupation with authenticity is markedly at odds with Atwood's own irreverent use of the Bard, which questions and parodies the canonical works; notably, Elaine's retrospective is being held at a gallery named Sub-Versions, paralleling Atwood's own approach to cultural authority. Atwood's use of Shakespeare is also at odds with the earnest desire for period fidelity and authenticity of the founders of the Stratford Festival (Groome 119), who viewed their productions as a means of educating and entertaining a Canadian audience through the works of the Bard while ideally cultivating a "distinctively Canadian comment on the classics" (Tyrone Guthrie, qtd. in Groome 126). The question of what a "Canadian Shakespeare" might be, however, remained amorphous. Canadian plays were not included at Stratford until 1960; by the 1970s, in the wake of a postcentennial revival of cultural nationalism, "Shakespeare and Stratford came increasingly under attack" for the focus on non-Canadian playwrights and limited support for either Canadian playwrights or directors (Makaryk 25). When Atwood revisits Shakespeare touring productions and the early years of the Stratford Festival, then, she is also thinking through vexed questions of nationalism and cultural capital.

The most multifaceted Shakespearean allusion in the play is Cordelia's own name. While her older sisters, named for the Shakespearean heroines Perdita and Miranda, are called by affectionate nicknames, Cordelia is always—and only—Cordelia (81). In fact, Atwood does not mention the character's last name at any point in the novel, while Elaine's other childhood friends are identified by their full names. Like her namesake, Cordelia is a youngest daughter who experiences conflicts with her father. But, as Bethan Jones points out, Atwood "mirrors, subverts, and parodies" the relationship between Lear and his daughters (34), since unlike in Shakespeare's work, *Cat's Eye*'s Cordelia is not a former favorite who is dramatically banished but is, instead, "gradually but relentlessly slighted" by her father (34). Julie Sanders suggests that Cordelia and the two other friends who torment Elaine are more akin to Goneril and Regan than Cordelia's own sisters are (*Novel Shakespeares* 224). Cordelia's silence is also repeated with a difference: Atwood writes that Cordelia is unable to speak up effectively at the dinner table to her father or compete with her older sisters in teasing him. The "give and take" of joking dialogue that Cordelia's father seeks is beyond her, because "she's frightened of not pleasing him"; Cordelia's fear is well warranted, Elaine observes, since "nothing she can say or do will ever be enough . . . she is somehow the wrong person" (281). Elaine concludes that Cordelia's name, rather than conferring on her a blessing, is a source of her misery: "Why did they name her that? Hang that weight around her neck? . . . The stubborn one, the rejected one, the one who was not heard" (295). In re-imagining Cordelia, and inserting her into additional Shakespeare contexts, notably her performance in *Macbeth*, Atwood gives her portrayal of child and adolescent female friendship tragic undertones while also pointing to Canada's protracted striving for cultural independence. As Elaine learns from an anglophile teacher in elementary school, "Because we're Britons, we will never be slaves." But the reality is more complicated, Elaine reflects: "we aren't real Britons, because we are also Canadians" (89).

Atwood grapples with Shakespeare's Canadian relevance even more directly in *Hag-Seed*, which was written as part of a series of contemporary reenvisionings commissioned by the Hogarth Press on the occasion of the four hundredth anniversary of the playwright's death (Gopnik). Atwood selected *The Tempest* as her foundation for a story about an acclaimed Shakespeare festival director, Felix Phillips. The character's name nods to the famed English director Robin Phillips, credited with revitalizing the Stratford Festival after his contentious appointment in 1975. Felix's position is usurped by his devious assistant while the director is mourning the death of his toddler daughter, Miranda. To his dismay, Felix's elaborate production of *The Tempest*, in which he himself was to appear as Prospero, is also abruptly canceled. Years later, Felix, who has retired to obscurity in the country, takes up a position as an English instructor at a men's penitentiary, where he initiates an annual Shakespeare production. Like Prospero on his remote island, the director has bided his time and now plans to seek revenge against his enemies by subjecting them to a nightmarish, drug-addled experience under cover of his imaginative *Tempest* production. Felix, who plays the role of Prospero, also effectively functions as Prospero within the world of the novel through his machinations (Tolan, "Margaret Atwood's Revisions" 118).

The Tempest is an intriguing choice for Atwood because, alongside the obvious analogy for artistic creativity in Prospero's magic (which she assesses in chapter 4 of *Negotiating with the Dead* [91–122]), it is the Shakespeare work most frequently interpreted as a colonial allegory, given Prospero's usurpation of authority over the island where he and his young daughter, Miranda, are shipwrecked. Prospero kills Sycorax, the witch who had controlled the island after subduing its original inhabitants, and effectively enslaves both her son, the monstrous Caliban, and Ariel, a fairy, whom Sycorax had imprisoned in a tree. Although Prospero has "no legitimate claims of ownership" to the island (Ridge 236), his magic gives him the upper hand. The performance of *The Tempest* by incarcerated men mirrors the various forms of imprisonment that Felix helps his students identify in the play, but while Felix had originally imagined emphasizing Caliban's abjectness by making him "a scabby street person—black or maybe Native—and a paraplegic as well" (Atwood, *Hag-Seed* 16), his prison production is more subtle in its casting choices and emphasizes Miranda's role.[1] This is consistent with Chantal Zabus's study of rewritings of *The Tempest* in Canada, which argues that, unlike their Indigenous and Quebec peers, "English Canadian writers have occluded the race discourse to focus on the gender issue": Miranda provides a "feminine trope of colonialism" through her subjection to her father (105).

The Tempest's production history in Canada includes multiple stagings that have emphasized Canada's colonization of Indigenous nations and other forms of internal colonialism. A college student production was set on Haida Gwaii and used Haida masks and performance techniques, although no Indigenous actors participated (Usher), whereas a professional production, directed by the noted Quebec filmmaker and theater practitioner Robert Lepage, involved collaboration with Wendat Nation members (Poll). In a 1982 St. John's production, *The Newfoundland Tempest* sought to explore the particularly marked relevance of the play for an isolated and rocky island province that didn't join the Canadian confederation until 1949 (Ormsby and King). In taking up *The Tempest* as her chosen work in the Hogarth series, Atwood thus aligns her project with a broader history of Canadian interest in the play as an allegory for Canada's relationship to Britain.

She also draws on the rich contemporary history of what has come to be known as "Prison Shakespeare." Despite the daunting challenges of potentially inaccessible language, length, and complexity, Shakespeare's works have been popular in prison productions around the world. As Rob Pensalfini explains, Prison Shakespeare has a tendency to emphasize rehearsing and workshopping over performance, and some programs eschew a final performance entirely (5); in part, this is because prison drama programs have been justified as educational rehabilitation or personal development for inmates, but there are also daunting security and logistical issues involved in preparing a live production before an audience, which Atwood's Felix addresses by filming his productions, which are broadcast throughout the prison.

Felix learns to work within the prison's constraints and innumerable rules, smuggling in cigarettes for the cast party and charming the prison guards into believing he is a harmless old man. His insistence that the inmates are capable of reading and understanding Shakespeare surprises Estelle, the university professor who coordinates the prison education program, who holds a stereotypical view that Shakespeare's work will be too difficult for this population, since "some of them can barely read" (Atwood, *Hag-Seed* 52). Pensalfini notes similarly that "there is an assumed mis-fit between Shakespeare and prisoners" based on a belief that "one must be highly literate" to cope with his works (16). But, as Felix argues in response to Estelle's concern, the actors and audience members involved in Shakespeare's productions were hardly erudite themselves; further, Felix has learned from his previous Shakespeare prison productions that his students are canny interpreters of the complex human motivations of the characters, drawing on their own challenging life experiences to animate their performances. For student readers, the initially hesitant and then enthusiastic actors model creative contemporary engagement with the text of *The Tempest* that can spark discussion about how to make canonical texts more broadly accessible and meaningful.

The figure of Miranda from Shakespeare's play is mirrored in Felix's lost daughter, who returns to him as a ghostly apparition while he is exiled in the country. Miranda also presents a key casting issue for Felix, who is sensitive to the ethical and pragmatic concerns of casting male prisoners in female roles. He elects to hire Anne-Marie, whose name reverses syllables in the name *Miranda*. She is a dancer and former gymnast whom he had originally cast for his festival production, and this incarnation of the character is anything but ethereal: when the inmate playing Ferdinand attempts to kiss her, she overpowers and chastens him. It is during a post-play class exercise that Miranda's vigor is most highlighted. Each small group who supports an actor playing a major character in the play has been tasked with imagining a post-epilogue afterlife for their character. While the Alonso group imagines the villain's murderous and rapacious rampage on board ship on the way back to Milan, Anne-Marie contradicts their assumption that Miranda could be so easily subdued, pointing out she was raised by Prospero and may possesses, along with the physical strength highlighted in the play, magical abilities. Through the figure of Miranda, Atwood engages in explicit feminist revisioning, imagining greater agency for a character often viewed as relatively passive, an approach at odds with her rethinking of Cordelia as a character who remains, in *Cat's Eye*, consigned to insufficiency and, ultimately, a decades-long absence from Elaine's life.

Shakespeare's plays present a formidable legacy to Canadian writers, and dozens of authors, ranging from Robertson Davies and Margaret Laurence to Suniti Namjoshi and Daniel David Moses, have taken up the task of rewriting his works in a Canadian context and for a contemporary sensibility. As *Cat's Eye* and *Hag-Seed* demonstrate, Atwood's characteristic achievement, accomplished through allusion and intertextuality, is her attentiveness to how issues of nation and gender can reinvigorate readings and rewritings of the Bard.

NOTE

1. This essay cites the Penguin edition of *Hag-Seed*.

Sea Changes: *Hag-Seed*, Shakespearean Adaptation, and Prison Representation

Gina Hausknecht

Margaret Atwood's *Hag-Seed* is equally a work of homage to Shakespeare's *The Tempest* and an adaptation about adaptation, a novel that burrows industriously, often gleefully, into the creative process. In a double-stranded borrowing from the play, the novel traces the redemptive emotional journey of a washed-up theater director, a Prospero figure, who avenges himself on his enemies through a production of *The Tempest* that organizes the story's narrative arc in a prologue, five acts, and an epilogue: the novel opens with Felix's dismissal as the artistic director of the Makeshiweg Festival (a genially sly nod to the Stratford Festival) as he prepares an extravagant staging of *The Tempest*, and it ends with his production of a different version of the play in a men's prison under the auspices of a prison education program. Underscoring the rich malleability of Shakespeare's works, the incarcerated actors generate their own alternative endings to the play as part of their coursework. Because half the novel's action takes place in a prison, *Hag-Seed* also serves, necessarily and uneasily, as a form of prison literature. This essay will consider *Hag-Seed* as Shakespearean adaptation and offer context for its uneven, sometimes troubling representation of prisons and Shakespeare prison programs. Both these frameworks provide accessible avenues of inquiry in the classroom: How do the creative approaches to *The Tempest* at the festival and in the prison fit into the ever-expanding field of adaptations of this play, and how might students contribute to this field themselves? How does the comic treatment of Felix's prison troupe resonate with real prison theater programs, and how does Felix's teaching compare to actual prison pedagogy?

Shakespearean Adaptation

The history of Shakespeare's amplification from popular Elizabethan playwright to revered linchpin of the Western literary canon is told through a long lineage of adaptations and appropriations. The "social and cultural tides that have swept and shaped Shakespeare's reputation" have given us his oeuvre in rewritings of all kinds: in the first couple of centuries, opera, dance, moral tales for children, aphoristic collections of his "beauties," painting, and then film and video, video games, memes, and Internet fan fiction and art (G. Taylor 374). *The Tempest* is among the earliest and most variously adapted of Shakespeare's plays, one of the first to be introduced to Restoration London audiences when the theaters reopened in 1660. In *The Tempest; or, The Enchanted Island*, first staged in 1667, John Dryden and William Davenant introduced new characters, including sisters for Miranda and Caliban and a girlfriend for Ariel, reflecting the new presence of women on the public stage, added music and a decidedly more comic tone, and rewrote much of the dialogue (Shakespeare et al.). An operatic 1674 version by Thomas Shadwell followed, and throughout the eighteenth-century *The Tempest* looked much more like these early rewritings than what we think of as Shakespeare's "original," the play printed in the First Folio of 1623, the closest text we have to the play as it was written or performed in his lifetime (G. Taylor 61, 200). Atwood's *Hag-Seed*, then, is a recent entry in a history almost as old as the play itself of imaginative retellings of *The Tempest*, animated at least as much by the values and aesthetics of the reteller as by those of the original playwright.

Over the twentieth century, *The Tempest* emerged as one of the most salient Shakespearean texts for probing the margins between past and present and investigating the impacts—whether violent, generative, or both—of centers on peripheries; Paul Brown describes this as a "discursive matrix" of colonial subjectivities (209). Postcolonial resistance and feminist skepticism have radically altered how *The Tempest* looks to us now. On page and stage, attention and sympathy shift from Prospero, the ostensible hero of Shakespeare's play, a duke and magician deposed by his malevolent brother, to other characters: Prospero's abused and abased servant Caliban, of Algerian descent, who asserts a hereditary right to the island which is the play's setting; Prospero's daughter, Miranda, the sole living female character on the island; the witch Sycorax, Caliban's mother, long dead when the play begins; the spirit Ariel, pining for his freedom, without whom Prospero cannot work his magic; and the Italian lords, courtiers, and servants who wander the island contemplating their own rule of it. In *Tempests after Shakespeare*, Chantal Zabus describes how the play not only reflects but also, "through its rewritings, has helped shape three contemporaneous movements—postcoloniality, postfeminism or postpatriarchy, and postmodernism" (1); Zabus charts the rise of what she calls "Calibanic postcoloniality" (9), feminist interrogations of patriarchal representations of women, and the return of fascination with Prospero as a controlling figure in increasingly resistant cultural contexts. Among the most influential postcolonial responses to the play was Aimé Césaire's play *A Tempest*, in which Prospero is a despotic white master falling apart under the moral strain of his own oppressive behavior, and Caliban and Ariel, explicitly identified as his slaves, choose different avenues of resistance. Caliban recurs in Caribbean literature as the face and voice of the resisting colonized subject, as in George Lamming's novel *Water with Berries* and as discussed in Rob Nixon's survey "Caribbean and African Appropriations of *The Tempest*." In Gloria Naylor's *Mama Day*, Miranda is the magic-wielding matriarch of a coastal island. If its title is the only direct reference to *The Tempest* in Rachel Ingalls's *Mrs. Caliban*, a novel about a lonely housewife's affair with a giant amphibious creature, that itself demonstrates the ubiquity of against-the-grain appropriations autonomizing the characters most under Prospero's control in *The Tempest*.

With her characteristic iconoclasm, Atwood, recentering her Prospero figure, treating the racial dynamics of the carceral setting only very lightly, and largely bypassing questions of oppression in both the play and the prison, veers away from this kind of inquiry into the nature and consequences of power. In the context of decades of postcolonial, feminist, and racially theorized productions and adaptations, *Hag-Seed*'s heroizing of Felix, however wry, can read as vaguely anachronistic (Ron Charles, in an early review, noted, "[T]his is, weirdly, a revision of 'The Tempest' in which the monster-slave is even more defanged than in the original story") or ideologically combative (Douglas M. Lanier assumes that "Atwood's interpretive emphasis seeks to rescue the play from recent critical trends" [244]). Although it uses a prison as one of its settings, the injustice that animates *Hag-Seed* is internecine squabbling for leadership of a theater company. It does not demonize the incarcerated men, to whom it is clearly sympathetic and even affectionate, so much as demote them; Felix is the novel's beating heart.

Atwood identifies the Caliban-centered postcolonial tradition as one of many available options, asking rhetorically in a *Guardian* piece describing the writing of *Hag-Seed*, "Is he a victim of colonial oppression, as he is frequently played these days?" and acknowledging, with her disarming frankness, "People have been redoing Shakespeare for a long time, often with odd results. And I too have redone Shakespeare, also with odd results" ("Perfect Storm"). Atwood's entire oeuvre is deeply referential, as Shakespeare's is; like Shakespeare, who mined for his own purposes everything he read, Atwood is an inveterate collector and recycler. *The Penelopiad* and *Hag-Seed* represent this on a large scale; on a smaller one are mischievous takes on *Hamlet* in the short stories "Gertrude Talks Back" (*Good Bones* 15–18) and "Horatio's Version" (*Tent* 115–20) and Shakespearean nods and asides throughout her work (see Atwood, "Margaret Atwood: Shakespeare in My Work"). As Jo Eldridge Carney points out in her chapter on *Hag-Seed* and *The Tempest*, Atwood herself has frequently adapted and been adapted: "Like Shakespeare, Atwood is on both ends of the borrowing cycle" (57). Atwood's works have been adapted for film and television, and, as with *The Handmaid's Tale*, readapted. That cycle itself, the churning of art into other art, is deeply embedded in *Hag-Seed*'s approach to the task set by the Hogarth Shakespeare project.

Hogarth Shakespeare

Hag-Seed was commissioned by the Hogarth Shakespeare series, which asked popular British, Canadian, and American novelists to write contemporary prose versions of Shakespeare's plays. With the series' debut novels timed for the quadrennial of Shakespeare's death in 2016, the project was conceived specifically as Shakespeareana. The seven titles that were published before the project petered out (Jo Nesbø's *Macbeth* was the last to appear, in 2018, and Gillian Flynn's version of *Hamlet* was announced but never published) were received with dutiful adulation, although the critics were divided on the Hogarth vision. Many of Shakespeare's readers and viewers are fiercely protective of the plays' special qualities or their author's special genius: "Shakespeare is a dramatic poet rather than a psychological novelist or a self-conscious critic of texts, and his imagination runs in broader, potent strokes that are not so much illuminated as belied by the inward-turning ironies of the modern psychological novel" (Gopnik). Others received the Hogarth series as an extension of Shakespeare's own creative process of adaptation and appropriation: Stephen Greenblatt notes that "[h]e was a great recycler of stories, and there's no reason why his stories shouldn't be recycled," and Jeanette Winterson, one of the series' authors, points out that "Shakespeare never invented a plot, he always went to an existing story or text and said, 'I'll have that.' . . . I think he would approve of what we're all doing" (qtd. in Alter). Lanier observes that in the absence of Shakespeare's language, the Hogarth series locates Shakespeare's literariness in narrative and in psychology, providing the characters "with extensive backstories and explicit chains of motivation that make their behavior plausible" (238). Students may enjoy charting how the parallels between Felix and Prospero both hew to the contours of the play and modernize it.

The first four Hogarth books are subtitled as retellings of their plays (e.g., *Hag-Seed: The Tempest Retold*). But what does it mean to retell a Shakespeare play? Fidelity is a notoriously vexed question in this four-hundred-year-plus context, even when deciding what the play itself is: editors since the early eighteenth century have debated whether to strive for the text as originally written, or performed, or intended, none of which is directly visible to us. For half of the Hogarth authors, the answer is plot: Anne Tyler's *Vinegar Girl* (*The Taming of the Shrew*), Edward St. Aubyn's *Dunbar* (*King Lear*), Tracy Chevalier's *New Boy* (*Othello*), and Nesbø's *Macbeth* transpose their plays' story to modern contexts, studiously mapping plot points and characters onto a decidedly contemporary setting. Othello, Iago, and Desdemona become the elementary school students Osei, Ian, and Dee; *Macbeth* is a crime thriller; Tyler's Kate is the misunderstood, socially awkward daughter of a negligent father; and St. Aubyn's Lear figure has left his media empire to his daughters with predictably unfortunate results. By contrast, *Hag-Seed*, Winterson's *The Gap of Time* (*The Winter's Tale*) and Howard Jacobson's *Shylock Is My Name* reach for more complex intertexts, asking not what the story of a Shakespeare play would look like in modern dress but how that play's thematic concerns show up in our lives now. In a recognizably Shakespearean way, *Hag-Seed* engages with *The Tempest* to tell its own story about the mechanisms of grief and rage, the complications of the desire for revenge and accountability, and the consolations of creativity.

Adaptation in Hag-Seed

Adaptation, like memory and haunting, makes present out of past; in *Hag-Seed*, adaptation evokes "the kinds of repetitive phenomena that define trauma"

(Zajac 325). Even as Felix adapts *The Tempest* at Fletcher for the purposes of his revenge, his central creative, compulsive reworking is adapting the narrative of his life to include his beloved dead daughter. Felix's Miranda may be a ghost or a projection of his grief or a trick of light and sound; in Yağmur Tatar's framing, Atwood "adeptly tinkers *Hag-Seed* into a mechanism that endlessly reflects the kaleidoscopic intertextuality of reality and illusion" (97). In casting himself as Prospero in the Fletcher production, Felix escalates the haunting: "By assuming the role of Prospero—or being possessed by it—Felix rehearses and rehashes his suffering" (Zajac 332). The profusion of the creative imagination is one of the novel's themes, the source both of Felix's original downfall—his creative excesses provide the pretext for his former partner, Tony, to remove him as artistic director of the festival—and his comeback: in the novel's climax, two shows happen simultaneously, one the videotaped production the students have rehearsed and the other the interactive performance piece that spills beyond the script.

Even when Felix has achieved his revenge, the art-making continues. Felix's students at Fletcher conclude each class with writing afterlives for their characters; Paul Joseph Zajac comments on the students' rewriting of the play's ending as a way the novel continues to defer its own ending, looping through one adaptation after another, even after Felix's story is seemingly resolved, a typically Atwoodian openness (338). In reimagining, resisting, and reshaping the play's original ending, they enter into a long lineage, and many of the Shakespeare prison programs mentioned below include this kind of creative exercise in one way or another; our students, too, may be encouraged to try their hands at imagining the characters' future lives or otherwise inhabiting their perspectives. Still, adaptation does not offer unlimited freedom, and in prison creativity is always conditioned by the carceral space, rife with "the tension inherent in generating original narratives that possess the power to subvert dominant narratives," as Nishevita Jayendran notes of Team Hag-Seed's invented ending for Caliban (20). Felix's response is to shut it down, summarily cutting off the class's enthusiastic response: "Felix stands up. This shouldn't get too far out of control" (Atwood, *Hag-Seed* 275).[1] He promptly assigns grades, ensuring that "the space that allows for creative expressions is moderated and mediated through discourses of power" (Jayendran 21). While the men get to write their own *Tempest* stories, the one that matters to Felix (and the novel) is his own; "an implicit hierarchy in meaning-making" is preserved (23). Inviting students to consider the power dynamics in this scene would open onto productive critical consideration of how Atwood represents prison education.

Shakespeare Prison Programs

Shakespeare-focused prison theater programs have been operating in Great Britain and North America since the 1980s; Rob Pensalfini's *Prison Shakespeare* and Amy Scott-Douglass's *Shakespeare Inside* provide helpful background, and Rowan Mackenzie's *Creating Space for Shakespeare* details the growing field of "applied Shakespeare." Although Shakespeare has long been performed in carceral settings, formal Shakespeare prison programs were first undertaken in England in 1982 by the Royal Shakespeare Company's Cicely Berry and in the United States in 1988 by Jean Trounstine, working in a women's prison in Massachusetts. The longest-running, most influential of the North American Shakespeare theater programs, Shakespeare Behind Bars, founded by Curt L. Tofteland in 1995 at the Luther Luckett Correctional Facility in Kentucky, continues to operate in both Kentucky and Michigan; it was the subject of a 2005 documentary, *Shakespeare Behind Bars*, which traces the Luther Luckett troupe over the course of a year as they rehearse and then perform *The Tempest*. This film, widely available, offers an excellent counterpoint to *Hag-Seed*; students reading the novel can watch a group of incarcerated men work closely with the play's language, themes, and central moral challenges around forgiveness and redemption. Many Shakespeare prison programs, including Prison Performing Arts, the Shakespeare Prison Project, Marin Shakespeare Company's Shakespeare for Social Justice, and Detroit Public Theatre's Shakespeare in Prison, along with Shakespeare Behind Bars, have active websites that students can explore for sample scenes and personal testimonies by participants.

Even as prison education in the United States contracted dramatically after the Violent Crime Control and Law Enforcement Act of 1994 revoked Pell grants for incarcerated students (J. M. Taylor 6), prison theater programs expanded both in number and mission: Shakespeare Behind Bars and Marin Shakespeare's program are among those that work with returning citizens and youth in juvenile corrections. Founded in 2012 at the University of Notre Dame, the Shakespeare in Prisons Network convened the first Shakespeare in Prisons Conference in 2013 and connects prison theater practitioners globally (shakespeare.nd.edu/service/shakespeare-in-prisons). As college-in-prison programs have re-emerged, Shakespeare has been regularly taught in literature courses. Although Felix stumbles into (and through) his gig teaching and directing Shakespeare at the Fletcher prison, his real-world counterparts have a wealth of professional resources, many of which students can easily consult.

Atwood briefly describes her research into prison literature and prison theater and educational programs in the acknowledgments of *Hag-Seed*. Although she clearly has a general sense of both the mechanics and the ethics of how these programs work, *Hag-Seed* forgoes the commitment to pedagogies that address and seek to repair the inequities and injustices of incarceration that characterize much prison education today. Atwood mentions as a particular source of inspiration Laura Bates's *Shakespeare Saved My Life*, nodding only in passing to Bard College. While the Bard Prison Initiative (bpi.bard.edu) has been a national leader in prison education as a systemic response to the ravages of mass incarceration, it is Bates's very personal memoir, focusing on the redemptive value of prison education for both the incarcerated participants and the instructor, that appears to inspire and guide Atwood. By contrast, Rebecca Ginsburg, in the introduction to her essay collection *Critical Perspectives on Teaching in Prison*, anatomizes the pitfalls of overfocusing on rehabilitation, starting with the default prioritization of "corrections" over learning: "Our job is not to reform our incarcerated students, any more than faculty on traditional campuses think of ourselves as engaged in student reform" (6). Even a quick look at the essays in Ginsburg's volumes—most particularly, perhaps, those by incarcerated and formerly incarcerated students—can provide valuable insight into the risks and rewards of prison education. Short, very readable essays by Jayme Yeo and Jean Howard explore a range of considerations Shakespeare teachers bring to their prison classrooms. The Alliance for Higher Education in Prison's highly browsable website offers a wealth of resources for a real-life Felix (www.higheredinprison.org). Students reading *Hag-Seed* certainly should know that prison programs typically do attend to how power saturates, organizes, and defines all relationships within carceral spaces: between instructor and incarcerated student, correctional officers supervising programs and incarcerated people receiving them, and educational systems and departments of correction.

Prison Representation in Hag-Seed

Hag-Seed is breezy and hopeful about these enmeshments. When Felix enters Fletcher, he observes his surroundings with brisk, confident detachment: "The smell of misery, lying over everyone within like an enchantment. But for brief moments he knows he can unbind that spell" (Atwood, *Hag-Seed* 75). He holds himself above the other teachers in the program and their "tut-tutting kind of moralizing that he finds obnoxious" (79). The two correctional officers who screen Felix each time he arrives are stock comic characters, jovial, enthusiastic, and unthreatening: "The guards have taken to watching the Fletcher Correctional performance videos along with everyone else. He gives a special talk about the play every year just for them, so they will feel included. It's always risky, the prospect that the prisoners might be having more fun than the guards. Resentments can build up, and that could cause problems for Felix" (75–76). However genial Felix's demeanor toward his charges, the director's self-interest is a given. Many of the characters are caricatures, in keeping with a busy, bustling novel featuring multiple, interweaving subplots and intertexts that seems only intermittently to need us to feel deeply about its protagonist. Yet caricaturing Felix's incarcerated students and the staff who work and volunteer at the prison resonates differently than comically sketching a solipsistic white male theater director steeped in privilege and self-pity. Prison is typically invisible to those who haven't themselves been or aren't connected to those who have been incarcerated. Because prison literature makes incarceration visible, representation matters. *Hag-Seed*'s Literacy through Literature program needs to be understood as an approximate, lightly drawn sketch; the resources mentioned above can help instructors and students contextualize Atwood's sometimes facile treatment.

Although many of the responses to the novel describe it as being set in a prison, we only see Fletcher through Felix's limited perspective. We never see it when he isn't there, and we never see what he doesn't: the life of confinement beyond the walls of the classroom. The instrumentalism of Felix's use of the class for his own ends, and his willingness to risk their safety and well-being, especially those of 8Handz, who is his Ariel and coconspirator, runs counter to how most prison educators understand what it means to volunteer in prison. The ways in which the novel's depiction of prison strains credulity undercut its nominal sympathy for the incarcerated students. *Hag-Seed* is alternately aware of the material constraints associated with going into a prison, as seen in the scrutiny Felix faces bringing in props and costumes, and blithe about those permissions, so that Anne-Marie brings baked goods and her knitting bag without incident. We presumably are meant to see Felix's winning over his students by smuggling in contraband cigarettes as an amusing, triumphant flouting of the prison rules, yet our rooting for his defiance erases the danger of doing so and the unlikelihood that a prison educator would run this risk, understanding that the consequences would be far more significant for the incarcerated students than for the instructor. What is further elided here is the inherent tension between education and incarceration: to participate in a prison program is at once to offer humanity and dignity and to comply with the fundamental inhumanity of the carceral system.

Hag-Seed lets the material reality of prison mostly recede into the background while repeatedly foregrounding the students' criminality for comic effect. In what is likely the most uneasy passage in the novel for prison educators, Estelle prepares Felix for each term by providing a cheat sheet on his students' criminal pasts (83), reprised when Felix passes information about the cast members' convictions onto Anne-Marie. He's blithely aware of the violation of trust in accepting and sharing the information despite having told the students he's uninterested in why they're at Fletcher and believing that "it would be disillusioning for his actors to find their criminal convictions spelled out" (137).[2]

Estelle's regard for the students in the program she considers her "special baby" seems thin at best: "You'll be teaching, well, convicted criminals. . . . Wouldn't you be rather wasted on them?" (49, 51). When Anne-Marie describes stringing WonderBoy along to get a good performance out of him (190), Felix dismisses his own mild concern with the essentializing and totalizing reflection that WonderBoy is "a con man, don't forget. A con man playing an actor. A double unreality" (191). This is despite Felix's earlier insistence on referring to his students as actors: "He refused to call them inmates, he refused to call them prisoners, not while they were in his theatre troupe" (71), a sensitivity that eventually seems more about him than them. (Many prison programs and, indeed, many departments of correction, prefer people-centered language like "incarcerated individual," minimizing use of terms, like *inmate*, *prisoner*, *convict*, or *felon*, that define people by their sentences.) Above all, *Hag-Seed* concerns itself with Felix's unfolding self-knowledge and healing; the prison and its inhabitants are props for that drama. In the novel's keenest, most accurate take on education in prison, government ministers plan to shut down the Fletcher program, characterizing it as "an indulgence, a raid on the taxpayer wallet, a pandering to the liberal elites, and a reward for criminality" (200). Painfully true to life, this passage does not exaggerate public discourse about prison educational and rehabilitative programs.

Hag-Seed is a tonally various novel, by turns silly and serious, treating Felix's self-involvement with forgiving mockery and barreling through its slightly absurd plot with sometimes madcap energy, but also probing the textures of grief and mourning and the challenges and consolations of art-making. Suited to Atwood-specific or contemporary fiction courses, the novel can also slip readily into a course or unit on Shakespearean adaptation and makes particular sense paired with the *Tempest*-focused documentary *Shakespeare Behind Bars*. The "writing beyond the ending" exercise that Felix sets his students in the fifth section, or "act," of the novel, would make an apt assignment, letting students experiment with how adaptation works and enter into the long-standing artistic dialogue with Shakespeare's plays. *Hag-Seed* can be usefully accompanied on a syllabus by any number of works by incarcerated people that speak compellingly to what it is like to live, study, and even perform Shakespeare in prison.[3] The ways in which the novel does not represent prison life and prison education realistically can provide the occasion to engage with how carceral systems do work and with the very question of why they are so hard for those on the outside to see clearly.

NOTES

1. This essay cites the Hogarth edition of *Hag-Seed*.

2. One way to approach the ethics of this choice is to assign the radio documentary "Act Five," an episode of *This American Life* that follows a group of incarcerated men in Missouri rehearsing *Hamlet* (Hitt). Jack Hitt, the interviewer, recounts both his decision to look up the men's crimes after they decline to reveal them to him and his recognition that doing so violated their trust, but the documentary treats that recognition only in passing. In my experience and that of other prison educators, students directed to Hitt's decision typically engage thoughtfully with it.

3. PEN America's Prison and Justice Writing program publishes imaginative literature by currently and formerly incarcerated writers on their website (pen.org/prison-writing). American Prison Writing Archive collects essays by incarcerated people (www.hamilton.edu/academics/open-curriculum/digital-hamilton/projects/american-prison-writing-archive). *Ear Hustle* (www.earhustlesq.com) and *Uncuffed* (www.weareuncuffed.org) are podcasts made within California prisons. A sampling of recent memoirs about the prison experience by formerly incarcerated people include Reginald Dwayne Betts's *A Question of Freedom*, Keri Blakinger's *Corrections in Ink*, Susan Burton's *Becoming Ms. Burton*, Ian Manuel's *My Time Will Come*, and Shaka Senghor's *Writing My Wrongs*.

Rethinking Archetypes in the High School Classroom with *The Penelopiad*

Marguerite Raymond

When my sophomore honors students enter my world literature classroom on the very first day of classes in August, the question "What makes someone a hero?" stares at them from the front board. As an icebreaker, they brainstorm in groups what characteristics would combine to make the perfect hero—for them, for school, for the city they live in, for the country, and for the world—and we begin planting the seeds of the idea that the definition of a hero can change according to need, perspective, and time. At first, there are some silly answers, like "a hero is someone who will give me the answers to the test" and other self-gratifying jokes, but then we start digging to find deeper answers, like "a hero is someone who advocates for those who cannot" and "a hero is someone who overcomes all obstacles." Once we have a range of ideas, we start narrowing the definition and considering how the proffered characteristics go together while continuing to deepen the discussion: Is a hero only someone who does something to benefit you or themselves? What does the journey they go through say about their character? What is the difference between a literary hero and those referred to as heroes in real life?

The course, which includes texts from all over the globe, begins with a traditional classics base. Throughout the fall semester, we learn about the roots of Western literary heroes with Joseph Campbell's *The Hero's Journey* and through different world mythology stories, Sophocles's *Antigone*, and Homer's *Odyssey*. This module gives students a common language they can use to discuss story elements and character development. It also prepares students to understand how mythic elements work and evolve from place to place or over time. Tracing Odysseus's and Telemachus's stories while focusing on archetypes and Campbell's steps helps students better understand how these characters influence one another through their archetypal functions and how most other characters in the myth are designed to help our hero reach the end of their journey.

After students are confident in their abilities to recognize and evaluate the hero qualities in these classic texts, we use excerpts from Margaret Atwood's *The Penelopiad* to reassess those traditional ideas of the hero. Atwood's focus on female characters that are neither victims nor heroes makes her short novel a perfect companion to the traditional black-and-white, good-guy-versus-bad-guy mentality of *The Odyssey*. In *The Odyssey*, Odysseus is the main hero of myth, the one that other heroes of myth and literature that come after him emulate. So, the students assume that everything that he does must be heroic. Usually, my class is not the first in which they have studied elements of the hero's journey, so the process of defining the epic hero builds on previous learning. It also involves breaking the definition apart, examining the reasons behind it, and rebuilding it together. *The Penelopiad* offers students a complementary counterpoint to *The Odyssey* by presenting a female perspective on the male-centered hero's journey, challenging traditional epic archetypes and trickster characteristics. In contemporary, relatable language, the *Penelopiad* encourages high school students to analyze how heroic mythoi influence one another and the stories we tell today.

The Storytelling of Penelope and the Chorus of Maids

In 2005, Canongate Books commissioned a series in which authors reimagined myths for more modern times. In addition to Atwood's version of *The Odyssey*, the series includes retellings of the stories of Atlas and Hercules, Samson, and Baba Yaga. Simon Goldhill in his *New Statesman* review of *The Penelopiad* recalls a common assignment in British curriculum, retelling ancient myths in modern settings, to set the premise of the Canongate Myths collection, which he calls "an intriguingly risky project in that it sounds so much like that primary school task, but wants to take an altogether more adult view of how the old stories remain part of our culture" (48). In some ways, this conception mirrors what teachers strive to do in the classroom: we begin with the primary task of retelling and understanding and then delve into the more mature thoughts and discussion that begin to stem from an activity so seemingly simple. The perspectives presented in *The Penelopiad* help students see *The Odyssey* anew, bringing to light questions about the text's definitions not only of the hero but of archetypes such as the trickster and the good wife—and, more broadly, about the acceptance of truth in storytelling. Atwood often writes about the theme of survival, and in *The Penelopiad* she writes not only of Penelope's survival but also the survival of myth. When we tell tales, what represents the "truth," and what should we leave behind? Who deserves to be listened to?

Atwood's Penelope is the primary narrator of her story (though, as discussed below, the twelve maids' commentary challenges her account as well as the canonical one). Throughout Penelope's narration, Atwood incorporates allusions to *The Odyssey* and Robert Graves's *The Greek Myths* to develop Penelope's character while complicating traditional depictions of it. For example, according to Graves's interpretation of the myth, when Penelope leaves her family home and her father begs her to stay, she covers her face with her veil in a display of modesty. However, Atwood's Penelope uses her veil to hide her laughter at her father (*Penelopiad* 49).[1] Unable to know whether either author has uncovered a truth in what is, after all, a myth, we must acknowledge the patterns of story-making, both in the myths that provide the foundation for many of our stories and in the histories we believe to be true.

As the story progresses, the reader becomes more aware that, although Penelope calls out Odysseus for the untruth of his stories, her own narrative may be unreliable as well. The maids, whom Penelope repeatedly insists that she loved and cared for, bring a different perspective on Penelope, too; they seem as angry at her as they are at Odysseus and Telemachus. The reader must eventually conclude that Penelope may be just as wily as Odysseus—foiling him as a trickster—and just as responsible as he was for the deaths of the maids. Students can evaluate her tale against what they have learned previously to determine what to believe while simultaneously acknowledging that Penelope is dismantling another story.

Rationale

Several Atwood texts use well-known Greek myths to subvert perspectives and make readers reconsider motivations, but *The Penelopiad* is particularly well-suited for the high school classroom because it reflects the traditional canon common to high schools across the country. *The Penelopiad* challenges these students to rethink a story that they are now familiar with. At this stage of their schooling, they have already been examined on this material and may believe they have more or less mastered it. But *The Penelopiad* invites them to revisit what they thought they knew and to think critically about heroism, empathy, and the value of reading literature.

This unit serves as a basic introduction to postmodernist thought by questioning traditional perspectives and examining how and why literature defines and frames characters. *The Penelopiad* prompts a class discussion on how archetypes, such as the good wife, have continued from the traditional canon to frame the stories we tell today; in chapter 1, "A Low Art," Penelope immediately rejects the archetype, telling her reader, "*Don't follow my example,* I want to scream in your ears—yes, yours!" (2). Atwood's direct address to the reader (which mirrors the mode of oral tradition) invites students to confront the texts more openly and begin to develop empathy for a more diverse range of perspectives. Atwood interacts with her readers in a way that is reminiscent of the oral tradition while still questioning the previous perspectives presented. The dual narrators, Penelope and the chorus of maids, give students a chance to examine historiography and consider who is telling the story and what their motivations might be.

The Penelopiad is a worthy companion piece to the traditional, hero-focused tale of *The Odyssey* because of the allusions, parallel themes, and postmodern techniques Atwood uses to reimagine the story of *The Odyssey* through the eyes of Penelope and the chorus of maids. In a study on the development of empathetic learners in the social studies classroom, Carolyn Casale and colleagues define historical empathy as follows: "the process of students' cognitive and affective engagement with historical figures to better understand and contextualize their lived experiences, decisions, or actions involves understanding how people from the past thought, felt, made decisions, acted, and faced consequences within a specific historical and social context" (4). Students spend half our block-scheduled class researching history and cultural information about ancient Greece, and in particular the roles of women. Then, in the second half of class, they start building their own empathetic abilities by discussing as a group why they think Homer would have portrayed the maids and Penelope as he did and debating why those women might have different feelings about their story.

The chapters from *The Penelopiad* that we focus on the most throughout our pairing with *The Odyssey* balance the voices of Penelope with those of her maids—namely, chapter 1, "A Low Art;" chapter 2, "The Chorus Line: A Rope-Jumping Rhyme;" chapter 12, "Waiting;" and chapter 26, "The Chorus Line: The Trial of Odysseus, as Videotaped by the Maids." In addition to or in place of using the novel, both "A Low Art" and "The Chorus Line: A Rope-Jumping Rhyme" are included in the Norton Critical Edition of *The Odyssey* with Emily Wilson's translation, which is the preferred version used in my classroom by virtue of its approachable language for high school students and its inclusion of other excerpts collected in the "Post-Classical Reception" and "Criticism" sections.[2]

Texts and Activities

After reading the introduction and invocation to the muse in Wilson's translation of *The Odyssey*, students look at and compare the introductions and invocations in Richmond Lattimore's and Robert Fagles's translations as well as Gareth Hinds's graphic novel interpretation. Then they read Atwood's introduction to Penelope in "A Low Art." Students focus on diction and translation, questioning why and how the four different writers chose different words and what the connotations of each of the choices means for the story as a whole. How does Fagles's calling Odysseus "the man of twists and turns" (77) or Wilson's describing him as "complicated" (5) change how the reader approaches his character? Then, how do those translations match with Penelope's description of him in *The Penelopiad*: "He was always so plausible. . . . I knew he was tricky and a liar, I just didn't think he would play his tricks and try out his lies on me" (2) or with the maids' claim that Odysseus "failed" and "killed" them (6)? Students consider the ambiguities and subtleties of translation and how the translator can change the meaning of a story through the connotations of the words chosen. In addition, they discuss the processes and responsibilities of translating works and decide whether it is more important to keep the translation as close to the original text as possible or to reflect the time of the translation itself. Throughout the unit, students analyze how the different translations and interpretations have evolved in meaning and relevance from the classical world to the world today.

In addition to Penelope's questioning of Odysseus's truthfulness, we compare her immediate rejection of the good wife archetype in Homer, where Penelope serves as an ideal representation of a woman that self-sacrifices, remains loyal to her husband, and provides a home for our hero to return to. However, in *The Penelopiad*, Penelope addresses this weight early on:

> And what did I amount to, once the official version gained ground? An edifying legend. A stick used to beat other women with. Why couldn't they be as considerate, as trustworthy, as all-suffering as I had been? That was the line they took, the singers, the yarn-spinners. *Don't follow my example,* I want to scream in your ears—yes, yours! (2)

Some of the students were surprised by this take on Penelope and even noted, "The tone is tense and slightly angry as Penelope acknowledges the hardships of being a woman in this time period and speaks about the wrongdoings surrounding her." In contrast, in the first book of *The Odyssey*, Penelope, introduced as "looking like a goddess," is upset by a song about the cursed Greeks (including her husband), and says, "I can hardly bear my grief. I miss him [Odysseus] all the time" (12). Telemachus scolds her for interrupting the poet and establishes his place above her as a man, although he is her son. Penelope supposedly "took to heart her son's deliberate scolding" and left to weep (12). This weepy Penelope that bends to the will of men around her does not sound like the same woman screaming at the beginning of Atwood's version. Students compare and contrast the introductions of Penelope, debate the shortcomings of associating characters with archetypes, and discuss how point of view influences readers' perception of a character.

Students also analyze various translations of book 9, where Odysseus tells of his exploits with the Cyclops as well as Penelope's version of the events. Specifically, students are instructed to compare and contrast the figurative language used in the different iterations as well as the connotations of the translators' diction. While Homer dedicates an entire book to the problems that Odysseus had to overcome for his crew with the "road of trials" in the hero's journey, Atwood reduces the exploit to a third of a sentence in chapter 12, "Waiting," immediately dismissing the tale's heroic aspects: "Odysseus had been in a fight with a giant one-eyed Cyclops, said some; no, it was only a one-eyed tavern keeper, said another, and the fight was over non-payment of the bill" (*Penelopiad* 83). In addition to severely truncating the exploit, Atwood casts doubt on the accepted version of events by following it with other, less noble possibilities.

Next, we look at the entirety of Atwood's chapter 12 and the alternative plausibilities Penelope presents there for Odysseus's exploits and the adventures that have made him a "hero." After reading the chapter, students then consider the question "The cliché is that history is written by the victors, so how much are we heroes in our own minds, yet the villain of someone else's story?" This question opens their discussions up to considering disagreements with their friends and families and imagining pop culture stories told through the lens of a different character (leading to an interesting defense of Scar from Disney's *The Lion King*).

With this notion in mind, students create a presentation explaining which version of the book 9 stories they prefer and why. Many note that *The Penelopiad* influenced their interpretation of some of the descriptions in Homer's tale. For example, more were able to recognize the trickster connotations describing Odysseus, such as in Wilson's translation, where he addresses himself as "Odysseus, Laertes' son, known for my many clever tricks and lies" (96), after reading Atwood and Penelope's accounts. Another student expanded their perspective to the Cyclops, commenting:

> I don't think Odysseus or the Cyclops are in the wrong. It just depends on what point of view you look at. To the Cyclops, Odysseus and his men are just strangers who have invaded his home. He doesn't know any better, and all he is doing is protecting his house. Odysseus didn't mean to cause any harm, but the Cyclops was unwilling to hear him out, so Odysseus had to harm him to save himself.

Because they had looked at another point of view with *The Penelopiad*, they were able to apply an alternative lens to other characters in *The Odyssey* to consider what their story might have been as well.

As a class, one of the things we debate is the nebulousness of defining the Western canon, which typically includes *The Odyssey*. In the Norton Critical Edition of Wilson's translation of *The Odyssey*, two excerpts from *The Penelopiad* are included in the "Post-classical Reception" section. In addition to *The Penelopiad*, students can see other texts that have been inspired by *The Odyssey*, such as works by Ovid, Tennyson, and Edna St. Vincent Millay as well as more contemporary authors like Ocean Vuong and Madeline Miller.

After reading Odysseus's version of events concerning the Phaeacians with the sirens, Cyclopes, and others, we return to chapter 1 of *The Penelopiad*, "A Low Art" (the same passage included in the Norton edition): "He was always so plausible. Many people have believed that his version of events was the true one, give or take a few murders, a few beautiful seductresses, a few one-eyed monsters" (Atwood, *Penelopiad* 2). In terms of considering a fictionalized epic as the "truth," students begin the unit confident that Homer's *Odyssey* offers a "plausible" blend of history and mythology. However, as the unit progresses and students look at how different translations can change the theme or tone or wording of certain events, they become savvier in taking the epic's claims with a grain of salt. Additionally, after this practice in seeing how perspective changes tone, students examine Joseph Brodsky's poem "Odysseus to Telemachus," Ocean Vuong's poem "Telemachus," and an excerpt from Madeline Miller's *Circe* (*Odyssey* 337–38, 356, 357) and identify specific allusions to parts of *The Odyssey* and ways in which the tone of each work influenced their changing perspectives about characters. Discerning in *The Penelopiad* excerpt that Penelope's tone was tense and at times angry, students discussed whether her anger was directed solely toward Odysseus or represented a more general frustration with the patriarchal nature of the time, which allowed Odysseus freedoms it denied his wife or any woman. After this activity, one student remarked:

> It is interesting to read from the perspective of other characters aside from the hero, because it provides a unique perspective of events from a different angle, that could possibly paint the "hero" in a completely different light. I enjoyed this activity because it showcased Penelope's internal struggle of trying to believe her husband was faithful and good, but also her constant fear that he either died or just ditched his life in Ithaca; this wasn't very touched upon in *The Odyssey*—obviously, since it's about Odysseus and to a certain degree Telemachus. It was just refreshing to analyze a different character's perspective in depth.

Another student mused: "My perspective of *The Odyssey* has changed after reading parts of *The Penelopiad* because before I saw Penelope as Odysseus's wife and nothing more. . . . The excerpt about the different stories told about Odysseus's journey and the grief and longing that Penelope felt allowed me to connect with her in a way." Penelope's emotions and reactions to Odysseus's stories had not factored into students' reading of *The Odyssey* to this point. Other students noted that Penelope's story had a different theme to it than Odysseus's did: "The main themes [in *The Penelopiad*] are class and patriarchy, as the text speaks about how Penelope had little say in what was done, but the maids, who were below her, had absolutely no say. Men, on the other hand, could do practically whatever they wanted, particularly regarding the treatment of women."

One of the most popular activities we do comes toward the end of the unit. After reading book 22 of *The Odyssey*, where Odysseus and Telemachus hang the maids, students read chapter 26 of *The Penelopiad*, "The Chorus Line: The Trial of Odysseus, as Videotaped by the Maids," and compare the maids' tones and motivations. Then students are grouped in teams representing the prosecution, defense, witnesses, judge, and jury to stage a mock trial themselves. Students research specific laws and "precedents" to support their clients and use various interpretations and evidence from both *The Odyssey* and *The Penelopiad* to support their side. After the activity, one of the students remarked, "The Chorus Maid's trial activity is tied for my favorite activity we ever did in class. . . . I learned how to better search for, collect, and present evidence under a very limited amount of time, and it strengthened my overall ability to look for important information in books, but also to articulate my thoughts on the fly."

Interestingly, most classes acquit Odysseus of any wrongdoing in hanging the maids, frequently basing their argument on a line from the Judge in that chapter of *The Penelopiad*: "Also, I do not wish to be guilty of an anachronism" (182). Like Atwood, the students have also come to realize that there is a gray area between the good guys and the bad guys and that it is possible to be at once a hero for some and a villain in the eyes of others. Odysseus, Penelope, and the chorus of maids each provide a different perspective on the event, and it is difficult to judge history without being influenced by the perspectives of our own time.

By the time we have finished our *Odyssey* unit in class, students are able to move beyond the gathering of knowledge and really begin to evaluate these characters through the mock trial. *The Odyssey* has given them the archetypes, Atwood has given them another view or two, and now they can judge on their own. Furthermore, students are able to combine the multiple perspectives with the themes of class and gender oppression in ancient Greek society that they had researched and discussed. One student noted on a reflection of this activity that

> I have very strong opinions, and being a woman, I feel that many things are still overlooked towards us. One of the biggest things is rape. Equality between men and women is a lot closer now than when the Odyssey was written, and it's a little infuriating seeing that what happened to the maids was a common thing then, and they thought there was nothing wrong with it. Rape is a touchy subject, and doing this activity in class was a mature way to discuss its reality.

After adding *The Penelopiad* to my curriculum in 2019, I saw a marked difference in the depth of my students' discussions about *The Odyssey* as well as an ability to understand a more nuanced character that they apply to other novels throughout the year. Reflecting on their experience, about three out of four students that year affirmed that reading the excerpts from *The Penelopiad* changed their opinions and perspectives about *The Odyssey*'s story. For example, one student stated, "It led me to believe that no one is perfect, and that all heroes have their flaws," and predicted that when analyzing literature in the future, they will be looking at the objectives and goals of the authors of those stories in relation to the heroes that they write. Another appreciated the practice of looking at a story from a different point of view as a tool that would help them with evaluating literature in the future as well as growing their own abilities to empathize with others: "Now, I try to think more of what a character's thoughts are instead of just looking at how the book portrays them."

Some students continue their study of Penelope and the maids in their formal research papers, searching for additional scholarly information on how these and other characters have been represented in other works. One even chose to read *The Penelopiad* in full for our independent-choice reading project the following semester. Even if they took nothing else away from it, most students enjoyed the excerpts from *The Penelopiad*: "I really liked *The Penelopiad*! It really sheds light on *The Odyssey* in a different way, changing viewpoints and also making it a tad bit more modernized in a sense." For the high school classroom, sometimes just enjoying the reading is enough to make it worthwhile. When that experience changes how they think and approach literature going forward, it is irreplaceable.

NOTES

1. This essay cites the Canongate edition of *The Penelopiad*.
2. Throughout this essay, references to *The Odyssey* cite the Norton Critical Edition.

Retracing Homer's *Odyssey* (Differently): Teaching *The Penelopiad* in the Two-Year College

Lisa Tyler

Funny and moving, Margaret Atwood's *The Penelopiad* is a retelling of the story of Homer's *Odyssey* by Penelope, Odysseus's faithful and long-suffering wife, who waits patiently for twenty years for her husband to return from the Trojan War. Also given voices are Penelope's twelve maids, who narrate portions of the story as a traditional Greek chorus using such nontraditional forms as a sea shanty, a scholarly anthropology lecture, and a videotaped criminal trial. Published in 2005, Atwood's short novel is part of a series of literary works drawing on Greek mythology and published in the United States, Canada, Germany, and the United Kingdom. Atwood explains, "The idea was to ask writers from around the world to retell a myth, any myth, each in his or her own way and in his or her own language, at a length of roughly 100 pages" ("Myths Series"). Mihoko Suzuki suggests that Atwood's more specific objective in this work is to "redefine the relationship of women readers and women writers to canonical texts" (274).

The Penelopiad works beautifully in the community college literature classroom on multiple levels. In addition to being an estimable work of literature in its own right, it introduces students to *The Odyssey*, one of the classic texts of Greek mythology, in a highly accessible way. Atwood both transforms this core humanities text and celebrates its fresh relevance for a very different time. As Atwood herself has observed of myths, "We will never know exactly what they meant to their ancient audiences. But myths can be used—as they have been, so frequently—as the foundation stones for new renderings that find their meanings within their own times and places" ("Myths Series").

Atwood is remarkably faithful to Homer's *Odyssey* and generally has Penelope note explicitly where she deviates from her husband's version of events. I have taught the book in two different introductory English courses: Mythology in Literature and Great Books of the Western World. I know that at least some of my students come to me having already read *The Odyssey* (or at least excerpts from it) in high school. For the benefit of those completely unfamiliar with *The Odyssey* and those who just need a refresher, I direct students to review the short version of Homer's work posted at the free website *Mythweb*, which devotes a paragraph of summary as well as a cartoon to each of *The Odyssey*'s twenty-four books and offers students a quick way to acquaint themselves—or reacquaint themselves—with the major events of the myth ("Odysseus"). Then we spend a class period reviewing the events of *The Odyssey* to make sure students have done the reading. I also review the definition of *epic*—a long narrative poem, originally oral, involving heroes and gods, grand adventures, and often the establishment of a nation—so that students understand the tradition to which Atwood is responding.

In both courses where I have taught this novel, I divide the book in half (breaking after chapter 13) and begin each class with a brief quiz to encourage students to read before coming to class. After the quiz is completed, I ask students questions from a list distributed in the previous class period. To help students who may hesitate to respond feel more comfortable, I generally begin with factual questions about the course content and then shift to deeper concerns: First, what happened? And then, what does that mean? For example, I start with "Who tells this story?" and "Where is Penelope as the story opens?" and later move on to questions such as "Discuss the advice Penelope's mother gives her. What does it mean?" In my experience, student engagement and retention of material are both much better after class discussions than after lectures, and the Socratic method of asking students questions and then asking them to elaborate on their answers often touches on all the major points I would have raised in a lecture anyway.

Community college students are often wildly disparate in terms of reading ability. Some of the readings in my mythology course are demanding works, such as *The Epic of Gilgamesh* and Sophocles's *Oedipus the King* (both included in Thury and Devinney). But Atwood's funny, colloquial writing style appeals to students whose lives are busy and whose reading skills are uneven. I generally assign the novel as the last major reading of the term, and depending on the course, we typically spend about one to two weeks—that is, two to four seventy-five-minute class sessions—on it altogether. Along with it, I typically assign two poems as readings in the Mythology in Literature class: Alfred, Lord Tennyson's dramatic monologue "Ulysses" and Edna St. Vincent Millay's lyric poem "An Ancient Gesture," both of which are also revisions of *The Odyssey* and are readily available online. Atwood, who studied Victorian literature during her graduate work at Harvard (Oates), quotes Tennyson in *The Penelopiad* in Odysseus's line "That which we are, we are" (172).[1]

Nationwide, community college students are more likely to be female ("2022 Fast Facts"). In part because *The Penelopiad* is Greek mythology recounted from a female and distinctly feminist perspective, as even the order of Atwood's subtitle—*The Myth of Penelope and Odysseus*—indicates, it appeals to most of my students to a greater degree than the other course texts, almost all of which are told from a male perspective (Ingersoll 111). "The title, *The Penelopiad*, directly imitates the formation of the title of the *Odyssey* after Odysseus, stating quite unambiguously that this is the story of Penelope," explains Emily Hauser (12). As such, it is a correction of the record: "And what did I amount to, once the official version gained ground? An edifying legend. A stick used to beat other women with. Why couldn't they be as considerate, as trustworthy, as all-suffering as I had been? . . . *Don't follow my example*, I want to scream in your ears . . ." (2). As Coral Ann Howells notes of Penelope's revision of *The Odyssey*, "[T]his is her story of resistance to all those other stories, both the eulogies and the scandals, which have been imposed upon her" ("Five Ways" 10).

The students in Mythology in Literature have already read in our other course text, Eva M. Thury and Margaret K. Devinney's *Introduction to Mythology*, about the typical age differences in Greek marriages in classical times and about the marital tensions caused by age and power differentials within those marriages. Thury and Devinney draw on the work of the sociologist Philip Slater in explaining that while Greek men generally married only once they were financially secure, often around age thirty, girls in ancient Greece generally married between the ages of fourteen and eighteen. Girls were also unlikely to be educated outside the home. As a result, "women were closer in maturity and experience to their children than to their husbands" (32). Atwood brings that dry information to life when Penelope tells us that at the age of fifteen (38), "I was handed over to Odysseus, like a package of meat" (39). Understandably, Penelope sounds more than a little bitter: "What a fool he made of me, some say. It was a specialty of his: making fools. He got away with everything, which was another of his specialties: getting away" (2).

The women in my classes generally tend to identify with Penelope, in part because they are closer in age and experience to her than they are to her older husband. They also typically enjoy her self-deprecating wit, and they frequently identify with her resentment of her glamorous cousin and rival, Helen of Troy, whom she calls a "septic bitch" and "poison on legs" (131, 79). Penelope even titles one chapter "Helen Ruins My Life" (71–80). A classic "mean girl," Helen is what feminists used to characterize as "male-identified," meaning that she values men and their activities highly while devaluing women and their activities. Because my students tend toward conservativism in their politics and in their reading strategies, I generally wait for them to point out the feminist themes inherent in Atwood's novel, and then I respond by offering them the vocabulary of feminist discourse and further developing the ramifications of ideas they have raised themselves. Students are often more receptive to feminist theory if the ideas evolve organically from their own discussions (especially in response to very general questions, such as "How does Penelope describe Helen?" and "How does Penelope describe marriage?") than if I try to introduce those ideas in a lecture or initiate those discussions directly.

Students don't always immediately recognize that *The Penelopiad* is also a work in which the reliability of the narrator comes into play. So I call their attention to the moments when Penelope herself acknowledges her own unreliability, as for example when she tells the reader after Odysseus's return, "The two of us were—by our own admission—proficient and shameless liars of long standing. It's a wonder either of us believed a word the other said" (173). Even her opening sentence is revealed to be a lie: "*Now that I'm dead I know everything*," she tells us, but then immediately afterward concedes, "That is what I wished would happen, but like so many of my wishes it failed to come true" (1). Therefore, when Atwood draws on what one critic has called "the scandalous alternate tradition of a promiscuous Penelope" (Suzuki 274), readers are left to debate this problematic protagonist's virtue: "Atwood declines to resolve the question of whether we are to believe Penelope's self-defense or the maids' accusation. As the maids themselves say, 'The truth, dear auditors, is seldom certain'" (Suzuki 274). Penelope herself acknowledges, "It was hard to know what to believe" (91). That makes this an especially fun work to teach; one of my discussion questions asks whether Penelope remains faithful to Odysseus, and while some students valiantly defend her virtue, others concede that the answer is unclear.

Equally unclear for my students is the question of Penelope's complicity in the deaths of the twelve maids. Odysseus and his son ultimately hang them, and Atwood is deeply troubled by these killings, as she makes clear in her introduction: "I've always been haunted by the hanged maids; and, in *The Penelopiad*, so is Penelope herself" (xv). In fact, it's Atwood's entry point into the story. Stymied for some time by writer's block, she had asked her agent about the possibility of returning the advance and abandoning the project and was told that the publisher would be "gutted":

> I did not want to be responsible for gutting anyone. "Give me a couple of weeks, then," I said. Desperation being the mother of invention, I then started writing *The Penelopiad*. Don't ask me why, because I don't know. Let's just say that the hanging of the 12 "maids"—slaves, really—at the end of *The Odyssey* seemed to me unfair at first reading, and seems so still; and that my brain was addled early in life by reading Robert Graves's *The Greek Myths*. ("Myths Series")

As Susanna Braund tells us, Atwood "challenges us to reassess the consequences of the identifications we make when we read modern retellings of ancient myth" (203).

To help students in my Great Books class understand and appreciate the role of the chorus of maids, I have sometimes shown them the National Theatre's thirteen-minute video "The Ancient Greek Chorus in Historical Context," available on *YouTube*, before they read the first book of the semester, generally either *Antigone* or *Oedipus the King*. In the professionally produced video (complete with helpful subtitles), a Durham University assistant professor of ancient Greek literature describes the origins and historical development of the classical Greek chorus, which was typically composed of twelve to fifteen men. The narrator also details the role the chorus plays in various classical Greek dramas, and photographs from productions of those dramas in the twenty-first century demonstrate the continuing relevance of these texts. That brief video enables my students to understand the traditions Atwood invokes in her novel and see how she uses "the dramatic form of the Greek chorus" "as a response and a means of 'talking back' to the authoritative epic narrative" (Suzuki 275).

While Penelope begins the novel by explaining, "The difficulty is that I have no mouth through which I can speak" (4), the maids end the novel saying, "We had no voice" (195). While the class differences remain—unlike Penelope, the maids have voices only after death, and even then their voices are filtered by Penelope's—the obvious implication of these parallels is that these women nevertheless have more commonalities than differences. Like her maids, Penelope has no power and is entirely dependent upon powerful men (Collins 65). The maids seem to recognize this inequality; they certainly treat Penelope and Odysseus very differently. Penelope recalls her unsuccessful attempts to confront the maids in Hades: "'Why can't you leave him alone?' I yell at the maids. I have to yell because *they won't let me get near them*" (190, italics added). But the maids tell Odysseus, "Look over your shoulder! Here we are, walking behind you, close, close by, close as a kiss, close as your own skin" (193). The maids haunt Odysseus but evade Penelope, suggesting that they ultimately do not hold Penelope responsible for what they perceive as Odysseus's sins.

But while Penelope and her maids may be alike in their seeming powerlessness at the hands of Odysseus and Telemachus, Atwood also offers an alternative vision, one in which what initially seems powerless is actually powerful and even unstoppable. As Penelope's mother, a semidivine water nymph known as a Naiad, advises her,

> Water does not resist. Water flows. When you plunge your hand into it, all you feel is a caress. Water is not a solid wall, it will not stop you. But water always goes where it wants to go, and nothing in the end can stand against it. Water is patient. Dripping water wears away a stone. Remember that, my child. Remember you are half water. If you can't go through an obstacle, go around it. Water does. (43)

The implication is that Penelope's vaunted patience and the maids' relentlessness through the ages are themselves forms of feminist resistance. As Penelope observes after acknowledging the difficulty of making herself understood, "But I've always been of a determined nature. Patient, they used to call me. I like to see a thing through to the end" (4). The maids in their quest for vengeance are equally determined, telling Odysseus, "We're the serving girls, we're here to serve you. We're here to serve you right. We'll never leave you, we'll stick to you like your shadow, soft and relentless as glue" (193).

The prominence given to the murders of the maids—who, as Atwood acknowledges, were in fact enslaved—also introduces class issues into our discussion of the story: "Through their collective 'we,' the maids are witty and energetic satirists of the dominant order, which sacrificed their bodies and normalized their hanging" (Massoura 401). Several discussion questions ask about the role of the maids, their tone, their function as a chorus, and the significance of their words. It was particularly interesting to teach the story during the spring 2011 quarter, when a hotel maid's accusation of rape at the hands of the French politician Dominique Strauss-Kahn—then managing director of the International Monetary Fund and a potential presidential candidate in France—was in the news. My students, many of whom work in retail and food service, are generally quite cynical about the prospect of justice for the maids in the novel and in the real world. Even in their afterlife, the maids must unite as one to be heard—their voices are not distinctly articulated, as Penelope's is—and they are never able to obtain the justice they seek.

My classes' enthusiasm for this novel is high. Students, especially women students, frequently report finishing its 198 pages in one sitting, and this is the only work studied all term that yields multiple perfect scores on the quiz. Students are as enchanted as Atwood is by Penelope's story. In the Mythology in Literature course, studying this brief contemporary novel introduces students to *The Odyssey* through a book they generally perceive as fun to read. Atwood's novel reminds students that Greek mythology remains central to Western culture and vitally important to our culture's best storytellers. For students in my Great Books in Western Culture course, Atwood's novel reaffirms the lasting significance of classical literature like *The Odyssey* while also acknowledging the limitations of the great books tradition in terms of its failures to consider gender and class. *The Penelopiad* is an intellectually rigorous literary work that allows community college students to grapple with an important Western tradition in a critical and thoughtful way.

NOTE

1. This essay cites the Canongate edition of *The Penelopiad*.

Cadets Weaving Connections: Teaching Conflict and Leadership through *The Penelopiad*

Katja Pilhuj

To those unfamiliar with The Citadel, The Military College of South Carolina, the choice to attend a four-year university with a military structure and all that entails—physical training, inspections, marches, uniforms, and the like—may seem hard to understand. And for those who do choose to matriculate, there is rarely one reason that compels them to forgo a more conventional college experience. The motivations include family tradition, alumni connections, and a desire for structure, but a large portion of the students attend the university to pursue a military career; still others will become civilian workers in the US defense industry. Essentially, if you teach at The Citadel, you will be teaching students likely to find themselves working in some leadership capacity, often in a military setting, both during their time at university and after. The issues of war and its effects, from weaponry to strategy, heroism to trauma, often permeate the curriculum, not merely because the students are already interested but also because they will need the insight and skills derived from such topics. And the humanities are not exempt: literature has long grappled with conflict and its inheritance. Margaret Atwood's *Penelopiad* marks a relatively recent exploration of one of the oldest literary conflicts, the Trojan War. Atwood's irreverent version of the events of *The Iliad* and *The Odyssey* offers an opportunity for students not only to better understand classical texts and think critically about literary depictions but also to question the ideals of leadership and the characterization of great leaders in literature, in the curriculum, and in their future careers.

Through passages from Atwood, the Homeric poems, and other adaptations both ancient and modern, students learn the skills of close reading, analyzing literary tropes, and using critical lenses like feminism to question ideas about martial glory and the aftermath of war beyond the stereotypically stoic warrior. Formulating new ideas from multiple and varied sources prepares these students for military and civic roles that continue to evolve toward increasing complexity and inclusion. With Atwood's text in particular, students can consider the strategies that Penelope employs with constrained resources on the home front to successfully hold off the suitors and maintain the kingdom. This essay explores how students can deeply consider these issues and eventually develop new interpretations of leadership and conflict that will better serve them and those they may lead.

Students at The Citadel, usually called cadets, do undertake a curriculum in their major like students at universities across the United States. But alongside this traditional curriculum are required classes and activities involving military history and practices. These practices permeate all aspects of campus life: sorted into squads and platoons, students live in barracks, wear uniforms every day, and march and drill throughout the semester. In these ways and more, the cadets are immersed in military life. Their Reserve Officers' Training Corps (ROTC) classes complement this routine. Each week, cadets attend these ROTC classes, taught by active-duty and retired service members. Contracted students, who will become officers after graduation, take an ROTC class every semester, for a total of eight, in addition to their full academic schedule. Even noncontracted cadets are required to take at least four ROTC classes, enrolling in an additional four courses that address some aspect of leadership before they graduate. Most of the ROTC classes focus on the history, organization, and practices of a particular branch of the military, and one class of the first four in a cadet's progression addresses leadership strategies specifically. This approach is undoubtedly helpful for students who will be commissioning after graduation. In the training of military leaders, it is worth considering how information related to personnel management and conflict resolution can be learned and retained—or not. The sharing of instructors' own professional experience, for example, may resonate strongly or not at all, depending on the speaker's intention, forethought, and storytelling gifts. One cadet recounts an experience in which "[m]y professor was a particularly reserved aviator. . . . Most of his stories were regarding how they developed incentive systems. . . . There were no [examples] interesting enough for me to have held on to." Attention and retention are challenges in any class, but particularly in those that must relay a set of general policies and rules and use examples dependent on the instructor's own experience, which will vary in each course.

Although the ROTC classes provide information necessary to prepare cadets for military careers, they are not the only ones that do so. The humanities, and literature-based courses in particular, can compel students to consider conflict and how to act using memorable stories from both text and film. Even the classical texts upon which Atwood's text is based (which are included in my class alongside her novel) can resonate with students despite their antiquity. The writer and director Bryan Doerries demonstrates how effective these stories can be for a modern audience, and the class will read and discuss excerpts of his ideas. Doerries uses performances and discussions of ancient plays dealing with soldiers and war in order to encourage active-duty soldiers and veterans to articulate their feelings not only about their deployment experiences but also about navigating post-military life. Doerries views these plays as dynamic and living texts that still have relevance if we ask the right questions—namely, "What do we recognize of ourselves and our struggles in these stories?" (8). Doerries inverts the conventional approach that asks what messages these texts have for us, putting the reader and viewer in the more active subject-position to look for themselves and their circumstances in the text. He asserts, "It is by actively recognizing our behaviors and actions in these ancient stories that we imbue them with significance" (24). Whether readers are soldiers, veterans, or, I argue, students, seeing themselves in texts makes them more confident and eager to engage with the work and develop their critical thinking and writing skills. Thus students become more likely to see the study of literature, no matter its provenance, as relevant to their lives.

The focus on war and heroes found in much of ancient Greek literature already has some built-in appeal for the cadets at a military college. But all my students already have an idea of these texts thanks to their continual adaptation in popular culture, as in films like *Troy* and *300*. The class in which Atwood's text is covered takes advantage of this familiarity, asking students to consider the original ancient texts in comparison with the contemporary ones with which they feel more comfortable. The texts and films I teach feature recurring characters in similar situations that foster comparative discussions. Students' familiarity with the more contemporary versions of figures like Odysseus and Achilles also makes them curious to compare them with the original sources. Discussion and writing assignments focus on the ways that Achilles, Agamemnon, Hector, and Odysseus grapple with martial conflict to help students articulate more detailed and complex claims about the ways these warriors lead their men. Students develop their thoughts on these characters through class debate and discussion, moving to written assignments that ask them to choose from different leadership criteria, explain why those standards are important to effective leadership, and describe how in certain passages those characters are shown to fulfill (or fail to attain) these leadership qualities. Students define and consider various categories of leader attributes, from physical prowess to creative problem-solving to compassion for subordinates. The discussions and shorter writing assignments encourage cadets to move past some of the more general and simpler statements they initially make about "good" or "ineffective" leadership.

Atwood's *Penelopiad* affords an opportunity to move beyond the clang of bronze on the battlefield, bringing to the forefront conflicts of a very different nature as well as individual characters and issues that can be easily overlooked in the ancient passages. In *The Penelopiad*, Odysseus's wife tells her own story, addressing the perspectives and constraints that women face when immersed in warrior culture. Students begin to see how Penelope's strategies and partial victories, accomplished in difficult situations and within the constraints of expectations of feminine behavior, represent a new and nuanced way of achieving objectives beyond smashing their opponents. Such lessons teach cadets in a mostly male student body to consider perspectives beyond the conventionally masculine. The discussions lead all students to carefully evaluate characters' choices and actions in multiple types of conflict, often placing themselves in those situations, as suggested by Doerries, and deriving ideas about their potential approaches and what makes leadership effective or principled. The careful critical analysis that students are encouraged to undertake in these discussions can carry over to their written assignments; weekly prompts ask them to compare only one or two specific aspects of the ancient and contemporary versions of one character, a focus that necessitates refining their language to carefully differentiate between depictions of the same characters by different authors.

For example, one student writes, "This cleverness presented by Odysseus can also be perceived as deceitfulness in *The Penelopiad*. Odysseus can be deceitful and manipulative in order to gain what he wants in a situation." The student's assertion demonstrates how he has begun to view both versions of the character in a more complex way. Rather than simply stating that Odysseus is smart, the student now considers how the character's choices, while based on intellect, can be perceived in drastically different ways.

In class discussions, students reveal how these assignments broaden their scope of consideration in terms of leadership and its effects while also narrowing their argumentative focus to produce more nuanced claims. While students may initially assert simply that Homer's Odysseus is brave and Penelope is loyal, the introduction of Atwood's versions of these characters compels students to reevaluate not only their original appraisals of these characters but also their conceptions of leadership and conflict. Students and cadets in particular often focus first on the feats of martial prowess in *The Iliad* and *The Odyssey*, with some consideration of Odysseus's use of strategic stealth. Discussions and assignments on the ancient texts can be useful in developing students' abilities to evaluate these texts critically; prompts require the use of specific passages to further delineate, for example, what makes *The Iliad*'s Odysseus a thoughtful leader. By the time the class discusses *The Penelopiad*, students possess a comfortable familiarity with the epic's characters and can speak more authoritatively about them, so they are ready to spot differences and similarities between Homer's and Atwood's versions. The comparative activities I employ move students past the simplistic assertions often encountered in first- or second-year writing: that the characters in a work are distinguished from one another by many differences but are also united by some similarities or that one character is a good leader while another is an evil villain. In class, students are directed toward specific passages, first in the Atwood text and then in the original, and prompted to list specific adjectives that could apply to the depictions. Students then choose terms from the generated lists and compose justifications of their characterizations for homework, quoting from the passages to support their choice of these adjectives. Students then often use these assignments to create supporting body paragraphs in their later argumentative essay.

The use of *The Penelopiad* necessitates a more in-depth consideration of the epic's characters, with the focus naturally on Penelope. Atwood's version of the story, existing as it does in two time periods—ancient Greece and the twenty-first-century present—forces students to consider a more expansive context for Penelope in the original era. Atwood highlights the societal restrictions confining an upper-class ancient Greek woman like Penelope, including scrutiny of her body. Atwood details how Penelope's movements are constrained because her value lies in the maintenance of her chastity. Before her marriage, Penelope explains, "[the maids] never left me unattended, I was a risk until I was safely married" (24).[1] But even after her marriage, this control continues, since "whenever I went out I had to take two of the maids with me—I had a reputation to keep up, and the reputation of a king's wife is under constant scrutiny" (56). With passages like these, students begin to understand the ideologies that restrict both versions of these characters and better comprehend Penelope's strategies for maintaining the safety of Ithaca and herself. That Penelope recognizes the importance of her wifely loyalty is made clear when Atwood relates her reasoning for elucidating her fidelity and her love for a still supposedly absent Odysseus, even when she is fully aware that the disguised beggar to whom she speaks is he: "better he should hear all this while in the guise of a vagabond, as he would be more inclined to believe it" (107). Her actions are based solidly on an awareness of the idea that her bodily continence is continually expected and valued. Even after Odysseus defeats the suitors and "reveals" himself to her, she remains strategically skeptical. She explains to the reader, "The hardness of my heart was a notion I was glad to foster, however, as it would reassure Odysseus to know I hadn't been throwing myself into the arms of every man who'd turned up claiming to be him" (132). These passages, when analyzed by students, foster a deeper understanding of how both Penelopes effectively navigate the expectations placed upon them. As a cadet explains, "Atwood's depiction may have altered the perception of the original depiction because it is told through the eyes of Penelope and the Maids and focuses on the challenges of life as a woman in ancient times in Greece." The more forthright declarations by women found throughout Atwood's narrative encourage student analysis of the intelligence exhibited by both Penelope and the maids in the face of restrictive gender hierarchies in both versions of the tale.

This intelligence ultimately generates a greater appreciation of alternative means of conflict resolution and thus leadership through these texts, issues that cadets and any students can find productive. Rather than the slash-and-burn strategies that so many of the epic heroes employ (as Atwood's Penelope dryly notes of Odysseus, "That was his style; stealthy when necessary, true, but he was never against the direct assault method when he was certain he could win" [106]), cadets appreciate the tactics that Penelope uses in both versions. One cadet writes, "This enhanced version of Penelope solidifies my original perception of Penelope as intelligent, but it also adds a new dimension to her character that Homer's depiction did not explore: her tact and ability to remain calm and maintain her composure." As in this assertion, students note that Penelope's seeming inaction at times can instead be seen as careful observation and assessment, arguably helpful skills when encountering conflict. In her best-known conundrum after Odysseus leaves for war, when the suitors arrive, Penelope astutely recognizes her isolated position, observing, "By *alone* you will understand that I mean without friends or allies" (61). Penelope is a lone female leader in this male world, responsible for her household and especially for the maids, who help form a mutual resistance against the suitors but whose vastly different status exacerbates Penelope's singular position. Ultimately, Penelope's limited choices as a woman in ancient Greece compel her to consider options other than direct confrontation. She explains, "I knew it would do no good to try and expel my unwanted suitors, or to bar the palace door against them. If I tried that, they'd turn really ugly and go on the rampage and snatch by force what they were attempting to win by persuasion" (83). Cadets will remember the suitors' murderous intentions toward Penelope's son Telemachus, and their generally belligerent attitude, and will agree with this assessment, appreciating Penelope's unique challenges and responses as a singular woman leader.

Seeking options, Penelope remembers her mother's advice, seemingly cryptic and given long ago:

> Water does not resist. Water flows. When you plunge your hand into it, all you feel is a caress. Water is not a solid wall, it will not stop you. But water always goes where it wants to go, and nothing in the end can stand against it. Water is patient. Dripping water wears away a stone. Remember that, my child. Remember you are half water. If you can't go through an obstacle, go around it. Water does. (34)

Atwood draws on ancient traditions that make Penelope's mother a Naiad, a water nymph, and her speech's use of water affords cadets an extended metaphor to unpack and apply to Penelope's situation. Cadets are asked to consider, both in discussion and in writing, how the Naiad's conception of water can be mapped onto Penelope's patient and quiet resistance of the suitors, including her weaving and unweaving of the shroud, garnering gifts from the suitors, and drawing out and relying on the uncertainty of her status as wife or widow. Cadets can visualize the qualities of patience, circumspection, and judgment to work around obstacles, as opposed to taking them head on. Penelope's leadership of the kingdom and the household (including the maids)—places her in a complex and tenuous position, a situation where cadets are encouraged to consider the competing assumptions, needs, and restrictions Penelope must contend with. With the maids in particular, Atwood illustrates how all these women, not just Penelope, are hampered by restraints of both gender and status. In one of their first appearances, the maids explain how they must navigate the strictures of gender and their status as enslaved to achieve some measure of agency:

> As we grew older we became polished and evasive, we mastered the secret sneer. We swayed our hips, we lurked, we winked, we signalled with our eyebrows, even when we were children; . . . Between the bright hall and the dark scullery we crammed filched meat into our mouths. We laughed together in our attics, in our nights. We snatched what we could. (12)

The maids negotiate, with some success, the world that keeps them low in the social hierarchy.

Penelope becomes a kind of leader of these maids, and the students see her adopting similar tactics: in addition to the well-known strategy of the shroud, this Penelope encourages twelve of her maids to take advantage of the expectation that the suitors, like many ancient Greek male guests, would take sexual interest in the household servants. During these interactions, the maids learn useful information and relay it back to Penelope. Both strategies make effective use of the limited resources of women, conforming to the expectation that a wife will weave for the house and oversee its servants as well as the presumed defenselessness of a household's women in regard to male visitors. Cadets can see how Penelope as an effective leader marshals her scant means to protect the kingdom and keep the suitors as bay. However, her tactic of using the maids ends in tragedy when they are hanged by a returned Odysseus and Telemachus for their supposed insubordination and disloyalty. Penelope is unable to inform her husband of their loyal complicity in her plans. Even before this conclusion, Penelope details the terrible price the maids pay as spies: "Several of the girls were unfortunately raped, others were seduced, or were hard pressed and decided that it was better to give in than to resist" (90). Though she comforts the women and explains to the reader her restrained circumstances, through her desperation, and ultimately her remorse and grief, Penelope shows how her leadership choices are not always successful, especially given the disadvantages of gender. Allowing the maids a voice affords students an opportunity to evaluate Penelope's choices: Was she right or justified in her choice to use the maids? What other options should have been considered? Shouldn't the particular vulnerability of the maids have been taken into account? The students conclude that at times there may be no good options, but that all the potential variables in a situation must be taken into consideration. The story of this Penelope and the maids expands the scope of cadets' reflections when operating in a leadership capacity to include assumptions and expectations of gender and status, individual personalities, potential harm, and any other competing factors. Cadets can connect these literary ideas to their own experiences, both at the university and in their professional careers, military or otherwise.

In terms of leadership and conflict, cadets will also make insightful connections between the versions of Odysseus from Homer and Atwood. The novel highlights the numerous physical confrontations that Odysseus undertakes as Atwood casts doubt on the character's fabled heroic leadership, suggesting that his exploits might have just been chaotic bar fights:

> Odysseus had been in a fight with a giant one-eyed Cyclops, said some; no, it was only a one-eyed tavern keeper, said another, and the fight was over non-payment of a bill. . . . Some of the men had been eaten by cannibals, said some; no, it was just a brawl of the usual kind, said others, with ear-bitings and nosebleeds and stabbings and eviscerations. (65)

Students have already examined these two episodes in Homer's poem; the encounter with the man-eating Laestrygonians and Polyphemus, the Cyclops, results in violent loss of life among Odysseus's crew. Although the escape from the Cyclops features some of Odysseus's clever strategizing, both disasters, students often note, are a result of the epic hero's unconsidered curiosity. Landing on the Laestrygonian beach and with supplies successfully restocked, Odysseus insists on sending men "to find out what people lived / and ate bread in this land" (bk. 10, lines 101–02).[2] Even in one of the story's most memorable examples of Odysseus's clever leadership, the episode with the Cyclops, Odysseus takes his crew from their temporary camp on a safe island with plentiful freshwater and game to explore the nearby Cyclops island. Once within the empty cavern home of Polyphemus, he rejects his men's pleas to leave before the owner's return, asserting, "But I / refused. I hoped to see him, and find out / if he would give us gifts" (bk. 9, lines 227–29). In these and other cases, students are reminded that despite the clever ways Odysseus extricates himself from these situations, his insistent curiosity, greed, and self-interest cause him to lose sight of the best interests of the men he leads and the overall mission of returning home. They will often assess Odysseus as a poor leader, one who at various times places his selfish desires above the greater good of the mission and his men's welfare. Such considerations can help cadets recognize and define traits disadvantageous in leadership in addition to beneficial ones.

In both the traditional text and Atwood's version, cadets can see how Odysseus plunges headlong into confrontations, with little concern for observation, plan, or strategy, and more focus on personal glory, causing fatal consequences for his crew. Considering these shortcomings leads to fruitful comparisons to the leadership of Atwood's Penelope. Although her careful and subtle strategies are not entirely successful—the maids who assist and spy for her are still horrifically murdered—Atwood's Penelope preserves herself, increases Odysseus's estate, and protects the bulk of her household with limited resources and authority. Cadets are left with a changed perspective of the epic hero, seeing his exploits more as pointless brawls than as effective problem-solving. One cadet writes that the comparison reveals of Odysseus "that his stories weren't as glorious as they seem." Students begin to question the initial ways that Homer describes his leader as well as their former readings of those ancient descriptions. Comparing the stories of *The Odyssey* with the new depictions in *The Penelopiad* helps students thoughtfully reexamine the original poem and its ideas of leadership.

The comparisons also help students foster a broader perspective on the specific circumstances that affect the reader's perception of characters, especially of leaders or heroes. The conceptions and constraints of gender, in the ancient poem and today, become important points of discussion. One cadet sees how Atwood's novel represents considerations of "realities" including gender:

> [In] rejecting the male perspective of *The Odyssey* and developing a female-perspective-based version of the original tale[, Atwood] openly criticizes *The Odyssey* and retells the story of Odysseus' overdramatized journey, where Odysseus is murderous, selfish, and unfaithful. Atwood

> recognizes the realities of Greek tragedies instead of [just] the appreciation of the heroes. She includes examples of rape and arranged marriage to support her ideas. Atwood's modernization of the ancient tale examines how much society has changed and how much it has remained the same.

Extending beyond the male-centered ancient Greek context, Atwood's novel encourages students and Citadel cadets in particular to start applying their assessments of these leadership examples to their own lives. For cadets, who are continually challenged to learn about and exhibit principled leadership, the novel and its characters afford examples and vocabulary that help them articulate their present-day realities. Illustrating how Penelope is constrained by her culture's valuing of women's physical beauty and chastity and its dismissal of their intelligence, Atwood's novel can demonstrate to students the specific gender-based challenges present both in the texts and in the world around them. After considering the choices Odysseus and Penelope make in defense of their people, students more closely examine their own realities, including uneven perceptions of the abilities of men and women in the military and in the workplace as well as the understanding of gender and sex as a male-female binary. Students discuss the different expectations of men and women working toward or in leadership positions, noting that these leaders, like Penelope, must choose to directly confront or more subtly circumvent any conflicts that arise. Women leaders, they note, are judged by gendered assumptions that are often unfortunately not that distant from those in the ancient Greek epics. The practice of considering more of an individual character's unique context carries over to real-life situations where cadets, who must deal with their superiors and lead groups of individuals from varying backgrounds, can use contextual information to determine the best course of action.

By reading and analyzing Atwood's *Penelopiad*, students develop a deeper appreciation for Penelope, who emerges from a role they originally considered minor. Agonizing over the danger to her son after he has gone searching for news of his father, listening to the raucous suitors below, Homer's Penelope feels trapped. "Her mind," the narrator says, "was like a lion caught by humans, / terrified, as they throng and circle round him, / trying to trap him" (bk. 4, lines 791–93). The description is easily glossed over on a first reading, but revisiting it after reading Atwood's depiction of Penelope's resolve reveals the power inscribed in the metaphor. Penelope is not just any animal but a lion, and this lion has not been defeated yet, though she is surrounded. The image is a kind of cliff-hanger where the hero, represented by a formidable predator, is left in a seemingly hopeless situation, and the reader must wait to see how they will eventually triumph. And this Penelope, a pacing lion who holds off and manipulates the suitors until she can maneuver the mysterious "beggar" into a contest that only Odysseus can win, will triumph—she even arms him with the weapons he needs.

Considering Atwood's Penelope and comparing her to the Homeric one can generate these types of rich analyses where students can incorporate broader contextual information about gender and culture to create more complex assessments of leadership. One of the more striking student examples of these arguments is expressed by a cadet who writes:

> Ultimately, Atwood depicts her character as a prefiguring of the modern hero. Combining the elements of Penelope's physical will, devious intelligence, and devotional fidelity, her heroism is generated through the mark of virtue rather than through conquest and feats. This distinction conveys the separation of the modern and ancient heroes; where Odysseus is associated with the imagery of turbulent currents and storms, Penelope is compared to a gentle yet interminable stream—flowing passion directed toward resolve over the creation of strife.

This argument recognizes a distinction between the types of leadership that Odysseus and Penelope represent and how they might be aligned to their respective time periods. Following Atwood, the student uses the figure of water to reflect his understanding of how things he once considered fixed now seem more fluid. This demonstrates how Atwood's epic broadens and complicates students' definitions of heroism, conflict resolution, and leadership, with applications to their own lives. Ancient Greek literature no longer seems so remote as Atwood highlights issues of gender and cultural norms that affect how potential leaders can act and be seen in challenging situations. A comparative study using *The Penelopiad* affords opportunities for in-depth exploration of these issues, especially valuable for students who will soon be immersed in stressful contexts and given responsibility for multiple individuals at a relatively young age. Cadets and students alike can ultimately learn how literature can be useful beyond the classroom, preparing them to consider what type of leader they want to be.

NOTES

1. This essay cites the Grove edition of *The Penelopiad*.
2. This essay cites the 2018 Norton edition of the translation by Emily Wilson.

Reproductive Ransom and Self-Recovery: Mothering in *The Handmaid's Tale* and *Wild Seed*

Tarshia L. Stanley

When pairing the work of the preeminent speculative fiction authors Margaret Atwood and Octavia E. Butler, it seems natural to read *The Handmaid's Tale* with *Parable of the Sower.* Both texts occupy unique spaces in early-twenty-first-century culture as prophetic insights into late-stage Western capitalism, gender inequities, and human-inspired environmental devastation. Both books have seen a resurgence in popularity and have an almost continual presence in the lexicon of social media's "necrofuturistic" techno-pundits (Canavan, "If the Engine"). *The Handmaid's Tale* has garnered a new global audience with the television production based on the text, and Butler's book has experienced a posthumous rise to the top of the *New York Times* Best Sellers List and a litany of producers who would like to prepare her work for the screen. However, for instructors interested in engaging students in critique of lesser-known works, pairing the immensely popular *The Handmaid's Tale* with Butler's *Wild Seed* will create room for new and unique readings.

The Handmaid's Tale and *Wild Seed* focus on mothering and reproductive bodies in ways that are familiar to students but still offer enough unexplored material for them to move beyond the more obvious critiques. On the surface, each text features a female character who is seemingly defined by her physical and psychological body as a mother; however, it is possible to see in "Offred" and Anyanwu an engagement with their mothering selves that does not diminish who they are as individuals and perhaps even enhances their self-efficacy. Even deeper reflections exhume and examine the sociocultural and economic structures that dictate that the enactment of mothering is the necessary negation of the characters' individual selves. It may be that in each of them there is a personhood that is not diminished but enhanced by motherhood. Students may find evidence of this even when these protagonist mothers are under duress; in fact, the character's familiarity with empathy and nurture and their need for family and community may even enhance their self-efficacy.

Both *The Handmaid's Tale* and *Wild Seed* were published just as the second wave of feminism was expanding its borders beyond the traditional center. Some feminist readings of motherhood still set it at odds with women's individuality and access to economic and political power. The late-twentieth-century culture wars were beginning while Atwood and Butler were building out their woman-centered speculative worlds. Central to questions of womanhood are a woman's role as a procreating body and the limitations that are seemingly inherent within that designation. Both Atwood and Butler take up this question in the literal and figurative bodies of their protagonists. Offred exists in a dystopian America in which sexual slavery (for white, abled, fertile women) has become the norm. Offred's physical body and the physical bodies of the other fertile women, or Handmaids, have become the property of the state. The affront is double, for in the world before Gilead, Offred determined her own reproductive margins, was married, and had a child. In fact, much of the control of Offred's behavior has to do with the promise that she will see her kidnapped daughter if she behaves and produces offspring for the Commander and his wife.

Predicated on the biblical concept of appropriating the bodies of powerless female servants for procreation, the Republic of Gilead is a nightmare for both the Handmaids and all the other women who fall into its different categories of use and abuse. The Aunts are the Republic's psychosocial handmaids who maintain the system. These women, who are past the age of childbearing and seen as sexually undesirable, make sure the Handmaids are subservient and follow the rules. The Marthas similarly are not used as breeders and instead perform the domestic functions that make the households run. However, the Wives, seemingly at the top of the female hierarchy, are also at the mercy of the men. Handmaids invade their homes, their marriages, and their marital beds at the command of the husbands. The world of Gilead is a feminist nightmare where women police one another and vie for esteem and significance by means of their fertility or marital status.

Wild Seed begins on the continent of Africa in 1690. The disembodied spirit Doro accidentally discovers the protagonist, Anyanwu. The narrative posits Doro and Anyanwu as immortals searching for other long-lived beings like themselves. Anyanwu is also a shape-shifter, a healer, and a consummate earth mother, whereas Doro must constantly kill to survive. Thus, life and death meet and pair in order to produce the thing for which they both long: children who will not die. Doro persuades Anyanwu—or rather coerces her—to accompany him to the new world where he has collected people with special gifts and bred them together in an effort to create immortal progeny. They set out, seemingly on the same sacred journey, but unbeknownst to Anyanwu, Doro intends to use her body much as the Handmaids are used in Atwood's Gilead. Doro will breed Anyanwu with those men he deems special. He is after her offspring, and he is not concerned with Anyanwu's thoughts, her desires, or her autonomy. The story crosses continents, oceans, and centuries as we see their struggle play out across time and through the bodies of the supernaturally gifted children they sire.

One question to ask when teaching *The Handmaid's Tale* and *Wild Seed* is, Are there multiple ways to read motherhood? For both Offred and Anyanwu, initial critiques of motherhood represent mothering as their entire being. Their children and future children do indeed take up much of their inner thought processes and energy. However, their desires and longings for human relationship and interaction are not limited to the reproduction of children. In essence, the action of producing children is not the sum of who they are or all they want to do. They live under patriarchal constraints that attempt to reduce their existence to only reproduction. The system under which they live threatens their positions as mothers and even their lives if they do not produce offspring, and it puts each of them in the position of having to resist that totalizing depiction.

In "Gender, Ontology, and the Power of the Patriarchy: A Postmodern Feminist Analysis of Octavia E. Butler's *Wild Seed* and Margaret Atwood's *The Handmaid's Tale*," Aisha Matthews posits that both Offred and Anyanwu "are supposed to capitulate entirely to the biological imperative" (654). It is of course true for Offred that the Republic owns her body and therefore much of her will because she must make sacrifices to survive. However, there are multiple ways in which Offred continues to push for and nurture her own sense of self. For example, she takes meticulous note of her surroundings. Offred is a witness, a historian who carefully observes her situation, parsing its signs and storing her analyses for the time she will record them. And Offred knows what it is to be free to mother her child, and reunion with that child is one of the things that is used to control her. From the opening paragraph of the novel, Offred is still in control of her intellect and imagination as she describes not just her present place but its connection to the past and the present: "We slept in what had once been the gymnasium. The floor was of varnished wood, with stripes and circles painted on it, for the games that were formerly played there; the hoops for the basketball nets were still in place, though the nets were gone" (Atwood, *Handmaid's Tale* 3).[1] The protagonist is more than a body or a womb; she is a mind resisting her circumstances in the only safe way she can in that moment. In her analysis, place and time collide to allude to the game, the artificial painted onto the natural, the nets that are not really gone, the lines that must not be crossed and the circles to which she now belongs. Offred goes on to describe the "old sex," the "loneliness," and the "expectation" present in the gym where she and the other Handmaids are forced to gather. She denotes the Aunts, with the "electric cattle prods slung on thongs from their leather belts" (3–4). Her use of phallocentric symbols and language opens up numerous opportunities for the study of semiotics. Both introductory and advanced literature classes can move beyond the study of simple symbolism to understanding social and cultural semiotics through the images in Atwood's and Butler's texts. The language in each is filled with signs and referents that support studies of patriarchy, feminism, race, class, and even sexual identity.

Although Offred's body is not free, her mind is engaged in a struggle for autonomy. Further analysis of the way the narrative is broken up into chapters suggests both a shopping list and an ethnographic study. The chapter titles cover Offred's observation and assessment of Gilead and the Handmaids' place in it. Of the fifteen chapters, seven are titled "Night." From her description of sleeping in the gym, Offred moves to an understanding of the night as her time for unfettered thoughts and dreams: "The night is mine, my own time, to do with as I will, as long as I am quiet. . . . [T]he night is my time out. Where should I go?" (37). Offred's nights continue as she remembers her old life, as she contemplates how to use the night to get some of what she needs from the Commander, and as she is first compelled, then chooses, to sleep with Nick.

Yet even in the worst moments meant to dehumanize her, Offred is thinking; she is assessing; she is being. There are times Offred is anxious, bored, afraid, desirous, and pleasure-seeking. Whether it be the pleasure of flowers or of sex with Nick, the character's constant analysis of her situation, her acknowledgment that she is still a human being, that she still needs and dreams and hopes, works against a simplistic reading of her as merely a body—at least for the reader. While she may be primarily a body to her captors, we see even in her limited circumstance that Offred is still a friend, a woman, a mother, and, perhaps most importantly, an eyewitness.

It is at the very end of the book, in the chapter titled "Historical Notes," that Offred's role as eyewitness is best understood. The Gileadean Research Association is holding a conference in the year 2195. The subject of this conference is the validity and value of an oral history of Gilead from a person whom we understand to be Offred. Academics with surnames like Pieixoto, Crescent Moon, Running Dog, and Chatterjee from departments of Western philosophy and universities in the Republic of Texas provide a rich context for students to engage Atwood's treatises on colonialism, nationalism, authoritarianism, and so on. The tone of the final chapter, as has often been pointed out, negates the seeming progress made in the future. Even though, as the text explains, world maps have been redrawn to exclude white patriarchal enclaves like Gilead as the center, Professor Pieixoto is still able to make disparaging remarks about Professor Maryann Crescent Moon. Being chair of the department of Caucasian anthropology does not protect Professor Crescent Moon from the tongue-in-cheek banter of academicspeak that Professor Pieixoto uses to verbally "enjoy" her, both sexually and as food. Like Offred, she remains a body to be consumed.

This chapter is perhaps the most important of all in that it reiterates Atwood's contract with the reader. *The Handmaid's Tale* is not a fairy story with a happy ending but a call to action for its readers—both those in the diegetic space and those outside it. Atwood declares that patriarchy will not change, especially when perpetuating systems nurture and support it; rather, it must be undone. There is action readers of Offred's account must take, both those within the world of the novel and those in the world outside, if the isms that *The Handmaid's Tale* warns about are to be overcome. Students can act by writing about the systems of government, economics, culture, education, and history that are apparent in the final chapter to determine how they are sustained both in the Gilead that Offred suffers and the post-Gileadian world that readers witness.

It is in the final chapter that readers are given evidence to corroborate Offred's testimony and see her endorsed as more than a reproductive body. Pieixoto spends his lecture debating whether the woman's account on the cassette tapes (thirty of them) can be entrusted with the label *history*. He takes for granted the validity of the partially ciphered diary written by a man named Limpkin, which in a myriad of ways supports the story told by the woman's voice on the cassette tapes. Students can examine the academy's relationship with history and its legitimation of the male voice and the written word as truth. As the readers with whom Atwood is having a discussion, students will need to ponder the survival of Offred's voice and the other reasons her legacy might be up for debate by the Gileadean Research Association. Here it might be useful to ask students to spend time with the epilogue and critique the conference that takes place. Students can ask themselves questions like who speaks first, who speaks at all, and what voice is truly at the center of inquiry. They should spend some time deciphering the layered meanings of Pieixoto's words and even the construct of the conference itself.

If reproduction and the birthing body are premises in the novel, then students might ask who or what is being reproduced at the conference. While generally the ending is read as reinforcing Offred's role as passive and a victim—she is literally disembodied in the last chapter—counterreadings will see her voice as the center of the narrative. Reading between and beyond the lines can render Offred as both witness and "herstorian." Her greatest act of reproduction and resistance is to tell the story. Rather than more children, Offred reproduces the story of Gilead. Her skills as a mother are used to birth the story, the testament, the witness—and that is her progeny.

Offred's posthumous selfhood is evidence of both her survival, once she is taken from the Commander's home, and her positioning as more than a breeder and repository for the desires of the patriarchy. Likewise, Anyanwu repeatedly demonstrates her ability to be more and to do more than Doro, a metaphor for the patriarchy, would condone. Doro first motivates Anyanwu to leave Africa by threatening to find and enslave or kill the many offspring she has produced in her three-hundred-year life. Anyanwu could try to flee, but she is too invested in the lives of her children to endanger them. Her culture posits children as more valuable than money. Also, Anyanwu finds herself intrigued by the idea that she might partner with Doro to one day create children who are immortal like herself. She allows herself to be drawn into a relationship with Doro, who may see her primarily as the perfect breeder, because she longs for extended companionship both from children and from a lover. Students will find it intriguing to look at the metaphorical difference between Anyanwu (which means "Sun Woman") and Doro (a dark death spirit), who can only exist by stealing the bodies of the living. Anyanwu wants a family whereas Doro requires subjects. There is a world of difference between their desires, although it is the same set of people who can satisfy them both.

Throughout the novel, Anyanwu constantly identifies herself not just as a mother but also as a healer. Along with her shape-shifting abilities, Anyanwu can manipulate her cellular structure and chemical composition to manufacture medicines. She combines her metaphysical ability with her psychosocial prowess to become the ultimate therapist and physician. It is ultimately this quality that stops Doro from killing her when he finds her again in 1840. Posing as a white, male plantation owner, Anyanwu has gathered misfits with special abilities in much the same fashion that Doro built his settlements of breeders. Again, students will find it interesting to compare the ways Doro and Anyanwu treat their people. They can highlight the intelligence, autonomy, and tenacity it takes for Anyanwu not only to elude Doro for more than a century but also to refrain from using her extraordinary power to become like him. Anyanwu gathers those with special abilities to her without enslaving them and subverting their wills. Instead, she creates a safe space in which they develop and grow, demonstrating her ability to mother and her ability to lead. She recognizes the personhood of each of the people she gathers and thereby recognizes her own.

When she and Doro first meet, Anyanwu is intrigued and hopeful that she may finally have found a life partner. However, Doro makes it clear that, to him, she is something to be directed and owned as well as a means to an end. He threatens to kill Anyanwu's children if she will not submit to him, and he likens Anyanwu herself to a child in need of instruction in making that threat: "Sometimes only a burn will teach a child to respect fire" (Butler, *Wild Seed* 13). Next, he tells her clearly who and what he is: "I kill, Anyanwu. That is how I keep my youth, my strength. I can only do one thing to show you what I am, that is kill a man and wear his body like a cloth" (13). Anyanwu agrees to participate in a terrible game in hopes of winning a family and a community, but she learns that she and Doro are adversaries rather than mates. Anyanwu is quickly forced to reckon with the fact that Doro is not like her. She cannot rescue or change him as she is used to doing with her misfits. His long life as a killing spirit has left him without empathy and even humanity—characteristics that Anyanwu possesses in abundance. Although he refers to the people that he forces into being as his children, Doro is not a father. His work is not about nurturing a family, growing a community, or even building a nation; it is about domination. We as readers feel frustration as we wait for Anyanwu to fully realize Doro's deficiencies.

In the latter half of their struggle of wills, after Anyanwu has run for her life, Doro tracks her to the Louisiana plantation. Anyanwu tries once again to be Doro's partner—this time in business. She agrees to care for his troubled children until he brings her one who murders her son Steven. Yet it is not the murder that alone causes Anyanwu to want to give up. Doro also decides to take the body of a woman he had brought her to protect. Anyanwu can no longer tolerate the easy way Doro kills or the fact that the only constant she has ever found in her long life—or may ever find—is death.

Students will find the endgame between Doro and Anyanwu complicated. Doro begins to experience feeling, if not of love, then at least of spiritual longing rather than just hunger. He begs Anyanwu not to die. Allowing Anyanwu into his process of joining another spirit until it is consumed by him and stopping short of killing her has somehow changed him. As he begs her not to die, he realizes he has no control over Anyanwu. His ultimate weapon was fear of death, but she has evolved past that. As he collapses into a sobbing heap and begs her to live, she sees potential. Anyanwu begins to care for him as if he were one of her misfits, and when he wakes, they reach a compromise, one that Doro promises not to breach because he has come so close to being without her. However, Anyanwu is not so lonely, not so much a nurturer, that she harbors hope that the emptiness in Doro can forever be held at bay. He accuses her of not trusting him and she responds: "You are still the leopard. . . . And we are still the prey" (253).

It is true that "[b]oth Anyanwu and Offred face patriarchal attempts at definition that presume a woman's emptiness, underscoring the assumption that womanhood is complementary to manhood, thereby relegating womanhood to the position of manhood's shadow" (Matthews 646). However, it is the women's reactions to the attempts at emptying them of selfhood that are ripe for contemplation. As limited as some of the ways they resist seem to be, there is indeed resistance and even some recovery of selfhood or, more accurately, some new definitions of self. For Offred, the fact that her voice and vision—her perspective—survives can be read as the one example of the feminine selfhood possible in Gilead and beyond. For Anyanwu, the decision to be in family and community and then to cease being in those relationships if it frees her from Doro represents her choosing the best selfhood possible when the devil is both her nemesis and her partner.

Students will find many fruitful themes when comparing Atwood's and Butler's construction of fictional worlds and the way these worlds shape womanhood and motherhood in the texts. The totalitarian society of Gilead tries to empty women of intellectual, emotional, and bodily autonomy. The theocratic Doro attempts to focus Anyanwu's intellectual, emotional, and bodily autonomy in a kind of worship. Gilead does not want its women to think for themselves. Doro wants his woman to only think of him. Gilead centers reproduction as the right of the state and controls it to maintain power and patriarchy. Doro is at the center of his own world and uses reproduction as his tool for shaping his empire.

Neither Gilead nor Doro admits the power women have as the sole proprietors of reproduction. Neither openly acknowledges that the coercion, manipulation, and violence they perpetuate is in direct proportion to the strength of mothering they so desperately attempt to control. In the end, they cannot contain motherhood because it cannot be contained. Motherhood itself is a reproduction of the mother. Offred never completely disappears. She reproduces her story as a future text. Anyanwu reproduces her mothering for Doro—becoming an anchor that keeps him from total destruction. Both Offred and Anyanwu make choices about how and when they mother.

Students might spend time exploring the idea of mothering in spaces wherein the female body is owned by the state and analyzing circumstances wherein motherhood is owned by the individual. Each text provides a space in which to look at mothering not just as the anti-feminist sacrifice of self but as a recovery of selfhood in patriarchal systems designed to abuse women's desire or right to mother. Students can write journal entries as both Offred and Anyanwu to determine how each handles her lack of autonomy and to discover where they each find power. Students may compare Anyanwu's shape-shifting with Offred's disembodied voice at the end of *The Handmaid's Tale* to consider whether these characters are powerful only when they do not physically inhabit the female body.

The texts are also useful for looking at the power of speculative fiction to illuminate contemporary issues. Both characters are caught up in an apocalypse—an ending. Offred must survive the end of her society, and Anyanwu's world in Africa ends. For each woman a new way of living has to emerge if they are going to survive. Assignments that look at survival in new and hostile worlds are possible with these texts. Another approach might examine the sociocultural world in which both Atwood and Butler wrote. The early and mid–1980s were times of great individualization and an unabashed move toward free-market economies and laissez-faire capitalism. Politics became increasingly divisive, and technology became accessible for many. Reading *The Handmaid's Tale* and *Wild Seed* against the backdrop of the times in which they were written opens up a wealth of possibilities of reading motherhood and the female body.

Pairing the texts will promote deep critical inquiry: students can read numerous examples of critiques of Atwood's text and still have room to create new interpretations of Butler's lesser-known *Wild Seed.* No matter the approach, reading the texts in tandem offers numerous possibilities for student inquiry. Each text asks pertinent questions about the past and the future and the woman's role as mother and female body across those spaces.

NOTE

1. This essay cites the 2017 Anchor edition of *The Handmaid's Tale.*

The Handmaid's Tale as Campus Book Pick: Dystopia, Dominance Feminism, and Satire

Helen Thompson

> The Court finds that the right to abortion is not deeply rooted in the Nation's history and tradition.
>
> —*Dobbs v. Jackson Women's Health Organization*

Among the events I helped organize as faculty chair of my university's annual campus-wide reading program, One Book One Northwestern, was a visit from the feminist human rights lawyer Catharine MacKinnon. I had been invited to chair One Book after the book had already been selected. The academic year was 2018–19; the book was Margaret Atwood's *The Handmaid's Tale*. MacKinnon gave her talk, "Butterfly Politics," at Northwestern in April 2019. After seven months of intense thought about Atwood's text among many constituencies, I was struck during the Q and A by MacKinnon's response to a softball question asking her opinion of Atwood's dystopia. Gilead, MacKinnon replied, focuses on reproduction, not sexual violence. Therefore, MacKinnon intimated, *The Handmaid's Tale* did not resonate with the presentation she had just delivered: a full-throated affirmation of the transformational impact of the Me Too movement and the even miraculous prospect that women's harassment—whose structural depth and breadth were only beginning to be exposed—could be challenged and widely perceived as intolerable. The dissonance seemed clear. Harassment, rape, and the problematics of consent—the latter, in MacKinnon's view, a preemptively misogynist standard of feminine sexual acquiescence—defined a dystopia whose epitome was the pervasive, pornographic coercions revealed by Me Too. *The Handmaid's Tale*, with its puritanical red gowns and blinkered bonnets, was not the right dystopia for a reckoning driven by Me Too. The dire forecast voiced by Offred's second-wave-feminist mother—"As for you, she'd say to me, you're just a backlash. Flash in the pan. History will absolve me" (Atwood, *Handmaid's Tale* 121)—had become, it seemed, moot.[1]

After the overturn of *Roe v. Wade* in June 2022, I take MacKinnon's expression of distance from Atwood's dystopia as an occasion to reassess the relation of *The Handmaid's Tale* to second-wave and 1980s feminism. This essay explores *The Handmaid's Tale*'s eviscerating portrait of dominance feminism, the movement helmed by MacKinnon and her colleague Andrea Dworkin, with whom MacKinnon cowrote anti-pornography ordinances for Minneapolis, Indianapolis, Los Angeles, and Massachusetts in the 1980s and early 1990s. Dominance feminism also includes second-wave coalitions like Women Against Pornography. MacKinnon's essay "Sex and Violence" articulates one of the movement's driving aspirations, which syncs with the baseline premises of Me Too: to "ask a series of questions about normal, heterosexual intercourse and attempt to move the line between heterosexuality on the one hand—intercourse—and rape on the other" (MacKinnon 89).

The core diagnostic advanced by MacKinnon and Dworkin concerns women's pervasive, oppressive exposure to sexual coercion, harassment, and assault. This precise insight is claimed by Gilead's founders as a license for anti-feminist reaction that enforces women's subordination under the guise of protection and redress. But Atwood's dystopian extrapolation of pseudo-protectionist patriarchy does not exhaust *The Handmaid's Tale*'s feminist significance. My essay concludes with feminist valences of *The Handmaid's Tale* illuminated by my stint as faculty chair. Ultimately, I locate *The Handmaid's Tale*'s complex feminism not only in its engagement with the anti-pornography and anti-rape movements but also in the counterrepressive analytical energies solicited by its genre: satire. Atwood conjures the prospect of satire as potentially feminist form from the very conditions of censorious anti-feminist dystopia.

Sex Wars: Dominance Feminism and Protectionist Dystopia

The Handmaid's Tale's hostility to dominance feminism is anticipated by an early, isolated flashback: the protagonist and narrator Offred's recollection of an episode "in a park . . . with my mother." Even though her mother "said we were going to feed the ducks," the daughter realizes she has been brought to the park for a different reason:

> But there were some women burning books, that's what she was really there for. . . .
>
> There were some men, too, among the women, and the books were magazines. They must have poured gasoline, because the flames shot high, and then they began dumping the magazines, from boxes, not too many at a time. Some of them were chanting; onlookers gathered.
>
> Their faces were happy, ecstatic almost. Fire can do that. Even my mother's face, usually pale, thinnish, looked ruddy and cheerful, like a Christmas card; and there was another woman. . . .
>
> You want to throw one, honey, she said. How old was I? . . .
>
> The woman handed me one of the magazines. It had a pretty woman on it, with no clothes on, hanging from the ceiling by a chain wound around her hands. I looked at it with interest. It didn't frighten me. I thought she was swinging, like Tarzan from a vine, on the TV.
>
> Don't let her *see* it, said my mother. Here, she said to me, toss it in, quick. (Atwood, *Handmaid's Tale* 38–39)

Because Offred speaks in the voice of her childhood self, this passage resists signification as evidence of Atwood's own feminist politics. Offred's inescapably particular narrative vantage in *The Handmaid's Tale*, which tethers the reader to her domestic, unheroic encounter with totalitarian theocracy, here serves to transmit her past analysis of a scene in which her firelit mother resembles "a Christmas card" and a woman in bondage gear seems to be "swinging, like Tarzan from a vine, on the TV." Such efforts of analogical understanding highlight the limits of Offred's juvenile comprehension. By restricting Offred's cognitive capacities to those of a young child, Atwood deploys the satirical technique called defamiliarization, animated through the voice of a narrator—often a traveler encountering a radically different place—characterized by extreme inexperience. The "pretty woman . . . with no clothes on, hanging from the ceiling" exemplifies this literary device and its semiludic demand on the reader, whom Atwood presumes will decipher the naive reference to pornography. Most trenchantly, as seen through child-Offred's eyes, her mother is—and, indeed, she *is*—"burning books." Offred's mother participates in the endeavor negatively defined, at least since the sex wars of the 1980s, as the means and ultimate end of anti-pornography feminism: censorship.

What Offred's childish description—whose dim pastness Atwood flags with the query "How old was I?"—most centrally enables is the evacuation of any substantive feminist reference from this scene. Atwood is thus reticent about not just its topicality—although, again, the reader is cued to recognize it—but her judgment of its political implications. Perhaps "happy, ecstatic almost" faces reflect the febrile obsession of dominance feminists with pornography and their fanatical fixation on its legislative banishment. Perhaps "Don't let her *see* it" telegraphs the insoluble paternalism of the latter project. But child-Offred is unable to entertain such thoughts. Atwood's indictment of the strand of dominance feminism defamiliarized by the phrase "burning books" resides instead in that feminism's utility to those who justify Gilead's coup.

Also at a preliminary moment in *The Handmaid's Tale*, Offred's indoctrinator Aunt Lydia condenses the logic by which claims of pornographic harm provide cover for Gileadean repression:

> The sidewalks here are cement. Like a child, I avoid stepping on the cracks. I'm remembering my feet on these sidewalks, in the time before, and what I used to wear on them. Sometimes it was shoes for running, with cushioned soles and breathing holes, and stars of fluorescent fabric that reflected light in the darkness. Though I never ran at night; and in the daytime, only beside well-frequented roads.
>
> Women were not protected then.
>
> I remember the rules, rules that were never spelled out but that every woman knew: Don't open your door to a stranger, even if he says he is the police. . . . Don't stop on the road to help a motorist pretending to be in trouble. . . .
>
> Now we walk along the same street, in red pairs, and no man shouts obscenities at us, speaks to us, touches us. No one whistles.

> There is more than one kind of freedom, said Aunt Lydia. Freedom to and freedom from. In the days of anarchy, it was freedom to. Now you are being given freedom from. Don't underrate it. (24)

Even if Offred initially prompts the reader to regress (step on a crack, break your mother's back), this passage, unlike the park episode, features a retrospective narrator aware that she is sundered from "the time before." Offred's evocation of "shoes for running" may be just as descriptively vivid as her childhood recollection of combusting porn magazines, but it is not as naive. Most critically, "cushioned soles and breathing holes, and stars of fluorescent fabric" take for granted the inclusivity of athletics, the mundane instrumentality of commodities sold to persons who work out, assured in America in 1972 by passage of Title IX, federal civil rights law prohibiting sex-based discrimination in federally funded schools. The physical attributes of Offred's sneakers thus incarnate the attributes of her physically liberated body. Yet viewed from Offred's position as a Handmaid, the same details—namely, the shoes' fluorescent stars—reflect the circumstances that, despite Title IX, failed to make gender extraneous to one's right to athletic pursuit. Offred never needed glow-in-the-dark footwear because she obeyed restrictions of space and time dictated by the threat of harassment and rape—the same threat MacKinnon and Dworkin identify as the ongoing mechanism of women's oppression well after Title IX was ratified.

In the history of modern Western feminism, the acknowledgment that women's full access to three-dimensional space is crucial to their realization as athletes and as persons dates to Simone de Beauvoir's *The Second Sex*. Yet when Offred yokes this insight to the immobilizing impact of collectively internalized "rules" to avoid rape, her narrative voice mutates. Even before she cites Aunt Lydia on "freedom to" versus "freedom from," Offred makes a pronouncement seemingly true to the reality of the time before and consistent with the dogma to come: "Women were not protected then." One hint that this assessment blurs into Gileadean doctrine lies in its aphoristic closure, which elides the nuance of Offred's prior musing on soles and holes. More to the point, in this pivot away from her powers as an "I" who runs, Offred, shifting into the grammatical passive voice, insinuates the ominously unspecified necessity of a protector. When Offred affirms the structuring force of sexual violence in the time before, her narrative voice enters a thought-world already shaped by Gilead's rationale for her unfreedom. In that light, the "freedom from" that Aunt Lydia touts is no infringement of "freedom to" but rather welcome deliverance from formerly inescapable harassment: "no man shouts obscenities at us, speaks to us, touches us. No one whistles." Offred's Gileadean recall of the time before—"Women were not protected"—isolates the preemptive mandate of protection from whistles, obscenities, and unwanted touch as the pseudo-feminist rationale for Atwood's anti-feminist dystopia.

In Handmaid times, Offred inhabits the dystopian achievement of her protection. By extrapolating this dire apotheosis of "freedom from," Atwood joins the side of the sex wars that abjures MacKinnon and Dworkin for, as their pro-sex opponents argue, claiming vulnerability not only as the key determinant of womanhood but also as the rationale for legal redress that will further entrench women's victim position. As enshrined by dominance feminists, victimhood defines its constituency, according to the political theorist Wendy Brown, as the product of "injury-forming identity" (21). Brown worries that institutional foreclosure of potential harm, like the redress promised by MacKinnon and Dworkin's anti-pornography ordinances, "powerfully legitimizes law and the state as appropriate protectors against injury and casts injured individuals as needing such protection by such protectors" (27). By summoning the law to prevent present and future injury from porn, Brown argues, MacKinnon catalyzes an injury-identity-protection loop whereby "law and the state" collude with a feminism invested in weakness as essence: "the construction of femininity is the making of female vulnerability and violation as womanhood" (81). Writing in 1995, ten years after *The Handmaid's Tale* was published, Brown offers an unwittingly apt synopsis of the protectionist premise voiced by Aunt Lydia—and an injury-identified Offred herself—when Brown argues that "MacKinnon aims to compel the law . . . to recognize and rectify relations of domination among its subjects—in particular, by making it recognize gender as a relation of domination rather than a benign or natural marker of difference" (130). *The Handmaid's Tale* anticipates and speculatively enacts this scenario. As assured by a nightmarish instantiation of the law, the censorious activism performed by Offred's mother is continuous with, and even solicits, Aunt Lydia's protectionist warrant for the legislative enforcement of "gender as a relation of domination."

More recently, feminist concern that statutory protections cement female victimhood has been sparked by the still thwarted promise of Offred's sneakers' reflective stars. In April 2011, the US Department of Education published a "Dear Colleague" letter (now rescinded) extending Title IX's prohibition of discrimination on the basis of sex in education to define "sexual violence, including rape, sexual assault, sexual battery, and sexual coercion" as "forms of sexual harassment" that "create a hostile environment" (United States, Department of Education). The media scholar and cultural critic Laura Kipnis, a keen observer of Title IX's expanded institutional uptake, greeted this development with poignant testimony to Brown's warning that feminine injury might become a site of identitarian cathexis. Armed with digital correspondence fleshing out anterior relationships in two Title IX cases at Northwestern, Kipnis aimed to show that the vulnerability espoused by their female complainants was retroactively caused by Title IX itself. For Kipnis, these formerly agential actors metamorphosed into "passive damsels" (53), enticed by Title IX's protectionist enablers into a state of "aggrieved passivity" (90). For Kipnis as for Brown, dominance feminists, epitomized by MacKinnon, partner "themselves with Christian conservatives to fight the demon pornography" (Kipnis 19) to collude in a reactionary articulation of sex that conscripts women into "the endangered damsel–powerful predator story" (Kipnis 55). In the quasi-consensual ambit of university hookup culture, the "story" to which Kipnis alludes is emphatically not a script for Handmaids. But Kipnis's passivity-inducing story does the same work as Gilead's expurgated, unsubtly patriarchal Bible: it resurrects gender roles that haunt the historical scene of their supposed obsolescence. It is not sexual violence, whose reality Atwood, Kipnis, and Brown do not deny, that reanimates and magnetizes such roles. Rather, dominance feminism embraces female vulnerability and the ensuing imperative of protection exploited by sex fundamentalists and overzealous Title IX administrators.

Brown and Kipnis unabashedly stigmatize weakness as the corollary of legal or administrative efforts to legislate women's equality. To counter the specter of such enfeeblement, Kipnis proposes a "grown-up feminism" (188) modeled by her empowerment in one self-defense class. In so doing, she appears to overlook MacKinnon's own long-standing expertise in martial arts, invoked in "Women, Self-Possession, and Sport" to motivate a feminist vision of physical capacity: "women as women have a distinctive contribution to make to sport that is neither a sentimentalization of our oppression as women nor an embrace of the model of the oppressor" (MacKinnon 123). This statement resonates with the utopian—not dystopian—impulse elaborated in such venues as second-wave anti-beauty-pageant activism, karate, and science fiction. But here I mean to foreground *The Handmaid's Tale*'s agreement with the pro-sex critique that casts dominance feminism as debilitating, prudish, and politically dangerous. Atwood limns such a portrait by underscoring the affinity of book-burning and the squeamish anti-sex ideology espoused by Aunt Lydia:

> The summer dresses are . . . pure cotton . . . though even so . . . in July and August, you sweat inside them. No worry about sunburn though, said Aunt Lydia. The spectacles women used to make of themselves. Oiling themselves like roast meat on a spit, and bare backs and shoulders, on the street, in public, and legs, not even stockings on them, no wonder those things used to happen. *Things*, the word she used when whatever it stood for was too distasteful or filthy or horrible to pass her lips.
>
> (Atwood, *Handmaid's Tale* 55)

Aunt Lydia's revulsion at the "spectacle" of sunbathing women's sensual pleasure is distilled in her radically objectifying gloss of their bodies as "roast meat on a spit." For Aunt Lydia, women's exposed corporeality solicits both sadism and Gilead's repressive sartorial codes. In this rendition of Gilead's protectionist premise, it is not pornography that incites and normalizes violence against women, as Dworkin and MacKinnon would have it, but women's own "bare backs and shoulders, on the street, in public." Aunt Lydia's repugnance fuses with a fundamentalist twist of the dominance feminist analytic to dictate the concealment of women's bodies from public view. A vector for anti-sex evangelism whose historical avatar Atwood locates in New England's repressive Puritan polity, Aunt Lydia animates the confluence of protectionism and gynophobic loathing. As Brown argues, this construction of femininity relocates the imminent threat of misogynist violence in female flesh, whose appeal to an always violating male gaze impels women's defensive containment in Handmaid garb. Aunt Lydia appears to riff on the objectifying scopic regime theorized in Laura Mulvey's influential essay "Visual Pleasure and Narrative Cinema" as the male gaze: "Modesty is invisibility, said Aunt Lydia. Never forget it. To be seen—to be *seen*—is to be—her voice trembled—penetrated. What you must be, girls, is impenetrable" (Atwood, *Handmaid's Tale* 28).

To retaliate, Offred animates Aunt Lydia's own dehumanized embodiment: "She blinked, the light was too strong for her, her mouth trembled, around her front teeth, teeth that stuck out a little and were long and yellowish, and I thought about the dead mice we would find on the doorstep" (55). But if here Offred caricatures the snaggle-toothed pallor of the anti-sex moralist, then *The Handmaid's Tale*'s ultimate representation of her capacity to refuse Gileadean injury-identity is far more equivocal. Unlike Brown's, Kipnis's concern with protectionism is less encroaching repression than the psychic lure of vengeful victimhood as an institutionally sanctioned route to some approximation of equity. For Kipnis, the simultaneously weak and vengeful posture of "aggrieved passivity" stunts injury-identified women by channeling their fury into a protectionist campus bureaucracy barely proximate to any juridical process (90). Atwood anticipates and exceeds this outcome with the gruesome incitement of aggrieved passivity known as Salvaging, illustrated in the text when a mob of Handmaids is encouraged by Gilead's police to rip apart an accused rapist. By placing a critical rejoinder to this charge in the mouth of a member of the Handmaid resistance—"He wasn't a rapist at all, he was a political. He was one of ours" (Atwood, *Handmaid's Tale* 280)—Atwood's dystopia comes full circle. Totalitarian patriarchy justified in the name of women's protection must fabricate the harm without which its subjects would no longer sustain their debilitating and deeply vengeful identity with their "freedom from."

In her 2017 introduction to *The Handmaid's Tale*, Atwood makes explicit the Gileadean regime's co-optation of "some of the stated aims of 1984 feminism—such as the anti-porn campaign and greater safety from sexual assault" (xvi). In fact, as a companion vignette—also insulated from political commentary—to the book-burning scene, a clip of Offred's mother marching in a Take Back the Night rally briefly appears among the snuff films featured in Offred's anti-pornographic conditioning. Anticipating the introductory clarification Atwood would append to her text over three decades later, Offred surmises that anti-rape activism ballasts Gilead's protectionist rationale: "is this a thing we're intended to see, to remind us of the old days of no safety?" (119). Conjured as a nightmarish extrapolation of anti-porn and anti-rape feminism's "stated aims," *The Handmaid's Tale* is a protectionist dystopia.

One Book Chair as Feminist Killjoy: Satire, Student Response, and Dystopia

The Handmaid's Tale moves from Offred's indoctrination to the seamier contradictions of Gilead—among them, Offred's discovery that the state runs a brothel staffed with sex workers to serve superiors in the regime. This revelation occasions a defamiliarizing tour de force. Brought into the sex workers' milieu for a night, Offred glimpses her former best friend, Moira. She is puzzled by Moira's outfit; it is some kind of costume or disguise, but Offred cannot intuit what Moira is meant to impersonate:

> She's dressed absurdly, in a black outfit of once-shiny satin that looks the worse for wear. It's strapless, wired from the inside, pushing up the breasts, but it doesn't quite fit Moira, it's too large, so that one breast is plumped out and the other one isn't. . . . There's a wad of cotton attached to the back, I can see it as she half turns; it looks like a sanitary pad that's been popped like a piece of popcorn. I realize that it's supposed to be a tail. Attached to her head are two ears, of a rabbit or deer, it's not easy to tell; one of the ears has lost its starch or wiring and is flopping halfway down. She has a black bow tie around her neck and is wearing black net stockings and black high heels. . . .
>
> The whole costume, antique and bizarre, reminds me of something from the past, but I can't think what. A stage play, a musical comedy? Girls dressed for Easter, in rabbit suits. What is the significance of it here, why are rabbits supposed to be sexually attractive to men? How can this bedraggled costume appeal? (Atwood, *Handmaid's Tale* 239)

For those not subjected to years of deprogramming, it is evident that Moira is dressed as a Playboy Bunny. The "strapless" bustier, exploded "sanitary pad" as cottontail, "bow tie," fishnets, heels, and "two ears, of a rabbit or a deer" combine to identify the still iconic bunny profile that Moira abjectly simulates. Yet the stakes of this defamiliarizing setup differ from those of the book-burning episode. Rather than feminism reduced to rank censorship by a naive viewer who tells it like it is, Moira's bunny costume is a trademark symbol of exploitation whose prior performance as real-life wage labor—though not, in that case, outright sex work—is relayed with deflating precision in Gloria Steinem's journalistic account of her undercover employment at a Playboy Club, "I Was a Playboy Bunny." The reader who guesses the referent of Moira's appended ears may also grasp this tableau's second-degree relation to Steinem's gritty, alienating exposé of the toil of Playboy pulchritude. Given these layers of reference, Offred's resolute, perhaps surprising failure to decode Moira's "antique and bizarre" masquerade operates to foreground the literary yield of Handmaid brainwashing: satire.

Offred is genuinely puzzled by her friend-turned-state-sex-worker's costuming as a "rabbit." The satirical payoff of Offred's anti-pornographic conditioning, it turns out, is perplexed estrangement from the epitome of 1970s American female sexiness, the Bunny. The carnivalesque decrepitude of Moira's lank ears and lopsided breasts may augment the effect, but Atwood transmits the critical force of this defamiliarizing exercise through the core rationality of Offred's bemused queries: "why are rabbits supposed to be sexually attractive to men? How can this . . . costume appeal?" Atwood closes Offred's description of Moira with an unexpected reward of Handmaid amnesia, Offred's failure to internalize normative—even in Gilead—sex stereotypes. As the result of censorious protectionism whose marked excesses include forced illiteracy, Offred musters a naively satirical take on mainstream pornographic misogyny.

Having taught *The Handmaid's Tale* in classes on second-wave feminism and feminist speculative fiction, I became aware, as faculty chair of One Book One Northwestern, that dystopia and satire coexist in some tension in Atwood's text. As the theorist Georg Lukács might suggest, contemporary dystopian blockbusters like *Divergent* and *The Hunger Games* marshal hyperlegible taxonomies of good and evil, rendering resistance an appurtenance of redundantly heroic character. Satire, by contrast, suspends the audience's easy recourse to moral judgment, tasking us with the work of referential decipherment as well as the vertiginous indeterminacy of our own prospective collusion. A dilemma early in the One Book year enhanced my sense of this tension. While my remit as faculty chair entailed feminist programming, which stands as shorthand for a dizzyingly rich range of activist, scholarly, and creative reflection, the administrative director of the One Book program enlisted undergraduate volunteers to draw as many students as possible to One Book events. After pondering options for *Handmaid's Tale*–themed entertainment, the latter team devised an escape room. Players would employ clues from Atwood's text to exit a closed space, proving their puzzle-solving chops as well as their grasp of Handmaid trivia. But the escape room never launched. Several members of the Northwestern community, braver than I, registered concerns that systemic misogynist abuse should not be thematized as a game.

Soon after the escape room debacle, I had the daunting opportunity to interview Atwood, an event followed by lively questions from undergraduate readers. Many students voiced queries piqued by the streaming release of the Hulu adaptation of *The Handmaid's Tale* (2017–25) and its implementation of race-blind casting. The latter decision, in the students' view, threw into relief the failure of Atwood's original to represent the racial determinants of American women's differential experiences of oppression. As these students knew, Atwood claims global historical precedents for Gilead's authoritarian tactics. Handmaid salvaging marks an exemplary instance: *The Philippine Collegian* reports in 1978 that "salvaging" is Philippine slang for the extrajudicial murder of political activists, among others, under Filipino martial law (Editorial Board). But the mechanism whereby an injury-identified horde of Handmaids inflicts their aggrieved passivity on a falsely accused rapist claims an even closer referential fit in America history. As Jacquelyn Dowd Hall has shown, in America in the 1920s and '30s, Jessie Daniel Ames led a movement to repudiate the paternalist pretense of protection sustaining an extrajudicial lynching regime fueled by false charges against Black men of sexually assaulting white women. This historical contrivance of white women's injury is rooted in American enslavement and regimes of racial supremacy. While my interpretive lens has been dominance feminism, the students who keenly queried Atwood were mobilized by intersectional feminist analytics. Grappling with *The Handmaid's Tale* in this campus forum affirmed that as America-become-Gilead, Atwood's protectionist dystopia cannot be insulated from the historically racist determinants of the value of the femininity whose vulnerability the regime cements and exploits.

The escape room fiasco saw, in Sara Ahmed's phrase, the dour "feminist killjoy" (11)—me—called in to stop the fun before it even started. Reflecting on the escape room in the wake of Roe, I realize that we missed the prospect of even more treacherous play somewhere else—in *The Handmaid's Tale* engaged not as dystopia but as satire. Atwood's satire includes slick, apposite gimmicks of protectionist theo-patriarchy, like "Soul Scrolls" and "Prayvaganzas" (Atwood, *Handmaid's Tale* 116, 21); but Atwood also satirizes hypocrisy that punctures the righteous pretenses of sex-panicked political profiteers, in Gilead as in America today. We cannot laugh at an impregnation Ceremony in which Atwood reminds us of the continuity of state-mandated reproduction with coercion and rape. But Atwood solicits, and only flimsily deflects, that very response: "He nods, then turns and leaves the room, closing the door with exaggerated care behind him, as if both of us are his ailing mother. There's something hilarious about this, but I don't dare laugh" (95). This is the insoluble textual and generic challenge of *The Handmaid's Tale* as a pick for campus programming. To wrestle with a satire of dominance feminism that may nonetheless, with the prospect of the defamiliarized Bunny, affirm some of that movement's deepest insights and aims, we need to "dare [to] laugh."

NOTE

1. This essay cites the 2017 Anchor edition of *The Handmaid's Tale*.

Teaching *The Handmaid's Tale* and *The Testaments* through the Theoretical Zeitgeist

Debrah Raschke

That Atwood is attuned to the contemporary zeitgeist is no secret—note the many "Make Margaret Atwood Fiction Again" signs in on-location and virtual protests (fig. 1). T-shirts, buttons, and a red cap bearing the acronym MAFA are also readily available. In her recent essay collection, *Burning Questions*, Atwood comments that she made "a rule" in writing *The Handmaid's Tale*, noting that she "would not include any detail that people had not already done, sometime, somewhere; or that they lacked the technology to do" (252). Likewise, theoretical perspectives do not emerge full-blown out of thin air. They are born from cultural phenomena. Thus, it makes sense that Atwood's writing would engage not just cultural artifacts but theoretical ones as well. In this light, it is not surprising to see theoretical interweaving in Atwood's work—an interweaving, moreover, that shifts with the theoretical zeitgeist. Wherein lies the theoretical resistance in Atwood's work? Where lies the means for change? These are the foundational questions I ask in teaching *The Handmaid's Tale* and *The Testaments*, each text then gesturing toward a different remedy that mirrors the theoretical temper in which it was produced.

The Handmaid's Tale was written during the height of post-structuralist theory—Jacques Lacan, Jacques Derrida, Jane Gallop, Hélène Cixous, Luce Irigaray, Julia Kristeva, Barbara Johnson, and so many others who produced a revolutionary rethinking of a cultural and metaphysical binary configuration that aligned anything not white or masculine with a position of untruth. There was something exhilarating about this cultural moment that sparked anticipatory change to an imprisoning hegemony. Thus, I encourage students to see these post-structuralist acts of resistance within the novel. Hilde Staels convincingly reads *The Handmaid's Tale* through Julia Kristeva's concept of a "poetic discourse" that "renovates language" and "breaks through governing laws and ideologies" to create "new meanings" ("Margaret Atwood's *The Handmaid's Tale*" 456). It is Derridean theory interwoven throughout the novel, though, that I have found to be most useful in challenging Gilead ideology. The damaging effects of presence, phonocentrism, and binary fixations, as well as the disrupting effects of *sous rature*—that which is under erasure—infuse the text. Deconstruction, in challenging the question of "what is," critiques "essentialism," seen as a "logocentric fiction of presence" (Payne 123)—what Gilead creates in equating the Handmaids to the singular definition of womb bearer. Disruption of such signification exposes a presumed fixity that is not at all fixed, a totality that is an illusion. Offred spends considerable time ruminating about the slippage of the sign. It is one of her favorite pastimes: "I sit in the chair and think about the word *chair*. It can also mean the leader of a meeting. It can also mean a mode of execution. It is the

Figure 1. Photograph by Leah Hogsten, published in "1,000 Rally for Women's March in Utah to Protest Anti-abortion Laws," by Paighten Harkins, *The Salt Lake Tribune*, 2 Oct. 2021. Photo courtesy of *The Salt Lake Tribune*.

first syllable in *charity*. It is the French word for flesh. None of these facts has any connection with the others" (110).[1] She muses further on the difference between *lie* and *lay*, on the slang with which *lay* was associated in pre-Gilead times (37), and on the various connotations of *Mayday* (a "beautiful May day" and a "distress signal," from *m'aidez* ["help me"]; 43–44). Derridean theory thus provides a conduit to understanding Atwood's *The Handmaid's Tale* in that it exposes Gileadean tyranny and, through Offred's narrative, provides alternative ways of resisting its entrapment.

Offred's musing on the multiple meanings of the word *chair* exemplifies this on a literal level and may seem nothing more than surface boredom, but it is much more. This meditation on the word *chair* directly precedes her meandering thoughts on her breakfast, in which the chain of signification moves from the egg she is served to the oscillating quality of light, then to the shell of the egg looking like the "craters on the moon . . . barren . . . , yet perfect," and finally to her redefining the concept of barrenness foisted upon her by the Gilead regime (110). The juxtaposition is important. What seems like a simple dislodging of the stability of the word *chair* becomes the foundation for her subsequent resistance to Gilead's defining her as uselessly barren. It too becomes important in how she reads the world around her, such as her encounter with the seemingly univocal placards or uniforms that define the enemies of the state hanging from the Wall: purple placards signifying gender treachery, black cassocks religious treachery, and a placard bearing the "drawing of a human fetus" identifying those doctors and nurses who aided women in ending a pregnancy "when such things were legal" (43, 32). Gilead attempts to impose what Derrida in *Of Grammatology* defines as the "philosophy of presence"—that which codifies the sign as nonnegotiable truth (12). I take a moment here to ask students to discuss (within their comfort zone) the effects of having a name with which they do not identify imposed on them and the effects of that linguistic violence. One student remarked that such totalizing is a stealing of self and agency. I then ask them to identify where this happens in the novel.

Janine's forced confession of having experienced a gang rape at the age of fourteen elucidates this process well when Aunt Lydia prods the other Handmaids for a response: "*Her* fault, *her* fault, *her* fault." It breaks Janine. A week later Janine remarks: "It was my fault. . . . It was my own fault. I led them on. I deserved the pain" (72). It is easy to dislike Janine, but what happens to her is an evisceration of self, one that comes from succumbing to the "positivity of the sign." She comes to see herself as Gilead sees her, thus making her a perfect pawn for Gilead's operations.

For Derrida, as the theorist Madan Sarup notes, "Signifiers and signifieds are continually breaking apart and reattaching in new combinations, thus revealing the inadequacy of Saussure's model of the sign" (33). Offred is good at this signifying reconfiguration. I ask a student to read aloud the passage referencing the bodies hanging on the Wall who are "like dolls" without faces, "scarecrows," bags "stuffed with some undifferentiated material" that amount to nothing—"zeros." They are "the heads of snowmen, with coal eyes and the carrot noses fallen out" and then not snowmen, but dissidents whose blood seeps through the "white cloth" (32). For Offred the bloodied "red smile" is the "same as the red of the tulips in Serena Joy's garden" (33). I then ask students to explore how Offred's observations tell a story not contained within the identifying placards. I have two goals in noting this scene and others like it: to give students practice in close textual reading and to accentuate how the presence of a single label not only fails to encompass experience but also dehumanizes and limits subjectivity.

This process of identifying the marginalized narrative reflects what Derrida means by the trace, arche-writing, supplementarity, or *sous rature* (Spivak, Translator's preface lxxi). This palimpsestic process is reflected well in the shopping scene, where the wording "Lilies of the Field" seeps through the image of the "golden lily" that identifies the store where the Handmaids now order their Gileadean dresses. Offred notes: "You can see the place, under the lily, where the lettering was painted out, when they decided that even the names of shops were too much temptation for us" (25). This pairs well with Derrida's "Exergue" in *Of Grammatology* and Gayatri Chakravorty Spivak's preface, both of which accentuate that which is hidden or in exile but nevertheless still present even in its marginalization. What does it mean not to be part of a text or history yet still to be part of it? As Offred comments, "We lived in the gaps between the stories" (57). Here I ask students to find those "gaps" or other stories in the novel and explore why they matter. Many will note the two missing theological virtues in Serena Joy's display of the singular "Faith" bedroom pillow (57) as well as Gilead's twisting of biblical passages, all of which unveil Gilead's power tactics. It is all about erasure.

I begin the "Historical Notes" performatively, pretending to brush them off. I point to them with seeming dismissiveness and then ask students: "Are there any questions?" And usually, there are none, thus mirroring the end of Professor Pieixoto's talk, which, in employing the same question, ends the novel. Only a blank space follows this question—enforced silence. We then discuss the "Historical Notes" in earnest, beginning with how the posed question shuts down conversation. In the light of our previous discussions, I ask students to identify what is not being said in Professor Pieixoto's conference talk. Most see the better-than-thou attitudes and sexist language that permeate the conference, and many see how Professor Pieixoto co-opts Offred's story—wishing she had written something else, that she had more "the instincts of a reporter or a spy" (310). Often not noted, though, is the shifting tenor of Professor Pieixoto's talk. The professor begins tentatively admitting that he and his colleague "held out no hope of tracing the narrator herself directly" (304), that the "other names in the document are equally useless for the purposes of identification and authentication" (306), and that what was discovered is "guesswork" (310). Then, suddenly, he shifts into a mode of certainty. By the end of his talk, Professor Pieixoto claims "authoritative certitude on a narrative extracted from unnamed and unnumbered tapes" (Raschke 262). Thus, what makes Gilead viable—a gradual suppression of alterity that then morphs into fixed meanings—is mirrored in the academic conference. I use this realization as a catalyst for a discussion of how academe forms life visions—when it is liberatory, when it is not, and what both visions look like in the classroom.

The pedagogical reception of *The Handmaid's Tale* has been particularly linked to the cultural and theoretical moment in which the novel is read. The work resonated well during the zenith of post-structuralism, when students were eager to understand theory and its connections to contemporary writing and when the restrictiveness of the Reagan years was still fairly close in cultural memory. When during the Obama years the political ambience became more progressive, the novel lost some of its zest. Many students found it far-fetched and highly implausible. It was at this point that I created an assignment requiring that students research unfamiliar cultural events. This improved the novel's cultural relevance, but the activity was still more like a treasure hunt than an informative exercise. Then there was the 2016 election and the release of the Hulu series in 2017; in the 2018 rendition of the course, I included the entirety of Hulu's first season. I assigned the first two episodes to students to watch at home and planned for us to watch the third episode in class together. When I asked students whether they would like to watch the third episode on their own as well, the resounding answer was "no," that they valued the communal viewing and the immediate discussion that followed. In the 2018 version, I needed a whistle. Students could not stop talking. The first class segment was initiated by a student who had prepared four or five questions pertaining to a single, short clip. The student played the clip and posed questions, replaying the scene as needed. The assignment, what I call a discussion prompt, is essentially a mini-teaching exercise. The second class segment was an open discussion focused on any observations from the first two episodes. The final segment, the communal viewing, allowed for spontaneous response. In this viewing, I asked students to note at least one scene for discussion. One of the many productive student-led discussions involved the use of water in season 1:

> In episode 1, "Offred," the first reference to water comes at marker 13:19, when June is having a flashback to a day at the beach with her husband and daughter. The water is calm and still, an indication of the contentment she feels in her life at this time. Moments later at marker 15:11, the viewer is introduced to the river that runs through Gilead. The river flows in churning swirls and rapids, starkly contrasting with the previous image of the calm and still ocean. The river that runs through Gilead in the series is a major location for some of the most emotionally heightened scenes throughout season 1. The swiftly coursing river is an indication of an impending change, as seconds after first seeing the river the screen depicts traitors of Gilead hanging from the Wall for their various offenses.
>
> The scene continues to another flashback to a happier time prior to the rise of Gilead, in which June visits the aquarium with her family. The tableaus presented are free of dialogue, replaced only with the sounds of being underwater and the flapping of jellyfish, which mimics the sound of a fetal heartbeat. The sound is accompanied by a tableau of June's daughter, Hannah, against a glass wall of the jellyfish tank surrounded by the

> blue water and repetitious beating sound. This image is later repeated in a subsequent episode, "Nolite Te Bastardes Carborundorum," at marker 15:49 when June visits the doctor and sees a pregnant Handmaid sitting in front of a fish tank, with a pulsing background noise that imitates the beating of a fetal heart, and rows of framed photos of Commanders and Wives holding "their" babies hangs on the wall above.

This observation prompted an insightful commentary on the shifting connotations of water and of Gilead's co-opting its positive inflections for its controlling purposes.

How then can Gilead be stymied? Phrased another way, how can the impulse toward totalitarianism ripe in this current political environment be stymied? *The Testaments* attempts to address this question. Atwood comments in *Burning Questions* that she "wanted to explore, at least in fiction, a turning in the other direction; a veering toward freedom, not away from it" (420). Nevertheless, *The Testaments* is not just a sequel or a "what-happened-next narrative," a technique often scrutinized in Atwood's oeuvre. It is better understood pedagogically by its relationship to Atwood's MaddAddam trilogy. Atwood also noted that *Oryx and Crake*, the first published novel of the trilogy, is a bookend to *The Handmaid's Tale* (*Conversations* 173), which I read as the bookending of two different theoretical moments.

The Handmaid's Tale's embrace of post-structuralist tactics mirrors the uncovering of alterities previously obscured. The beginning of the twenty-first century, however, witnessed a co-opting of progressive strategies, including post-structuralist and postmodern ones. What once created subversion became inundation: Did a particular event happen? Is it true? Jean Baudrillard's delineation of representational untethering, defined by his fourth stage of simulation, where representation "has no relation to any reality whatsoever," seems to be a mark of our times (6). In *Oryx and Crake*, Jimmy tells his friend Crake, the soon-to-be-mastermind of the apocalypse, that the online executions they are watching look like "simulations," to which Crake replies, "You never know. . . . What is *reality*?" (83). Such postmodernist inundations, critiqued in the trilogy, create a psychic paralysis. Futures stop being imagined.

The failure of postmodernist strategies to address current societal problems then lays the groundwork for *The Testaments*, which chronicles the lives of its key three narrators: Aunt Lydia and Offred's two daughters, from whom she has been separated, Agnes Jemima / Aunt Victoria and Daisy/Nicole/Jade. The question thus becomes how the theoretical tenor of *The Testaments* is different. In this light, *The Testaments* can be read as an attempt to re-tether the world. With the exception of the second concluding Gileadean conference, the novel's structure (mostly) returns to the significance of the written word, which regains some of its resistive powers. Configured by a holograph and two transcripts of witness testimonies, the structure lays claim to some semblance of reality, the holograph in its connections with last wills and testaments and the transcripts of witness testimonies through the supposed veracity that emerges from judicial proceedings. In other words, the details matter. True, the author of a holograph can lie, particularly to defend a personal life, and indeed one might question the degree to which "the cloth drape shrouding" Aunt Lydia's statue does not also metaphorically shroud her narrative (Atwood, *Testaments* 3). Nevertheless, the novel does gesture toward a world where narratives can be verified, where not everything can be written off as fake.

Both *The Handmaid's Tale* and *The Testaments* employ multiple narratives, but they do so to different effects. What happens to Luke in *The Handmaid's Tale* remains uncertain, serving thus as a challenge to closure. In contrast, in *The Testaments* the diegesis is revealed, but only incrementally, mirroring the process through which knowledge usually is acquired. The accounts depicting the death of the Gilead missionary Pearl Girl Adrianna dramatize this process. The Canadian police first report it as "suicide, self-strangulation" (55). The next two accounts emerge through Aunt Lydia's response to Gilead Commander Judd's replacing the official Canadian claim of "suicide" with the Gilead version of a cover-up in which the "depraved Mayday terrorists enabled by Canada's lax toleration of their illegal presence killed Aunt Adrianna." Before answering Commander Judd's inquiry, though, Aunt Lydia records, "I already knew the answer, but had no intention of sharing it" (138). What Aunt Lydia knows to be the answer is later corroborated by Aunt Sally's confession to Aunt Lydia that a fight transpired between her and Adrianna, during which she killed her (138–39); by a later police report indicating that suicide "had been ruled out" and that "foul play was suspected" (193); by Ada, who tells Nicole that Adrianna was "working" for their "source"; and by Elijah, who in the same conversation affirms that Adrianna was killed by her partner (198). This differs from *The Handmaid's Tale*, where the uncertainty of multiple narratives challenges the principle of totality by which totalitarianism functions. Here instead, the multiple narratives present a different task—finding the most plausible narrative, which then becomes a conduit to resistance. In the end, much can be discerned. It is Aunt Lydia's persistent attention to detail and to recording that finally brings Gilead down. "The Gilead News" dismisses the revealed events as "fake" until the claim becomes indefensible (398).

Agnes's piecing together of her origin story works in a similar fashion. Agnes's beliefs about her parentage begin with a fairy tale in which Tabitha (Agnes's Gilead mother) tells the story of how she rescued her from an "enchanted castle" where she and other motherless girls were "locked inside" and "under the spell of the wicked witches" (11). She relays how they ran through a forest in an attempt to escape the witches who were chasing them and how they had to hide "in a hollow tree." Agnes reports that she knew the story "by heart" but that she "liked to hear it repeated" (12)—recalling perhaps the MaddAddam trilogy's literal-minded Crakers.

Gradually realizing that the narrative Tabitha told is indeed a fairy tale, Agnes understands that the running through the forest happened, but not the rest: that "it hadn't been Tabitha's hand" she had "been holding" but the "hand" of her "real mother" and that "it wasn't witches chasing" them but men with guns (85). The narrative structure reveals the shattering of the fairy tale, a process repeated throughout the novel and one that yields an acerbic commentary on contemporary politics. This resistant observing further joins *The Testaments* to a concern underlying much of Atwood's oeuvre—the importance of understanding the entrapment of the fairy tale's lure. Here I would ask students to choose a cherished fairy tale and query its appeal, its influences on cultural perspective, its fissures, and the price of holding on to that fiction. This assignment asks students to push their fairy tale to its own *méconnaissance* or definitional shattering. The aim here is to accentuate how scrutinizing detail can dismantle a narrative's negative hold (in effect, Aunt Lydia's methodology in her holograph). Scrutinizing the details unhinges the fairy tale's power. In teaching this novel again, I would frame this discussion with an interview on *To the Best of Our Knowledge* with Maryanne Wolf, who connects the loss of deep reading with the ability to think complexly. More bluntly, this loss makes us more susceptible to control—a phenomenon endemic in our contemporary age.

The Testaments further accentuates the possibility of connection (as opposed to postmodern fragmentation) and does so in part by linking literary and cinematic worlds. Paula's tea parties resemble the blue-permeated scenes of the *Handmaid's Tale* series more than they do the original novel. Other examples that appear in the series before they find their way into the written word include Aunt Lydia's stint as a schoolteacher and the iconic signs reading "Baby Nicole Belongs in Gilead" (Atwood, *Testaments* 171, 45). The *Testaments* also interweaves allusions to Atwood's *Payback* and the MaddAddam trilogy. As for Aunt Lydia, does she not belong to a long line of bad girls who haunt Atwood's work—*The Robber Bride*'s Zenia, *Alias Grace*'s Grace Marks, and *The Blind Assassin*'s Iris Chase Griffen? All are storytellers and survivors.

Do I believe *The Testaments*' somewhat happy ending? Still suspicious of those fairy-tale endings in Atwood's work, I would have to say, not entirely, but more than I did initially. I still do not believe the happy ending at the close of the novel *MaddAddam*. But the trilogy belongs to a different time, one that is concerned with late postmodernism and late capitalism (among other things) gone wrong—as if to say, "Look at this dark path we are taking." There may be "hope" in the trilogy, as Gerry Canavan suggests, "but not for us" ("Hope" 154). *The Testaments* closes with Professor Pieixoto's description of a statue that honors Becka (Aunt Immortelle), who sacrificed her life so that Nicole and Agnes could retain theirs. This statue bears two Biblical inscriptions, both from the wisdom tradition. The first, from Ecclesiastes 10.20, reads, "A bird of the air shall carry the voice, and that which hath wings shall tell the matter." Biblically, this passage ostensibly warns against defying authority and advises holding one's tongue about those in power lest a bird, representing the powers of surveillance, tell of the deed. The lines first appear in the novel when Becka selects them as a handwriting exercise for her charges who are training as missionaries for Gilead. Nevertheless, the bird in *The Testaments* does morph from a guardian of power to an agent of liberation and protection, thus giving voice to those whom Gilead victimized. Such a transformation can be further read as an undercutting of biblical literality that was the bane of those ensnared by Gilead.

Whether this is an instance of the biblical manipulation so common in Atwood's work, an example of the ambiguities of Ecclesiastes itself, a jest, or something else, that is a question for future discussions—perhaps a future student project. The second inscription, from Song of Songs 8.6, "Love is as strong as death," emphasizes that the power of love competes fiercely with the vision of death. Here there seems to be an exigency to believe, one that emerges from positioning *The Testaments* in a different mindset from the MaddAddam trilogy. In a National Public Radio interview, Jon Raymond, the author of *Denial*, comments that the ways in which popular culture has depicted the annihilation of the earth have been "uncountable" and that such imaginings have thus ceased to serve as effective warnings: their proliferation "starts to feel really morbid," like a "death wish almost—humanity just in some obsessive repetition, compulsion, imaging a future that is not necessarily preordained." *The Testaments* seems to sense this shift in zeitgeist characterized by Raymond's reflections, gesturing toward the need for love and hope in this pandemic and violence-ridden world.

I taught *The Handmaid's Tale* again in 2022, this time including only selected episodes from Hulu's season 1. With the attempted January 6 coup at the US Capitol, the overturn of *Roe v. Wade*, and continued political unrest, the series had become too close to a world students were already inhabiting. Again, the cultural moment had changed. What resonated more this time for the class was Offred's Derridean wordplay, an interest that had previously waned as the popularity of post-structuralism declined. It was all too easy to become mesmerized by a cultural moment that seemed on the brink of imploding at any second. The return to a focus on language provided a respite from the fury of what occasionally seemed like an inevitable future, and it elicited hope in the recognition that resistance can actually occur.

NOTE

1. This essay cites the 1998 Anchor edition of *The Handmaid's Tale*.

NOTES ON CONTRIBUTORS

Melissa M. Caldwell is professor of English at Eastern Illinois University. Her research in adaptation studies spans notions of literary adaptation from the early modern period to the twenty-first century. Her recent contributions include "Poetry after Descartes: Henry More's Adaptive Poetics," in *Adaptation before Cinema* (2023) and "'The Isle Is Full of Noises': The Many Tempests of Margaret Atwood's *Hag-Seed*," in a special issue of *Comparative Drama* on Shakespeare and contemporary fiction (2023).

Heidi Tiedemann Darroch works on Canadian literature and writing pedagogy and teaches at the University of British Columbia in the Coordinated Arts Program. Her recent work has appeared in the journals *Canadian Literature* and *English Studies in Canada* and in the collections *Ethics and Affects in the Fiction of Alice Munro* (2018), *Canadian Culinary Imaginations* (2020), and *Not Hockey: Critical Essays on Canada's Other Sport Literature* (2024).

Danette DiMarco is professor of English at Slippery Rock University, where she teaches first-year writing and British and world literatures. She has received her institution's President's Award for Excellence in Teaching, President's Award for Scholarly Achievement, and President's Award for Service. She coedited *Avian Aesthetics in Literature and Culture: Birds and Humans in the Popular Imagination* (2022) and *Inhabited by Stories: Critical Essays on Tales Retold* (2012) and has published in journals and books like *Teaching Literature Online*, *Mosaic*, *Papers on Language and Literature*, *College Literature*, *Misfit Children: An Inquiry into Childhood Belonging*, *Teaching Multiethnic American Literatures*, and *Eloquent Images*.

Rebecca S. Dixon is professor of English in the department of languages, literature, and philosophy at Tennessee State University, where she teaches literature, history, and women's studies. Her current research is on W. E. B. Du Bois and African American literary tradition. Her recent publications include "Mission Conscious: On the Foundation, Development, and Problems in the Field of Black Studies," in *Transformations in Africana Studies*, edited by Adebayo Oyebade (2023).

Melissa J. Ganz is associate professor of English at Marquette University. Her research and teaching focus on eighteenth- and nineteenth-century British literature and culture, law and literature, and the history of the novel. She is the author of *Public Vows: Fictions of Marriage in the English Enlightenment* (2019) and editor of *British Law and Literature in the Long Eighteenth Century* (2025). Her essays have appeared in journals such as *Eighteenth-Century Studies*, *Eighteenth Century: Theory and Interpretation*, *Nineteenth-Century Literature*, *Review of English Studies*, and *ELH*. She also has an active interest in pedagogy and has contributed several essays to pedagogy collections. In 2024, her essay "Crime Logs and Commonplace Books: Creative Engagements with Legal- and Social Justice-Themed Literature" appeared in a special issue of *Keats-Shelley Journal+*.

Shoshannah Ganz is associate professor of Canadian literature at Grenfell Campus, Memorial University, and graduate officer in the School of Arts and Sciences' Master of Applied Literary Arts program, which she developed. She is the author of *Eastern Encounters: Canadian Women's Writing about the East, 1867–1929* (2017) and coeditor of *The Ivory Thought: Essays on Al Purdy* (2008). She has over seventy publications on Canadian and Japanese literature, articles on pedagogy, and poetry publications in books and journals in North America, Europe, and Asia and is coediting a collection of essays on Onoto Watanna with Rena Heinrich and Dominika Ferens for McGill-Queens University Press.

Olivia A. Guillet is an English teacher at Berkhamsted School in England. She has taught high school and college-level English for twenty-two years, and Atwood's novels have been a primary focus of her academic research. Her essay "The Patchwork Quilt Narrative and Reader as Quiltmaker: Narrative Structure in Margaret Atwood's *Alias Grace* and *The Handmaid's Tale*" was published in *Margaret Atwood Studies* in 2023.

Gina Hausknecht teaches early modern literature in the English department and courses on incarceration in the social and criminal justice program at Coe College and is director of Coe's Prison Learning Initiative. She has published and presented on Shakespeare, Milton, seventeenth-century literature and culture, pedagogy and higher education, and graphic novel memoir. She has taught in prison in eastern Iowa and is coeditor of the essay collection *Shakespeare in the Age of Mass Incarceration* (2025).

Patrick Thomas Henry is assistant professor and coordinator of creative writing at the University of North Dakota. He is the fiction and poetry editor for *Modern Language Studies*. His short story collection, *Practice for Becoming a Ghost* (2024), won the 2022 NeMLA Creative Writing Book Award. His book *The Work of the Living: Modernism, the Artist-Critic, and the Public Craft of Criticism* (2024) contends that modernism's artist-critics generate and sustain publics through their strategic use of creative and critical expression. His work has appeared in *West Branch*, *Carolina Quarterly*, *Lake Effect*, *Massachusetts Review*, *Michigan Quarterly Review* online, and many others.

Justin Omar Johnston is associate professor in the English department at Stony Brook University. His book *Posthuman Capital and Biotechnology in Contemporary Novels* (2019) examines how clones, animal-human hybrids, and toxic bodies have proliferated across a variety of internationally acclaimed literary texts during the twenty-first century, and he has published a chapter, "The Human Endeavor: Bioethics and Biocapitalism in Don DeLillo's *Zero K*," in the edited volume *Literature and Medicine* (2024). Johnston teaches a range of courses on anglophone and postcolonial literature, science and literature, twentieth-century literature, and critical theory.

Amanda Licastro (she/her) is head of digital scholarship strategies and visiting associate professor of English at Swarthmore College, pedagogical director of the Book Traces project, and an Andrew W. Mellon Senior Fellow in Critical Bibliography. She serves on the editorial collective of the *Journal of Interactive Technology and Pedagogy* and on several committees for the Modern Language Association. Her research explores the intersection of technology and writing, including book history, dystopian literature, and digital humanities. She is coeditor of *Composition and Big Data* (2021) and has been published in the *Visual Resources Association Bulletin*, *Interdisciplinary Digital Engagement in Arts and Humanities*, *Hybrid Pedagogy*, *Kairos*, and *Digital Reading and Writing in Composition Studies*.

Lauren Rule Maxwell is professor of English at The Citadel, The Military College of South Carolina; the director of The Citadel Distinguished Scholars Program; and a former president of the Margaret Atwood Society. In 2013, she received The Citadel's Faculty Excellence Award for Scholarship, Teaching, and Service, and in 2023 she was awarded the inaugural School of Humanities and Social Sciences Excellence in Teaching Award. She is the author of *Romantic Revisions in Novels from the Americas* (2013) and has published numerous articles in addition to chapters in *F. Scott Fitzgerald in Context* (2013), *A History of Virginia Literature* (2015), *Teaching Hemingway and Modernism* (2015), *Margaret Atwood's Apocalypses* (2015), *Approaches to Teaching the Works of Cormac McCarthy* (2022), and *Margaret Atwood's Aesthetics* (2025).

Katja Pilhuj taught at The Citadel, The Military College of South Carolina, for thirteen years. Her primary area of research is early modern drama and geography, and she is the author of *Women and Geography on the Early Modern English Stage* (2019). She is currently a lecturer in English literature at Coventry University in the United Kingdom.

Debrah Raschke is professor at Southeast Missouri State University. She has published on modernist and postmodernist literature and on contemporary literary theory, with much of her recent work focusing on Margaret Atwood. Exploring how shifts in metaphysics at the turn of the twentieth century are invariably intertwined with gender ideology, her book *Modernism, Metaphysics, and Sexuality* (2006) explores how these dramas play out in modernist texts. *Doris Lessing: Interrogating the Times* (2010), an essay collection Raschke coedited with Phyllis Perrakis and Sandra Singer, addresses Lessing's prescient commentary on contemporary issues. Raschke's teaching interests include modernist and contemporary anglophone literature, nineteenth-century literature, contemporary literary theory, and comparative mythology.

Marguerite Raymond teaches Advanced Placement / Dual Enrollment classes at Bishop Lynch High School in partnership with Dallas College. Her research focus is on postmodern literature and feminist criticism in Margaret Atwood's novels. She led a roundtable discussion on developing student inquiry through reading and writing at the 2019 NCTE Annual Convention and participated in panels with the Margaret Atwood Society at the 2020 and 2022 MLA Annual Conventions and at the 2021 PAMLA Annual Conference. Most recently, her essay discussing the role of memory as a survival technique for characters in Atwood's writings was published in *Margaret Atwood Studies*.

Theodore F. Sheckels is Charles J. Potts Professor of Social Science Emeritus and a professor of English and communication studies emeritus at Randolph-Macon College. The author of *The Political in Margaret Atwood's Fiction* (2012) and *Margaret Atwood and Social Justice* (2023), he has published widely on Canadian, Australian, and South African literature as well as on American political communication. He is a former president of the Margaret Atwood Society and founding editor of *Margaret Atwood Studies*.

Katherine V. Snyder is associate professor of English at the University of California, Berkeley. Her research addresses post-traumatic, post-9/11, and postapocalyptic fiction of the twenty-first century, and her teaching has encompassed science fiction, climate fiction, pandemic fiction, and many classes on Margaret Atwood's writing. Her first book, *Bachelors, Manhood, and the Novel, 1850–1925* (1999), considered the rise of British and American modernist narrative in relation to the history of masculinity, and her current project, "Novel Traces: Rewriting the Past in the Post-9/11 Present," identifies a hitherto unrecognized cluster of post-9/11 novels that extensively rewrite canonical works of literature from various historical moments.

Tarshia L. Stanley is provost and vice president for academic affairs at St. Olaf College. Her research interests include film, media studies, and African American speculative fiction. She edited the Modern Language Association's teaching volume *Approaches to Teaching the Works of Octavia E. Butler* (2019), which was the 2021 recipient of the Idaho State University Department of English and Philosophy's Teaching Literature Book Award.

Helen Thompson is professor of English at Northwestern University, where she has taught courses on second-wave feminism. She is author of *Ingenuous Subjection: Compliance and Power in the Eighteenth-Century Domestic Novel* (2005) and *Fictional Matter: Empiricism, Corpuscles, and the Novel* (2017). She was faculty director of Northwestern's One Book One Northwestern program for the academic year 2018–19, when the campus-wide reading selection was Margaret Atwood's *The Handmaid's Tale*.

Lisa Tyler has taught at Sinclair Community College since 1990. Her essay on Atwood's short story "Rape Fantasies" was published in *Teaching English in the Two-Year College* in 1998. She has published four books, including the edited collection *Wharton, Hemingway, and the Advent of Modernism* (2019) and *Understanding Marsha Norman* (2019), and more than fifty essays in academic journals and edited collections.

SURVEY RESPONDENTS

Shelley Boyd, *Kwantlen Polytechnic University*
Jenn Brandt, *California State University, Dominguez Hills*
Heidi Tiedemann Darroch, *University of British Columbia*
Danette DiMarco, *Slippery Rock University*
Denise Du Vernay, *Loyola University, Chicago*
Melissa J. Ganz, *Marquette University*
Gina Hausknecht, *Coe College*
Patrick Thomas Henry, *University of North Dakota*
Steven Hymowech, *Fulton-Montgomery Community College*
Timothy Jackson, *Rosemont College*
Karl Jirgens, *University of Windsor*
Justin Omar Johnston, *Stony Brook University*
Amanda Licastro, *Swarthmore College*
Catherine Mainland, *North Carolina State University*
Colin Martin, *Mount Royal University*
Dunja Mohr, *University of Erfurt*
Laura Nicosia, *Montclair State University*
Marguerite Raymond, *Bishop Lynch High School*
Robin Runia, *Xavier University, Louisiana*
Theodore F. Sheckels, *Randolph-Macon College*
Katherine V. Snyder, *University of California, Berkeley*
Helen Thompson, *Northwestern University*
Tina Trigg, *King's University*
Lisa Tyler, *Sinclair Community College*
Lara Vetter, *University of North Carolina, Charlotte*
Tracy Ware, *Queen's University*
Liang Ying, *Beijing Foreign Studies University*

WORKS CITED

Ahmed, Sara. *Living a Feminist Life*. Duke UP, 2017.

Alexander, Jonathan, and Sherryl Vint. "Feminism, Violence, and the Anthropocene in *The Handmaid's Tale*." *The Routledge Companion to Gender and Science Fiction*, edited by Lisa Yaszek et al., Routledge, 2023, pp. 26–32.

Alias Grace. Directed by Mary Harron, Netflix, 2017.

Alien. Directed by Ridley Scott, Twentieth Century–Fox, 1979.

Alison, Jane. *Meander, Spiral, Explode: Design and Pattern in Narrative*. Catapult, 2019.

Allardice, Lisa. "'I Can Say Things Other People Are Afraid To': Margaret Atwood on Censorship, Literary Feuds and Trump." *The Guardian*, 4 May 2024, www.theguardian.com/books/article/2024/may/04/i-can-say-things-other-people-are-afraid-to-margaret-atwood-on-censorship-literary-feuds-and-trump.

Alpert, Jonathan. "The Origin of Slavery in the United States—The Maryland Precedent." *The American Journal of Legal History*, vol. 14, no. 3, July 1970, pp. 189–221.

Alter, Alexandra. "Novelists Reimagine and Update Shakespeare's Plays." *The New York Times*, 5 Oct. 2015, www.nytimes.com/2015/10/06/books/novelists-reimagine-and-update-shakespeares-plays.html.

"The Ancient Greek Chorus in Historical Context." *YouTube*, uploaded by National Theatre, 24 Feb. 2022, www.youtube.com/watch?v=iRMc-u9Nj74.

Andriano, Joseph. "*The Handmaid's Tale* as Scrabble Game." *Essays on Canadian Writing*, vol. 48, 1992, pp. 89–96.

"'Artpolitical'—Margaret Atwood's Aesthetics." *Georg-August-Universität Göttingen*, www.uni-goettingen.de/en/647228.html. Accessed 6 Dec. 2024.

Ashcroft, Bill, et al. *The Empire Writes Back: Theory and Practice in Post-colonial Literatures*. Routledge, 1989.

Atasoy, Emrah, and Thomas Horan. "Prayer Had Broken Out: Pandemics, Capitalism, and Religious Extremism in Recent Apocalyptic Fiction." *Studies in the Novel*, vol. 54, no. 2, summer 2022, pp. 235–54.

Atwood, Margaret. "Act Now to Save Our Birds." *The Guardian*, 8 Jan. 2010, www.theguardian.com/books/2010/jan/09/margaret-atwood-birds-review.

———. *Alias Grace*. Doubleday, 1997.

———. *Alias Grace*. McClelland and Stewart, 1996.

———. *Angel Catbird*. Vol. 1, Dark Horse Books, 2016.

———. *Angel Catbird*. Vols. 2 and 3, Dark Horse Books, 2017.

———. *The Animals in That Country*. Oxford UP / Little, Brown, 1968.

———. *Anna's Pet*. With Joyce Barkhouse, James Lorimer, 1980.

———. *Bashful Bob and Doleful Dorinda*. Bloomsbury, 2004.

———. *The Blind Assassin*. Doubleday, 2000.

———. *Bluebeard's Egg*. McClelland and Stewart, 1983.

———. *Bodily Harm*. McClelland and Stewart, 1981.

———. *Book of Lives: A Memoir of Sorts*. McClelland and Stewart, forthcoming.

———. *Bottle*. Hay Festival, 2004.

———. *Burning Questions: Essays and Occasional Pieces, 2004 to 2021*. Doubleday, 2022.

———. "Canadian Monsters: Some Aspects of the Supernatural in Canadian Fiction." Atwood, *Second Words*, pp. 229–53.

———. *The Canlit Foodbook*. Totem, 1987.

———. *Cat's Eye*. McClelland and Stewart, 1988.

———. *The Circle Game*. House of Anansi Press, 1970.

———. "Comments." *University of Toronto Quarterly*, vol. 61, no. 3, spring 1992, p. 382.

———. *The Complete Angel Catbird*. Dark Horse, 2018.

———. *Conversations*. Edited by Earl G. Ingersoll, Ontario Review Press, 1990.

———. *Curious Pursuits: Occasional Writing*. Virago, 2005.

———. *Dancing Girls*. McClelland and Stewart, 1977.

———. *Days of the Rebels, 1815–1840*. Natural Science of Canada, 1977.

———. *Dearly*. HarperCollins, 2020.

———. *The Door*. Houghton Mifflin Company, 2007.

———. *Double Persephone*. Hawkshead, 1961.

———. *Eating Fire: Selected Poetry, 1965–1995*. Virago, 1998.

———. *The Edible Woman*. Anchor Books, 1998.

———. *Encounters with the Element Man*. Ewert, 1982.

———. "Flying Rabbits: Denizens of Distant Spaces." Atwood, *In Other Worlds* [Anchor], pp. 15–37.

———. *For the Birds*. Illustrated by John Bianchi, Earthcare Books, 1990.

———. *Good Bones*. Coach House, 1992.

———. *Hag-Seed:* The Tempest *Retold*. Hogarth Books, 2016.

———. *Hag-Seed: William Shakespeare's* The Tempest *Retold*. Penguin, 2016.

———. *The Handmaid's Tale*. Anchor Books, 1998.

———. *The Handmaid's Tale*. Anchor Books, 2017.

———. *The Handmaid's Tale*. Narrated by Claire Danes et al., Audible, 2012.

———. *The Handmaid's Tale: The Graphic Novel*. Illustrated by Renée Nault, Random House, 2019.

———. "Happy Endings." *Good Bones and Simple Murders*, by Atwood, Nan A. Talese, 1994, pp. 50–56.

———. *The Heart Goes Last*. Doubleday, 2015.

———. *I Dream of Zenia with the Bright Red Teeth*. Coach House, 2012.

———. "I Invented Gilead. The Supreme Court Is Making It Real." *The Atlantic*, 13 May 2022, www.theatlantic.com/ideas/archive/2022/05/supreme-court-roe-handmaids-tale-abortion-margaret-atwood/629833/.

———. *In Other Worlds: SF and the Human Imagination*. Anchor Books, 2012.

———. *In Other Worlds: SF and the Human Imagination*. Nan A. Talese, 2011.

———. *In Search of* Alias Grace*: On Writing Canadian Historical Fiction*. U of Ottawa P, 1997.

———. *Interlunar*. Oxford UP, 1984.

———. Interview. *Dialogue*, hosted by Marcia Franklin, *PBS*, 1 Nov. 2024, www.pbs.org/video/author-margaret-atwood-m9nw4m/.

———. Interview. *Wild Card*, hosted by Rachel Martin, *NPR*, 6 Oct. 2024, www.npr.org/2024/10/04/nx-s1-5137935/margaret-atwood-book-poetry-the-handmaids-tale-paper-boat.

———. "Interview with Margaret Atwood." *Readers Read*, May 2003, www.writerswrite.com/features/margaret-atwood-50120031.

———. *The Journals of Susanna Moodie*. Oxford UP, 1970.

———. *Kaleidoscopes Baroque: A Poem*. Cranbrook Academy of Art, 1965.

———. *Lady Oracle*. McClelland and Stewart, 1976.

———. *Life before Man*. McClelland and Stewart, 1979.

———. *MaddAddam*. Doubleday, 2013.

———. *Margaret Atwood Poems, 1976–1986*. Virago, 1991.

———. "Margaret Atwood Reveals She's Writing Her Memoir." Interview by Jenna Bush Hager. *YouTube*, uploaded by Today, 6 Mar. 2023, www.youtube.com/watch?v=YkbxuonSCcQ.

———. "Margaret Atwood: Shakespeare in My Work | Stratford Festival Forum 2015." *YouTube*, uploaded by Stratford Festival, 8 Aug. 2015, www.youtube.com/watch?v=md-4oLobu04.

———. "Margaret Atwood: Telling Tales from the Future." Interview by Silver Donald Cameron. *YouTube*, uploaded by The Green Interview, 25 July 2022, www.youtube.com/watch?v=gAP6Wi6YYps.

———. *Marsh, Hawk*. Dreadnaught, 1977.

———. *Moral Disorder*. McClelland and Stewart, 2006.

———. *Morning in the Burned House*. Houghton Mifflin, 1995.

———. *Moving Targets: Writing with Intent, 1982–2004*. House of Anansi Press, 2004.

———. "Murdered by My Replica?" *The Atlantic*, 26 Aug. 2023, www.theatlantic.com/books/archive/2023/08/ai-chatbot-training-books-margaret-atwood/675151/.

———. *Murder in the Dark*. Coach House Press, 1983.

———. "The Myths Series and Me: Rewriting a Classic Is Its Own Epic Journey." *Publishers Weekly*, vol. 252, no. 47, 28 Nov. 2005, p. 58, www.publishersweekly.com/pw/by-topic/columns-and-blogs/soapbox/article/37037-the-myths-series-and-me.html.

———. *Negotiating with the Dead: A Writer on Writing*. Anchor Books, 2002.

———. "Never Let Me Go." Atwood, *In Other Worlds* [Nan A. Talese], pp. 168–73.

———, editor. *The New Oxford Book of Canadian Verse in English*. Oxford UP, 1982.

———. *Notes towards a Poem That Can Never Be Written*. Salamander, 1981.

———. *Old Babes in the Wood*. Doubleday, 2023.

———. *Oryx and Crake*. Anchor Books, 2004.

———. *Paper Boat: New and Selected Poems, 1961–2023*. Alfred A. Knopf, 2024.

———. *Payback: Debt and the Shadow Side of Wealth*. House of Anansi Press, 2008.

———. *The Penelopiad*. Canongate, 2005.

———. *The Penelopiad*. Grove Press, 2005.

———. The Penelopiad*: The Play*. Faber and Faber, 2007.

———. "A Perfect Storm: Margaret Atwood on Rewriting *The Tempest*." *The Guardian*, 24 Sept. 2016, www.theguardian.com/books/2016/sep/24/margaret-atwood-rewriting-shakespeare-tempest-hagseed.

———. *Power Politics*. House of Anansi Press, 1971.

———. *Princess Prunella and the Purple Peanut*. Key Porter, 1995.

———. *Procedures for Underground*. Oxford, 1970.

———. Review of *Diving into the Wreck*, by Adrienne Rich. *The New York Times*, 30 Dec. 1973, www.nytimes.com/1973/12/30/archives/diving-into-the-wreck-by-adrienne-rich-rich.html.

———. *The Robber Bride*. Nan A. Talese, 1993.

———. *Rude Ramsay and the Roaring Radishes*. Bloomsbury, 2003.

———. *Second Words: Selected Critical Prose*. House of Anansi Press, 1982.

———. *Selected Poems, 1965–1975*. Houghton Mifflin Company, 1976.

———. *Selected Poems, 1966–1984*. Oxford UP, 1990.

———. *Selected Poems 2: Poems Selected and New, 1976–1986*. Oxford UP, 1986.

———. *Snake Poems*. Salamander, 1983.

———. *Speeches for Doctor Frankenstein*. Cranbrook Academy of Art, 1966.

———. *Stone Mattress*. McClelland and Stewart, 2014.

———. *Strange Things: The Malevolent North in Canadian Literature*. Clarendon Press, 1995.

———. *Surfacing*. McClelland and Stewart, 1972.

———. *Survival: A Thematic Guide to Canadian Literature*. House of Anansi Press, 1972.

———. *Talismans for Children*. Cranbrook Academy of Art, 1965.

———. *The Tent*. Bloomsbury, 2006.

———. *The Testaments*. Doubleday, 2019.

———. "Tightrope-Walking over Niagara Falls." Interview with Geoff Hancock. Atwood, *Conversations*, pp. 191–220.

———. *True Stories*. Simon and Schuster, 1981.

———. *Two-Headed Poems*. Simon and Schuster, 1978.

———. *Unearthing Suite*. Grand Union, 1983.

———. *Up in the Tree*. House of Anansi Press, 1978.

———. *Waltzing Again: New and Selected Conversations with Margaret Atwood*. Edited by Earl G. Ingersoll, W. W. Norton, 2006.

———. *Wandering Wenda and Widow Wallop's Winderground Washery*. Illustrated by Dusan Petricic, UNKNO, 2011.

———. *War Bears*. Illustrated by Ken Steacy, *Dark Horse*, 2018.

———. Waterstone's Poetry Lecture. 1995. *Poetry Dispatch and Other Notes from the Underground*, 2007, poetrydispatch.wordpress.com/2007/10/01/margaret-atwood-waterstones-poetry-lecture/.

———. *Wilderness Tips*. McClelland and Stewart, 1991.

———. *Writing with Intent: Essays, Reviews, Personal Prose, 1983–2005*. Virago, 2005.

———. *The Year of the Flood*. McClelland and Stewart, 2009.

———. *You Are Happy*. Harper and Row, 1974.

Atwood, Margaret, and Victor-Lévy Beaulieu. *Deux Sollicitudes*. Trois Pistoles, 2005.

———. *Two Solicitudes: Conversations*. McClelland and Stewart, 1998.

Atwood, Margaret, and Shannon Ravenel, editors. *The Best American Short Stories*. Houghton, 1989.

Atwood, Margaret, and Robert Weaver, editors. *The New Oxford Book of Canadian Short Stories in English*. Oxford UP, 1995.

———. *The Oxford Book of Canadian Short Stories in English*. Oxford UP, 1986.

Auden, W. H. "In Memory of W. B. Yeats." 1940. *Poets.org*, poets.org/poem/memory-w-b-yeats.

———. "Musée des Beaux Arts." 1940. *The Norton Anthology of Poetry*, edited by Margaret Ferguson et al., 6th ed., W. W. Norton, 2018, pp. 1536–37.

Bach, Susanne. "May I Laugh about Women's Lib? or, The Difficult Relationship of Humour and Feminism in Margaret Atwood, Caryl Churchill, and Helen Fielding." *Gender and Laughter: Comic Affirmation and Subversion in Traditional and Modern Media*, edited by Gaby Pailer et al., Brill, 2009, pp. 315–28.

Bain, Jennifer. "Atwood's Coffee Is (Literally) for the Birds." *Toronto Star*, 27 Jan. 2010, www.thestar.com/life/food-and-drink/atwood-s-coffee-is-literally-for-the-birds/article_61048f0a-d042-5f0f-a7f2-f69691afa6b9.html.

Baker, Mike, et al. "Unexplained Coronavirus Cases in Three States Raise Specter of Spread." *The New York Times*, 28 Feb. 2020, www.nytimes.com/2020/02/28/us/coronavirus-solano-county.html.

Barrett, Andrea. "Research in Fiction." *The Writer's Notebook II: Craft Essays from Tin House*, Tin House, 2012, pp. 43–56.

Bates, Laura. *Shakespeare Saved My Life: Ten Years in Solitary with the Bard*. Sourcebooks, 2013.

Baudrillard, Jean. *Simulacra and Simulation*. Translated by Sheila Faria Glaser, U of Michigan P, 1994.

Bauer, Liza B. "Reading to Stretch the Imagination: Exploring Representations of 'Livestock' in Literary Thought Experiments." *Multispecies Futures: New Approaches to Teaching Human-Animal Studies*, edited by Andreas Hübner et al., Neofelis Verlag, 2022, pp. 95–113. *Goethe Universität, Frankfurt am Main*, publikationen.ub.uni-frankfurt.de/frontdoor/index/index/docId/68914.

Beauvoir, Simone de. *Le deuxième sexe*. Éditions Gallimard, 1949. 2 vols.

"Behind the Scenes of *The Handmaid's Tale* Season 2 with Cast, Author Margaret Atwood." *YouTube*, uploaded by ABC News, 4 May 2018, www.youtube.com/watch?v=KjI2G9bSsaQ.

Benczik, Vera. "The (Post)Apocalypse in Hungary: American Science Fiction and Social Analysis." *Contemporary American Fiction in the European Classroom*, edited by Laurence W. Mazzeno and Sue Norton, Springer International Publishing, 2022, pp. 135–48. *Springer Nature Link*, https://doi.org/10.1007/978-3-030-94166-6_9.

Bennett, Eric. *Workshops of Empire: Stegner, Engle, and American Creative Writing during the Cold War.* U of Iowa P, 2015.

Beran, Carol L. *Living over the Abyss: Margaret Atwood's* Life before Man. ECW Press, 1993.

"The Best Moments from *Glamour*'s 2019 Women of the Year Awards." *Glamour*, 11 Nov. 2019, www.glamour.com/story/women-of-the-year-awards-2019.

Bethune, Brian. "Margaret Atwood Recasts *The Tempest* inside a Prison." *Maclean's*, 7 Oct. 2016, www.macleans.ca/culture/books/margaret-atwood-recasts-the-tempest-inside-a-prison/.

Betts, Reginald Dwayne. *A Question of Freedom: A Memoir of Learning, Survival, and Coming of Age in Prison*. Penguin Group, 2010.

Bhowmik, Sayan Aich. "Pandemic and the End of the World in Margaret Atwood's *Oryx and Crake*." *Literary Representations of Pandemics, Epidemics and Pestilence*, edited by Nishi Pulugurtha, Routledge, 2023, pp. 160–65.

The Bible. King James Version. Christian Art Publishers, 2013.

Bickford, Donna. *Understanding Margaret Atwood*. U of South Carolina P, 2023.

Blakinger, Keri. *Corrections in Ink*. St. Martin's Press, 2022.

Bloom, Harold. *Margaret Atwood*. Bloom's Literary Criticism, 2009.

———. *Margaret Atwood's* The Handmaid's Tale. Chelsea House, 2004.

Borrow, Emily. "She Was Pregnant with Twins during Covid. Why Did Only One Survive? Why Being Black and Giving Birth in New York during the Pandemic Is So Dangerous." *The New York Times*, 6 Aug. 2020, www.nytimes.com/2020/08/06/nyregion/childbirth-Covid-Black-mothers.html.

Bouson, J. Brooks. *Brutal Choreographies: Oppositional Strategies and Narrative Design in the Novels of Margaret Atwood*. U of Massachusetts P, 1993.

———. "'A Commemoration of Wounds Endured and Resented': Margaret Atwood's *The Blind Assassin* as Feminist Memoir." *Critique*, vol. 44, no. 3, 2003, pp. 251–69.

———. *Critical Insights: Margaret Atwood*. Salem Press, 2013.

———, editor. *Critical Insights:* The Handmaid's Tale. Salem Press, 2010.

———. "A 'Joke-Filled Romp' through End Times: Radical Environmentalism, Deep Ecology, and Human Extinction in Margaret Atwood's Eco-Apocalyptic *MaddAddam* Trilogy." *Journal of Commonwealth Literature*, vol. 51, no. 3, 1 Sept. 2016, pp. 341–57, https://doi.org/10.1177/0021989415573558.

"Bowman v. Monsanto." *Oyez*, www.oyez.org/cases/2012/11-796. Accessed 20 July 2022.

Braddon, Mary Elizabeth. *Lady Audley's Secret*. 1862. Edited by Lyn Pykett, Oxford UP, 2012.

Bradley, Laura. "*The Handmaid's Tale*: How Janine Became Its Most Important Supporting Character." *Vanity Fair*, June 2017, www.vanityfair.com/hollywood/2017/06/handmaids-tale-episode-9-janine-suicide-death.

Braund, Susanna. "'We're Here Too, the Ones without Names': A Study of Female Voices as Imagined by Margaret Atwood, Carol Ann Duffy, and Marguerite Yourcenar." *Classical Receptions Journal*, vol. 4, no. 2, 2012, pp. 190–208.

"The Bridge." *The Handmaid's Tale*, created by Bruce Miller, season 1, episode 9, Hulu, 2017.

"The Brilliant Mistake." *The Chair*, created by Amanda Peet and Annie Julie Wyman, season 1, episode 1, Netflix, 2021.

Brindle, Kym. *Epistolary Encounters in Neo-Victorian Fiction: Diaries and Letters*. Palgrave Macmillan, 2013.

Brown, Paul. "'This Thing of Darkness I Acknowledge Mine': *The Tempest* and the Discourse of Colonialism." The Tempest*: A Case Study in Critical Controversy*, edited by Gerald Graff and James Phelan, 2nd ed., Bedford / St. Martin's, 2009, pp. 205–29. Originally published in *Political Shakespeare: New Essays in Cultural Materialism*, edited by Jonathan Dollimore and Alan Sinfield, Manchester UP, 1985.

Brown, Wendy. *States of Injury: Power and Freedom in Late Modernity*. Princeton UP, 1995.

Browne, Simone. *Dark Matters: On the Surveillance of Blackness*. Duke UP, 2015.

Brownley, Martine Watson. *Deferrals of Domain: Contemporary Women Novelists and the State*. St. Martin's Press, 2000.

Bruegel, Pieter. *Landscape with the Fall of Icarus*. 1560, Royal Museums of Fine Arts of Belgium, Brussels.

Bryant, John. "Textual Identity and Adaptive Revision: Editing Adaptation as a Fluid Text." *Adaptation Studies: New Challenges, New Directions*, edited by Jorgen Bruhn et al., Bloomsbury, 2013, pp. 47–67.

Brydon, Diana, "Caribbean Revolution and Literary Convention." *Canadian Literature*, vol. 95, 1982, pp. 181–85.

Brydon, Diana, and Irena Makaryk, editors. *Shakespeare in Canada: A World Elsewhere?* U of Toronto P, 2002.

Burton, Susan, and Cari Lynn. *Becoming Ms. Burton*. New Press, 2017.

Butler, Judith. "Imitation and Gender Subordination." *The Lesbian and Gay Studies Reader*, edited by Henry Abelove et al., Routledge, 1993, pp. 307–20.

Butler, Octavia E. *Parable of the Sower*. 1993. Grand Central Publishing, 2000.

———. *Wild Seed*. Doubleday, 1980.

Byatt, A. S. *On Histories and Stories: Selected Essays*. Harvard UP, 2001.

Caldwell, Melissa. "'The Isle Is Full of Noises': The Many Tempests of Margaret Atwood's *Hag-Seed*." *Comparative Drama*, vol. 57, nos. 1–2, 2023, pp. 119–37.

Campbell, Joseph. *The Hero with a Thousand Faces*. 3rd ed., New World Library, 2008.

Canaan, Serena, et al. *Maternity Leave and Paternity Leave: Evidence on the Economic Impact of Legislative Changes in High Income Countries*. IZA: Institute of Labor Economics, Mar. 2022, docs.iza.org/dp15129.pdf.

Canavan, Gerry. "Hope, but Not for Us: Ecological Science Fiction and the End of the World in Margaret Atwood's *Oryx and Crake* and *The Year of the Flood*." *Literature Interpretation Theory*, vol. 23, no. 2, fall 2012, pp. 138–59.

———. "'If the Engine Ever Stops, We'd All Die': *Snowpiercer* and Necrofuturism in SF Now." *SF Now*, special issue of *Paradoxa*, edited by Mark Bould and Rhys Williams, vol. 26, July 2010, pp. 41–66.

Carey, Jonathan. "What's Part Cat, Part Owl, and Out to Save the World? Meet Angel Catbird." *Audubon*, 9 Sept. 2016, www.audubon.org/new/whats-part-cat-part-owl-and-out-to-save-world-meet-angel-catbird.

Carney, Jo Eldridge. *Women Talk Back to Shakespeare: Contemporary Adaptations and Appropriations*. Routledge, 2022.

Casale, Carolyn, et al. "Developing Empathetic Learners." *Journal of Thought*, vol. 52, nos. 3–4, 2018, pp. 3–18. *JSTOR*, www.jstor.org/stable/90026734.

Castellani, Christopher. *The Art of Perspective: Who Tells the Story*. Graywolf, 2016.

Césaire, Aimé. *A Tempest*. Translated by Richard Miller, Theatre Communications Group, 2002.

Chapple, Freda. "Toward a Pedagogy for Adaptation Studies." Cutchins et al., *Redefining Adaptation Studies*, pp. 55–70.

Charles, Ron. "Margaret Atwood Rewrites Shakespeare. Who Will Do It Next—Gillian Flynn? Yes." *The Washington Post*, 3 Oct. 2016, www.washingtonpost.com/entertainment/books/margaret-atwood-rewrites-shakespeare-whos-next--gillian-flynn-yes/2016/10/03/6869e7ba-8389-11e6-a3ef-f35afb41797f_story.html.

Chee, Alexander. *How to Write an Autobiographical Novel*. Mariner, 2018.

Chevalier, Tracy. *New Boy*. Hogarth Books, 2018.

Christ, Carol P. "Margaret Atwood: The Surfacing of Women's Spiritual Quest and Vision." *Sign*, vol. 2, no. 2, 1976, pp. 316–30.

Clark, Alex. "Visualised: Europe's Population Crisis." *The Guardian*, 18 Feb. 2025, www.theguardian.com/world/ng-interactive/2025/feb/18/europes-population-crisis-see-how-your-country-compares-visualised.

Coetzee, J. M. *The Lives of Animals*. Edited by Amy Gutmann, Princeton UP, 2016.

Colarusso, Dana M. "Rhyme and Reason: Shakespeare's Exceptional Status and Role in Canadian Education." *Shakespeare and Canada: Remembrance of Ourselves?*, edited by Irena Makaryk and Kathryn Prince, U of Ottawa Press, 2017, pp. 215–40.

Collins, Shannon Carpenter. "Setting the Stories Straight: A Reading of Margaret Atwood's *The Penelopiad*." *Carson-Newman Studies*, vol. 9, no. 1, fall 2006, pp. 57–66.

Conroy, Frank. "The Writer's Workshop." *On Writing Short Stories*, edited by Tom Bailey, 2nd ed., Oxford UP, 2010, pp. 82–90.

Cooke, Nathalie. *Margaret Atwood: A Biography*. ECW Press, 1998.

———. *Margaret Atwood: A Critical Companion*. Greenwood Press, 2004.

Cooper, Melinda. *Life as Surplus: Biotechnology and Capitalism in the Neoliberal Era*. U of Washington P, 2008.

Cooper, Pamela. "Sexual Surveillance and Medical Authority in Two Versions of *The Handmaid's Tale*." *Journal of Popular Culture*, vol. 28, no. 4, spring 1995, pp. 49–66. *ProQuest*, www.proquest.com.

Costello, Bonnie. *Shifting Ground: Reinventing Landscape in Modern American Poetry*. Harvard UP, 2003.

Couturier-Storey, Françoise, and Jeffrey Storey. "Re-writing a Woman's Crime: *Alias Grace* and the Absence of Truth." *Fiction, Crime, and the Feminine*, edited by Redouane Abouddahab and Josiane Paccaud-Huguet, Cambridge Scholars Publishing, 2011, pp. 49–61.

Cowdy, Cheryl. "Ravines and the Conscious Electrified Life of Houses: Margaret Atwood's Suburban *Künstlerromane*." *Studies in Canadian Literature*, vol. 36, no. 1, 2011, pp. 69–85.

Crenshaw, Kimberlé. "Mapping the Margins: Intersectionality, Identity Politics, and Violence against Women of Color." *Stanford Law Review*, vol. 43, no. 6, 1991, pp. 1241–99. *JSTOR*, https://doi.org/10.2307/1229039.

Cutchins, Dennis. "Bakhtin, Intertextuality, and Adaptation." *Oxford Handbook of Adaptation Studies*, edited by Thomas Leitch, Oxford UP, 2017, pp. 71–86.

———. "Why Adaptations Matter to Your Literature Students." Cutchins et al., *Pedagogy*, pp. 87–96.

Cutchins, Dennis, et al. Introduction. Cutchins et al., *Pedagogy*, pp. xi–xix.

———, editors. *The Pedagogy of Adaptation*. Scarecrow Press, 2010.

———, editors. *Redefining Adaptation Studies*. Scarecrow Press, 2010.

Damrosch, David, editor. *Teaching World Literature*. Modern Language Association of America, 2009.

Daniels, Jessie. "White Women, U.S. Popular Culture, and Narratives of Addiction." *CUNY Academic Works*, 1 Mar. 2018, academicworks.cuny.edu/cgi/viewcontent.cgi?article=1602&context=gc_pubs.

D'Antonio, Carla Scarano. "Transformation through Storytelling in Margaret Atwood's Latest Poetry." *British Journal of Canadian Studies*, vol. 35, no. 1, 2023, pp. 49–68.

Darroch, Heidi. "Hysteria and Traumatic Testimony: Margaret Atwood's *Alias Grace*." *Essays on Canadian Writing*, vol. 81, 2004, pp. 103–21.

Davidson, Arnold E., and Cathy N. Davidson, editors. *The Art of Margaret Atwood: Essays in Criticism*. House of Anansi Press, 1981.

Davis, Angela. "Reflections on Black Women's Roles in the Community of Slaves." *The Massachusetts Review*, vol 13, nos. 1–2, winter-spring 1972, pp. 81–100.

Delord, Marie. "A Textual Quilt: Margaret Atwood's *Alias Grace*." *Canadian Studies*, vol. 46, 1999, pp. 111–21.

Derrida, Jacques. *Of Grammatology*. Translated by Gayatri Chakravorty Spivak, corrected ed., John Hopkins UP, 1997.

Devitt, Amy J. "Generalizing about Genre: New Conceptions of an Old Concept." *College Composition and Communication*, vol. 44, no. 4, 1993, pp. 573–86. *JSTOR*, www.jstor.org/stable/358391.

Dickens, Charles. *Oliver Twist; or, The Parish Boy's Progress*. Edited by Philip Horne, Penguin Books, 2003.

Djwa, Sandra. "'Here I Am': Atwood, Paper Houses, and a Parodic Tradition." *Essays on Canadian Writing*, no. 71, fall 2000, pp. 169–85.

Doerries, Bryan. *The Theater of War: What Ancient Greek Tragedies Can Teach Us Today*. Vintage, 2016.

Donnelly, Dianne. *Establishing Creative Writing Studies as an Academic Discipline*. Multilingual Matters, 2012.

Drichel, Simone. "Regarding the Other: Postcolonial Violations and Ethical Resistance in Margaret Atwood's *Bodily Harm*." *Modern Fiction Studies*, vol. 54, no. 1, 2008, pp. 20–49.

Dubrofsky, Rachel E. *Feminist Surveillance Studies*. Duke UP, 2015.

Dundas, Deborah. "Birdwatching with Margaret Atwood." *The Star*, 3 June 2017, www.thestar.com/entertainment/books/2017/06/03/birdwatching-with-margaret-atwood.

Dvorak, Marta. "The Right Hand Writing and the Left Hand Erasing in Margaret Atwood's *The Blind Assassin*." *Commonwealth Essays and Studies*, vol. 25, no. 1, 2002, pp. 59–68.

Eckstein, Barbara. "Beloved in the Attic: Harriet Jacobs's Confinement." *Approaches to Teaching Jacobs's* Incidents in the Life of a Slave Girl, edited by Lynn Domina, Modern Language Association of America, 2024, pp. 146–50.

Editorial Board. "The Politics of 'Salvaging.'" *The Philippine Collegian*, 6 Sept. 1978, phkule.org/article/516/the-politics-of-salvaging.

Elliott, Kamilla. *Theorizing Adaptation*. Oxford UP, 2020.

Elton, Sarah. *Locavore*. HarperCollins Publishers, 2011.

Feldman, Lucy. "*The Handmaid's Tale* Was a Warning. Three Decades Later, Margaret Atwood Is Back with Another." *Time*, 3 Sept. 2019, time.com/5667821/margaret-atwood-the-testaments/.

Felstiner, John. *Can Poetry Save the Earth?* Yale UP, 2009.

Ferguson, Frances. "The Lucy Poems: Wordsworth's Quest for a Poetic Object." *ELH*, vol. 40, no. 4, winter 1973, pp. 532–48. *JSTOR*, www.jstor.org/stable/2872558.

Filtness, Emma. "'The End of The End': Ageing, Memory, and Reliability in Margaret Atwood's Fictional Autobiography, *The Blind Assassin*." *Enter Text*, vol. 11, 2014, pp. 42–57.

Firth, Simon. "The Future of Reading and Writing in the Age of Digital Media." *Stanford University*, 24 May 2016, scpd.stanford.edu/insights/future-reading-and-writing-age-digital-media.

Franklin, Sarah. *Dolly Mixtures: The Remaking of Genealogy*. Duke UP, 2007.

Freeman, Hadley. "Playing with Fire: Margaret Atwood on Feminism, Culture Wars and Speaking Her Mind." *The Guardian*, 19 Feb. 2022, www.theguardian.com/books/ng-interactive/2022/feb/19/margaret-atwood-on-feminism-culture-wars.

Frey, William H. "White and Youth Population Losses Contributed Most to the Nation's Growth Slowdown, New Census Data Reveals." *Brookings*, 1 Aug. 2022, www.brookings.edu/research/white-and-youth-population-losses-contributed-most-to-the-nations-growth-slowdown-new-census-data-reveals/.

Fulkerson, Richard. "Composition at the Turn of the Twenty-First Century." *College Composition and Communication*, vol. 56, no. 4, June 2005, pp. 654–87.

Gabbert, Elisa. "A Poem (and a Painting) about the Suffering That Hides in Plain Sight." *The New York Times*, 6 Mar. 2022, www.nytimes.com/interactive/2022/03/06/books/auden-musee-des-beaux-arts.html.

Gibson, Graeme. *The Bedside Book of Birds: An Avian Miscellany*. Nan A. Talese, 2005.

Gilbert, Teresa. "Haunted by a Traumatic Past: Age, Memory, and Narrative Identity in Margaret Atwood's *The Blind Assassin*." *Traces of Aging: Old Age and Memory in Contemporary Narrative*, edited by Marta Cerezo Moreno and Nieves Pascual Soler, Transcript: Verlag fur Kommunikation, Kultur und Soziale Praxis, 2016, pp. 41–64. Aging Studies 9.

Gilman, Sander L. "Black Bodies, White Bodies: Toward an Iconography of Female Sexuality in Late Nineteenth-Century Art, Medicine, and Literature." "*Race*,"

Writing, and Difference, edited by Henry Louis Gates, Jr., U of Chicago P, 1986, pp. 223–61.

Ginsburg, Rebecca. Introduction. *Critical Perspectives on Teaching in Prison: Students and Instructors on Pedagogy behind the Wall*, edited by Ginsburg, Routledge, 2019.

Goldhill, Simon. "The Wisdom of the Ancients." *New Statesman*, vol. 134, no. 4764, Oct. 2005, pp. 48–50. *EBSCOhost*, search.ebscohost.com.

Gopnik, Adam. "Why Rewrite Shakespeare?" *The New Yorker*, 17 Oct. 2016, www.newyorker.com/magazine/2016/10/17/why-rewrite-shakespeare.

Grace, Sherrill E. "In Search of Demeter: The Lost, Silent Mother in *Surfacing*." VanSpanckeren and Castro, pp. 35–47.

Grace, Sherrill, and Lorraine Weir. *Margaret Atwood: Language, Text, and System*. U of British Columbia P, 1983.

Graves, Robert. *The Greek Myths*. Combined ed., Penguin, 1992.

Greene, Gayle. "*Life before Man*: Can Anything Be Saved?" VanSpanckeren and Castro, pp. 65–84.

Groome, Margaret. "Stratford and the Aspirations for a Canadian National Theatre." Brydon and Makaryk, pp. 108–36.

Grosz, Elizabeth. *Time Travels: Feminism, Nature, Power*. Duke UP, 2005.

Guedon, Marie-Francoise. "*Surfacing*: Amerindian Themes and Shamanism." Grace and Weir, pp. 91–111.

Haining, Casey Michelle, et al. "The Unethical Texas Heartbeat Law." *Prenatal Diagnosis*, vol. 42, no. 5, May 2022, pp. 535–41. *National Library of Medicine*, pmc.ncbi.nlm.nih.gov/articles/PMC9320804/.

Hall, Grace Elizabeth. *Making Whiteness: The Culture of Segregation in the South, 1890–1940*. Vintage, 1998.

Hall, Jacquelyn Dowd. *Revolt against Chivalry: Jessie Daniel Ames and the Women's Campaign against Lynching*. Columbia UP, 1993.

Hall, Lynda. "'He Can Taste Her Blood': Dr. Jordan's Consuming Desires in *Alias Grace*." *Margaret Atwood Studies*, vol. 2, no.1, 2008, pp. 28–36.

"Handmaids in the City." *Saturday Night Live*, created by Lorne Michaels, season 43, episode 20, SNL Studios, 12 May 2018. *YouTube*, www.youtube.com/watch?v=RUCXD3_wW2w&t=19s.

The Handmaid's Tale. Adapted and directed by John Dryden, BBC Radio 4, 2000.

The Handmaid's Tale. Directed by Volker Schlöndorff, Cinecom Pictures, 1990.

"*The Handmaid's Tale* au Ballet royal de Winnipeg." *YouTube*, uploaded by La Liberté Manitoba, 11 Oct. 2018, www.youtube.com/watch?v=RGHvr6thzjM.

"*The Handmaid's Tale*—Excerpts (Filmed 2003, Edited 2022)." *YouTube*, uploaded by Norman Frizzle, 11 Sept. 2022, www.youtube.com/watch?v=G_8oPw_D5RQ.

"Handmaid's Tale (Fancy Parody) feat. Katja Glieson | SketchSHE." Written and directed by Shae Raven. *YouTube*, uploaded by School of Flow, 16 Sept. 2018, www.youtube.com/watch?v=y823YoYdr1Q.

"*Handmaid's Tale*: The Musical." *Vimeo*, uploaded by Marcia Belsky, 2019, vimeo.com/264110737.

"The Handyman's Tale." *YouTube*, uploaded by Auckland Law Review, 11 Sept. 2017, www.youtube.com/watch?v=4v1CZVyHqmw.

Han Kang. *The Vegetarian*. Translated by Deborah Smith, Hogarth Books, 2015.

Harrison, Chloe. "Ninety-Nine Ways to Retell a Story: The Styles and Functions of Narrator Reconstrual." *Style*, vol. 57, no. 2, 2023, pp. 163–86.

Harvey, R. C. "The Maus Effect." *Rants and Raves*, 8 Dec. 2014, gocomics.typepad.com/rcharvey/2014/12/bechdel-on-maus.html.

Hassan, Waïl S. "World Literature in the Age of Globalization: Reflections on an Anthology." *College English*, vol. 63, no. 1, 2000, pp. 38–47.

Hauser, Emily. "'There Is Another Story': Writing after the *Odyssey* in Margaret Atwood's *The Penelopiad*." *Open Research Exeter*, 26 July 2018, hdl.handle.net/10871/33551.

Haynes, Natalie. *Pandora's Jar: Women in the Greek Myths*. HarperCollins Publishers, 2020.

Hengen, Shannon. *Margaret Atwood's Power: Mirrors, Reflections, and Images in Select Fiction and Poetry*. Second Story Press, 1993.

Hengen, Shannon, and Ashley Thomson. *Margaret Atwood: A Reference Guide, 1988–2005*. Scarecrow Press, 2007.

Higginson, Thomas Wentworth. "Emily Dickinson's Letters." *The Atlantic*, Oct. 1891, www.theatlantic.com/magazine/archive/1891/10/emily-dickinsons-letters/306524/.

Hinds, Gareth. The Odyssey*: A Graphic Novel*. Candlewick Press, 2010.

Hitt, Jack. "Act Five." *This American Life*, hosted by Ira Glass, 9 Aug. 2002, www.thisamericanlife.org/218/act-v.

Hogan, William. "Roots, Routes, and Langston Hughes's Hybrid Sense of Place." *The Langston Hughes Review*, vol. 18, spring 2004, pp. 3–23.

Homer. *The Odyssey*. Translated by Robert Fagles, Penguin Classics, 1996.

———. *The Odyssey*. Translated by Emily Wilson, W. W. Norton, 2018.

———. *The Odyssey*. Translated and edited by Emily Wilson, Norton Critical Edition, W. W. Norton, 2020.

———. The Odyssey *of Homer*. Translated by Richard Lattimore, HarperCollins Publishers, 2007.

Howard, Jean E. "The White Shakespearean and Daily Practice." *White People in Shakespeare: Essays on Race, Culture, and the Elite*, edited by Arthur L. Little, Jr., Bloomsbury, 2023, pp. 265–76.

Howells, Coral Ann. *The Cambridge Companion to Margaret Atwood*. 2nd ed., Cambridge UP, 2021.

———. "*Cat's Eye*: Elaine Risley's Retrospective Art." *Margaret Atwood: Writing and Subjectivity*, edited by Colin Nicholson, St. Martin's Press, 1994, pp. 204–18.

———. "Five Ways of Looking at *The Penelopiad*." *Sydney Studies in English*, vol. 32, 2006, pp. 5–18. *The University of Sydney*, openjournals.library.sydney.edu.au/index.php/SSE/article/view/590.

———. *Margaret Atwood*. St. Martin's Press, 1996.

Hunt, Richard. "How to Love This World: The Transpersonal Wild in Margaret Atwood's Ecological Poetry." *Ecopoetry: A Critical Introduction*, edited by J. Scott Bryson, U of Utah P, 2002, pp. 232–44.

Hutcheon, Linda. *The Politics of Postmodernism*. 2nd ed., Routledge, 2002.

———. *A Theory of Adaptation*. Routledge, 2006.

———. *A Theory of Adaptation*. With Siobhan O'Flynn, 2nd ed., Routledge, 2012.

———. *A Theory of Parody: The Teachings Twentieth-Century Art Forms*. 1985. Reprint ed., U of Illinois P, 2000.

Hyttinen, Helena. "The Dead Are in the Hands of the Living: Memory Haunting Storytelling in Margaret Atwood's *The Blind Assassin*." *Margaret Atwood: The Open Eye*, edited by John Moss et al., U of Ottawa P, 2006, pp. 373–83.

Indiana Jones and the Last Crusade. Directed by Steven Spielberg, Lucasfilm and Paramount Pictures, 1989.

Ingalls, Rachel. *Mrs. Caliban*. Harvard Common Press, 1982.

Ingersoll, Earl G. "Flirting with Tragedy: Margaret Atwood's *The Penelopiad*, and the Play of the Text." *Intertexts* vol. 12, nos. 1–2, spring-fall 2008, pp. 111–28. *Humanities International Complete*, https://doi.org/10.1353/itx/2008.0010.

Ishiguro, Kazuo. *Never Let Me Go*. Vintage, 2005.

Jaber, Maysaa. "'I Am a Celebrated Murderess': Female Criminality and Multiple Personalities in Margaret Atwood's *Alias Grace*." *Journal of Modern Literature*, vol. 47, no. 2, 2024, pp. 2–16.

Jacobson, Howard. *Shylock Is My Name:* The Merchant of Venice *Retold*. Hogarth Books, 2016.

Jayendran, Nishevita. "'Set Me Free': Spaces and the Politics of Creativity in Margaret Atwood's *Hag-Seed* (2016)." *Journal of Language, Literature, and Culture*, vol. 67, no. 1, 2020, pp. 15–27.

Jeffers, Jennifer M. "Life without a Primary Text: The Hydra in Adaptation Studies." Cutchins et al., *Pedagogy*, pp. 123–38.

Jenkins, Henry. *Convergence Culture: Where Old and New Media Collide*. New York UP, 2008.

Jenkins, Henry, et al. *Participatory Culture in a Networked Era: A Conversation on Youth, Learning, Commerce, and Politics*. Polity, 2015.

Johnson, Kenneth. "Earle Grey's Lasting Romance with Shakespeare." *The Globe and Mail*, 28 June 1958, p. A10.

Johnson, Tara. "The Aunts as an Analysis of Feminine Power in Margaret Atwood's *The Handmaid's Tale*." *Nebula*, vol. 1, no. 2, 2004, pp. 68–79.

Jones, Bethan. "Traces of Shame: Margaret Atwood's Portrayal of Childhood Bullying and Its Consequences in *Cat's Eye*." *Critical Survey*, vol. 20, no. 1, 2008, pp. 29–42.

Jones, Ellen E. "The Handmaid's Race Problem." *The Guardian*, 31 July 2017, www.theguardian.com/tv-and-radio/2017/jul/31/the-handmaids-tales-race-problem.

Jones, Jason. "The Creepy Treehouse Problem." *The Chronicle of Higher Education*, 9 Mar. 2010, www.chronicle.com/blogs/profhacker/the-creepy-treehouse-problem.ProfHacker.

Jones, Meta Duewa. "Reframing Exposure: Natasha Trethewey's Forms of Enclosure." *ELH*, vol. 82, no. 2, summer 2015, pp. 407–29.

Jones, Nicholas, et al. "Improved Race and Ethnicity Measures Reveal US Population Is Much More Multiracial." *United States Census Bureau*, 12 Aug. 2021, www

.census.gov/library/stories/2021/08/improved-race-ethnicity-measures-reveal-united-states-population-much-more-multiracial.html.

Juhasz, Suzanne. *The Undiscovered Continent: Emily Dickinson and the Space of the Mind*. Indiana UP, 1983.

Kalenkoski, Charlene Marie, and Sabrina Wulff Pabilonia. *Teen Social Interactions and Well-Being during the COVID-19 Pandemic*. IZA: Institute of Labor Economics, 2023. *JSTOR*, www.jstor.org/stable/resrep57479.

Kaus, Alaina. "Liberalities of Feeling: Free Market Subjectivities in Margaret Atwood's *The Blind Assassin*." *Critique*, vol. 56, no. 4, 2015, pp. 369–82.

Keats, John. "On the Grasshopper and Cricket." 1884. *Poetry Foundation*, www.poetryfoundation.org/poems/53210/on-the-grasshopper-and-cricket.

Khuram, Muhammad, et al. "An Intersectional Feminist Study of *The Handmaid's Tale* by Margaret Atwood." *Jahan-e-Tahqeeq*, vol. 7, no. 1, 2024, pp. 1221–28.

Kipnis, Laura. *Unwanted Advances: Sexual Paranoia Comes to Campus*. HarperCollins Publishers, 2017.

Klooβ, Wolfgang. "Margaret Atwood's *Hag-Seed*: The Aesthetics of Retelling Shakespeare's *The Tempest*." *University of Toronto Quarterly*, vol. 92, no. 1, 2023, pp. 76–90.

Knowles, Ric. *Shakespeare and Canada: Essays on Production, Translation, and Adaptation*. Peter Lang, 2004.

Kolchin, Peter. *American Slavery, 1619–1877*. Hill and Wang, 2003.

Kristeva, Julia, and Toril Moi. *The Kristeva Reader*. Columbia UP, 1986.

Ku, Chung-hao. "Eating, Cleaning, and Writing: Female Abjection and Subjectivity in Margaret Atwood's *The Blind Assassin*." *Concentric*, vol. 30, no. 1, 2004, pp. 93–129.

Kuhn, Cynthia. *Self-Fashioning in Margaret Atwood's Fiction: Dress, Culture, and Identity*. Peter Lang, 2005.

Kuźnicki, Sławomir. *Margaret Atwood's Dystopian Fiction: Fire Is Being Eaten*. Cambridge Scholars Publishing, 2017.

Lamming, George. *Water with Berries*. Longman, 1971.

Lane, Sandra, et al. "Marriage Promotion and Missing Men: African American Women in a Demographic Double Bind." *Medical Anthropology Quarterly*, vol. 18, no. 4, Dec. 2004, pp. 405–28.

Lanier, Douglas M. "The Hogarth Shakespeare Series: Redeeming Shakespeare's Literariness." *Shakespeare and Millennial Fiction*, edited by Andrew James Hartley, Cambridge UP, 2018.

"Late." *The Handmaid's Tale*, created by Bruce Miller, season 1, episode 3, Hulu, 2017.

Leber, Jessica. "Margaret Atwood Insists Birds Matter to Everyone—Whether They Realize It or Not." *Audubon Magazine*, 25 Nov. 2019, www.audubon.org/news/margaret-atwood-insists-birds-matter-everyone-whether-they-realize-it-or-not.

Le Guin, Ursula K. Review of *The Year of the Flood*, by Margaret Atwood. *The Guardian*, 28 Aug. 2009, www.theguardian.com/books/2009/aug/29/margaret-atwood-year-of-flood.

Leitch, Thomas. "How to Teach Film Adaptations, and Why." Cutchins et al., *Pedagogy*, pp. 1–20.

Lerner, Ben. *10:04*. Faber and Faber, 2014.

Lewis, Randolph. *Under Surveillance: Being Watched in Modern America*. U of Texas P, 2017.

Link, Kelly. "The Weirdest Story Ideas Come from Your Own Obsessions." *Gizmodo*, 16 June 2010, gizmodo.com/the-weirdest-story-ideas-come-from-your-own-obsessions-5565717.

The Lion King. Directed by Roger Allers and Rob Minkoff, Walt Disney Feature Animation, 1994.

Litwack, Leon. *Trouble in Mind: Black Southerners in the Age of Jim Crow*. Random House, 1999.

Lopez, Maria J. "'You Are One of Us': Communities of Marginality, Vulnerability, and Secrecy in Margaret Atwood's *Alias Grace*." *English Studies in Canada*, vol. 38, no. 2, June 2012, pp. 157–77.

Lyon, David. *The Culture of Surveillance: Watching as a Way of Life*. Polity Press, 2018.

Mackenzie, Rowan. *Creating Space for Shakespeare: Working with Marginalized Communities*. The Arden Shakespeare, 2023.

MacKinnon, Catharine A. *Feminism Unmodified: Discourses on Life and Law*. Harvard UP, 1987.

Mad Max. Directed by George Miller, Warner Brothers, 1979.

Makaryk, Irena. Introduction. Brydon and Makaryk, pp. 3–41.

Mallon, Thomas. *Henry and Clara*. Ticknor and Fields, 1994.

"The Manmaid's Tale." By Tammy Golden, illustrated by Tom Richmond, *MAD Magazine*, vol. 10, 16 Oct. 2019, pp. 15–19.

Mann, Steve, and Joseph Ferenbok. "New Media and the Power Politics of Sousveillance in a Surveillance-Dominated World." *Surveillance and Society*, vol. 11, nos. 1–2, 2013, pp. 18–34, https://doi.org/10.24908/ss.v11i1/2.4456.

Mannon, Bethany Ober. "Fictive Memoir and Girlhood Resistance in Margaret Atwood's *Alias Grace*." *Critique*, vol. 55, no. 5, 2014, pp. 551–66.

Manuel, Ian. *My Time Will Come: A Memoir of Crime, Punishment, Hope, and Redemption*. Vintage, 2021.

Marantz, Kate. "Making It (In)Visible: The Politics of Absence in Margaret Atwood's *Bodily Harm*." *Studies in Canadian Literature*, vol. 41, no. 2, 2016, pp. 137–56.

"Margaret Atwood Papers." *University of Toronto Libraries*, fisher.library.utoronto.ca/collections/margaret-atwood-papers. Accessed 3 Mar. 2025.

Martin, Nina, and Renée Montagne. "Black Mothers Keep Dying after Giving Birth. Shalon Irving's Story Explains Why." *NPR*, 7 Dec. 2017, www.npr.org/2017/12/07/568948782/black-mothers-keep-dying-after-giving-birth-shalon-irvings-story-explains-why.

Marzec, Robert P. "Margaret Atwood's *Oryx and Crake* and *The Year of the Flood* as Cli-Fi." *Teaching the Literature of Climate Change*, edited by Debra J. Rosenthal, Modern Language Association of America, 2024, pp. 158–67.

Massoura, Kiriaki. "Space, Time, and the Female Body: Homer's Penelope in Margaret Atwood's *The Penelopiad*." *Contemporary Women's Writing*, vol. 11, no. 3, 2017. *Complementary Index*, https://doi.org/10.1093/cww/vpx027.

Matthews, Aisha. "Gender, Ontology, and the Power of the Patriarchy: A Postmodern Feminist Analysis of Octavia Butler's *Wild Seed* and Margaret Atwood's *The Handmaid's Tale*." *Women's Studies*, vol. 47, no. 6, Sept. 2018, pp. 637–56.

Maxwell, Lauren Rule. "'To See Clearly and without Flinching': Teaching the Works of Margaret Atwood." *Margaret Atwood's Aesthetics: The Artpolitical*, edited by Dunja M. Mohr and Kirsten Sandrock, Routledge, 2025, pp. 168–78.

McCabe, Sean Estean, et al. "Race/Ethnicity and Gender Difference in Drug Use and Abuse among College Students." *Journal of Ethnicity in Substance Abuse*, vol. 6, no. 2, 2007, pp. 75–95. *National Library of Medicine*, pmc.ncbi.nlm.nih.gov/articles/PMC2377408/.

McCarthy, Ultan, et al. "Global Food Security—Issues, Challenges and Technological Solutions." *Trends in Food Science and Technology*, vol. 77, 2018, pp. 11–20.

McCombs, Judith, editor. *Critical Essays on Margaret Atwood*. G. K. Hall, 1988.

McElya, Micki. *Clinging to Mammy: The Faithful Slave in Twentieth-Century America*. Harvard UP, 2007.

McGurl, Mark. *The Program Era: Postwar Fiction and the Rise of Creative Writing*. Harvard UP, 2009.

Meakin, Kam. "Restorative Nostalgia and Historical Amnesia in *The Handmaid's Tale* Protests." *The Routledge Companion to Gender and Science Fiction*, edited by Lisa Yaszek et al., Routledge, 2023, pp. 343–50.

Michael, Magali Cornier. "Rethinking History as Patchwork: The Case of Atwood's *Alias Grace*." *Modern Fiction Studies*, vol. 47, no. 2, 2001, pp. 421–47.

Millay, Edna St. Vincent. "An Ancient Gesture." *Edna St. Vincent Millay Society*, millay.org/2022/04/27/an-ancient-gesture/. Accessed 13 Feb. 2025.

Miller, Arthur. *The Crucible*. 1953. Penguin Classics, 2003.

Mitchell, W. J. T. *Landscape and Power*. U of Chicago P, 1994.

"Modern Daddy: Norway's Progressive Policy on Paternity Leave." *International Labour Organization*, 1 Aug. 2005, www.ilo.org/publications/modern-daddy-norways-progressive-policy-paternity-leave.

Mohr, Dunja. "Critical Hope: Relationalities in Twenty-First-Century Speculative Fiction and Art." Ostalska and Fisiak, pp. 61–77.

Mohr, Dunja, and Kirsten Sandrock. "The Politics of Literature in Margaret Atwood's Work." *Margaret Atwood Studies*, vol. 17, Jan. 2024, pp. 54–60.

Monet, Stephen, and Tina McCaffrey. "Regreening the Moonscape: Greater Sudbury's Remarkable Ecosystem Restoration." *Ontario Association of Landscape Architects*, 2024, www.oala.ca/ground-56-regreening-the-moonscape.

Moodie, Susanna. *Life in the Clearings versus the Bush*. Richard Bentley, 1853.

Moore, Marianne. "Poetry." 1920. *Poets.org*, poets.org/poem/poetry.

Morgan, Jennifer L. *Laboring Women: Reproduction and Gender in New World Slavery*. U of Pennsylvania P, 2004.

Morris, David. *Public Religions in the Future World: Postsecularism and Utopia*. U of Georgia P, 2021.

Moslimani, Mohamad, and Jeffrey S. Passel. "What the Data Says about Immigrants in the U.S." *Pew Research Center*, 27 Sept. 2024, www.pewresearch.org/short-reads/2024/09/27/key-findings-about-us-immigrants/.

Moss, Elisabeth. "I cannot ever express my gratitude to this woman to my satisfaction." *Instagram*, 19 Sept. 2017, www.instagram.com/p/BZNZqniDB_O/.

Mulvey, Laura. "Visual Pleasure and Narrative Cinema." *Screen*, vol. 16, no. 3, autumn 1975, pp. 6–18.

Munroe, Grant. "How Margaret Atwood and Graeme Gibson Built a Bird Sanctuary." *The Walrus*, 18 Aug. 2017, thewalrus.ca/how-margaret-atwood-and-graeme-gibson-built-a-bird-sanctuary.

Murray, Jennifer. "For the Love of a Fish: A Lacanian Reading of Margaret Atwood's *Surfacing*." *LIT: Literature, Interpretation, Theory*, vol. 26, no. 1, 2015, pp. 1–21.

———. "Historical Figures and Paradoxical Pattern: The Quilting Metaphor in Margaret Atwood's *Alias Grace*." *Studies in Canadian Literature*, vol. 26, no. 1, 2001, pp. 65–83.

Nakamura, Lisa. *Cybertypes: Race Ethnicity and Identity on the Internet*. Taylor and Francis, 2013.

Nargund, G. "Declining Birth Rates in Developed Countries: A Radical Policy Re-think Is Required." *Fact, Views and Vision in OBGYN*, vol. 1, no. 3, 2009, pp. 191–93.

Naylor, Gloria. *Mama Day*. Vintage, 1988.

Nesbø, Jo. *Macbeth*. Hogarth Books, 2018.

Nir, Sarah Maslin, and Jesse McKinley. "'Containment Area' Is Ordered for New Rochelle Coronavirus Cluster." *The New York Times*, 10 Mar. 2020, p. A1.

Nischik, Reingard M. *Engendering Genre: The Works of Margaret Atwood*. U of Ottawa P, 2009.

———, editor. *Margaret Atwood: Works and Impact*. House of Anansi Press, 2002.

Nixon, Rob. "Caribbean and African Appropriations of *The Tempest*." *Critical Inquiry*, vol. 13, no. 3, 1987, pp. 557–78.

Noble, Safiya Umoja. *Algorithms of Oppression: How Search Engines Reinforce Racism*. New York UP, 2018.

Nussbaum, Emily. "A Cunning Adaptation of 'The Handmaid's Tale.'" *The New Yorker*, 15 May 2017, www.newyorker.com/magazine/2017/05/22/a-cunning-adaptation-of-the-handmaids-tale.

Oates, Joyce Carol. "Margaret Atwood's Tale." *The New York Review of Books*, 2 Nov. 2006, www.nybooks.com/articles/2006/11/02/margaret-atwoods-tale/?lp_txn_id=1369367.

"Odysseus." *MythWeb*, www.mythweb.com/Odyssey/index.html. Accessed 20 July 2022.

Oerlemans, Onno. *Poetry and Animals: Blurring the Boundaries with the Human*. Columbia UP, 2018. *EBSCOhost*, search.ebscohost.com.

"Offred." *The Handmaid's Tale*, created by Bruce Miller, season 1, episode 1, Hulu, 2017.

O'Neill, John. "Dying in a State of Grace: Memory, Duality, and Uncertainty in Margaret Atwood's *Alias Grace*." *Textual Practice*, vol. 27, no. 4, 2013, pp. 651–70.

Ormsby, Robert, and Michelle King. "*The Newfoundland Tempest*: Theatre of the Cultural Revival, the LSPU Hall, and Shakespeare." *Newfoundland and Labrador Studies*, vol. 35, nos. 1–2, 2020, pp. 7–50.

Ostalska, Katarzyna, and Tomasz Fisiak, editors. *The Postworld in-between Utopia and Dystopia: Intersectional, Feminist, and Non-binary Approaches in Twenty-First-Century Speculative Fiction and Literature*. Routledge, 2021.

"Other Women." *The Handmaid's Tale*, created by Bruce Miller, season 2, episode 4, Hulu, 2018.

Parker, Emma. "You Are What You Eat: The Politics of Eating in the Novels of Margaret Atwood." *Twentieth Century Literature*, vol. 41, no. 3, 1995, pp. 349–68.

Payne, Michael. *Reading Theory: An Introduction to Lacan, Derrida, and Kristeva.* Blackwell, 1993.

Pensalfini, Rob. *Prison Shakespeare: For These Deep Shames and Great Indignities.* Palgrave Macmillan, 2016.

Poll, Melissa. *Robert Lepage's Scenographic Dramaturgy: The Aesthetic Signature at Work*. Routledge, 2018.

Porter-Ladousse, Gillian. "The Retreating Sign: The Obsolescent Bridge in Margaret Atwood's *Cat's Eye*." *Commonwealth Essays and Studies*, vol. 17, no. 1, 1994, pp. 51–57.

Pundir, Leena. "Rennie's 'Massive Dis-involvement' in Margaret Atwood's *Bodily Harm*." *New Academia*, vol. 2, no. 4, 2013, pp. 1–9.

"Racial and Ethnic Disparities Continue in Pregnancy-Related Deaths: Black, American Indian / Alaska Native Women Most Affected." *Centers for Disease Control and Prevention*, 6 Sept. 2019, www.cdc.gov/media/releases/2019/p0905-racial-ethnic-disparities-pregnancy-deaths.html.

Rak, Julie. "Margaret Atwood and Sexual Assault." *Canadian Literature*, vol. 250, winter 2022, pp. 79–111.

Rao, Eleonora. "'It Always Takes a Long Time / To Decipher Where You Are': Uncanny Spaces and Troubled Times in Margaret Atwood's Poetry." *Humanities*, vol. 6, no. 3, summer 2017, www.mdpi.com/2076-0787/6/3/63.

Raschke, Debrah. "Margaret Atwood's *The Handmaid's Tale:* False Borders and Subtle Subversions." *Literature Interpretation Theory*, vol. 6, 1995, pp. 257–68.

Raymond, Jon. "The Future of the Earth under Climate Change Is 'Denial.'" Interview by Ayesha Rascoe. *Weekend Edition Sunday*, NPR, 24 July 2022.

Reed, Alison. "Disembodied Hands: Structural Duplicity in Atwood's *The Blind Assassin*." *Margaret Atwood Studies*, vol. 3, no. 1, 2009, pp. 18–25.

Reissenweber, Brandi. "Before the First Draft: Cultivating Inspiration in the Creative Writing Classroom." *Journal of Creative Writing Studies*, vol. 3, no. 1, article 9, 2018. scholarworks.rit.edu/jcws/vol3/iss1/9/.

"Remarkable Women Awards: Margaret Atwood Wins Icon of the Year Award." *Stylist*, 2020, www.stylist.co.uk/people/margaret-atwood-handmaids-tale-icon-award-remarkable-women-awards/369868.

Renfro, Kim. "Here's Why Serena Joy Is Much Younger in Hulu's Version of *The Handmaid's Tale*." *Business Insider*, 27 Apr. 2017, www.insider.com/handmaids-tale-why-serena-joy-is-young-2017-4.

Reynolds, Margaret. *Margaret Atwood: The Essential Guide to Contemporary Literature*. Vintage, 2002.

Rich, Adrienne. "Diving into the Wreck." 1973. *Poets.org*, poets.org/poem/diving-wreck.

Ridge, Kelsey. "'This Island's Mine': Ownership of the Island in *The Tempest*." *Studies in Ethnicity and Nationalism*, vol. 16, no. 2, 2016, pp. 231–45.

Ridout, Alice. "'Without Memory, There Can Be No Revenge': Iris Chase Griffen's Textual Revenge in Margaret Atwood's *The Blind Assassin*." *Margaret Atwood Studies*, vol. 2, no. 2, 2008, pp. 14–25.

Ritzenhoff, Karen A., and Janis L. Goldie, editors. The Handmaid's Tale: *Teaching Dystopia, Feminism, and Resistance across Disciplines and Borders*. Lexington Books, 2019.

Rogerson, Margaret. "Reading the Patchworks in *Alias Grace*." *Journal of Commonwealth Literature*, vol. 33, no. 1, pp. 5–22.

Rolls, Alistair. "Telling Tales: The True Story of *The Handmaid's Tale*." *Studies in Canadian Literature*, vol. 47, no. 1, 2022, pp. 95–116.

Rose, Marilyn. "Under/Cover: Strategies of Detection and Evasion in Margaret Atwood's *Alias Grace*." *Detecting Canada: Essays on Canadian Crime Fiction, Television, and Film*, edited by Jeanette Sloniowski and Rose, Wilfrid Laurier UP, 2014, pp. 205–26.

Ross, Nicola. *Healing the Landscape: Celebrating Sudbury's Reclamation Story*. Regional Municipality of Sudbury, 2001.

Rubenstein, Roberta. "Pandora's Box and Female Survival in Margaret Atwood's *Bodily Harm*." *Journal of Canadian Studies*, vol. 20, no. 1, 1985, pp. 120–35.

Sabin, Janice A. "How We Fail Black Patients in Pain." *AAMC*, 6 Jan. 2020. www.aamc.org/news/how-we-fail-black-patients-pain.

Saenz, Rogelio, and Kenneth M. Johnson. "White Deaths Exceed Births in a Majority of US States." U of Wisconsin, Madison, 2016, apl.wisc.edu/data-briefs/natural-decrease-18.

Sahin, Sevgi, and Laurence Raw. "Toward a Pedagogy for Adaptation Studies." Cutchins et al., *Redefining Adaptation Studies*, pp. 71–84.

Salesses, Matthew. *Craft in the Real World: Rethinking Fiction Writing and Workshopping*. Catapult, 2021.

Sandefur, Gary D., et al. "An Overview of Racial and Ethnic Demographic Trends." *America Becoming: Racial Trends and Their Consequences*, edited by Neil Smelser et al., National Academy Press, 2001, pp. 40–102.

Sanders, Julie. *Adaptation and Appropriation*. 2nd ed., Routledge, 2015.

———. *Novel Shakespeares: Twentieth-Century Women Novelists and Appropriation*. Manchester UP, 2001.

Santos, Sofia Ferreira, and Mark Easton. "Net Migration Could Push UK Population to 72.5m—ONS." *BBC*, 25 Jan. 2025, www.bbc.com/news/articles/c05l9y56773o.

Sarup, Madan. *An Introductory Guide to Post-Structuralism and Postmodernism*. U of Georgia P, 1988.

Scott-Douglass, Amy. *Shakespeare Inside: The Bard behind Bars*. Continuum, 2007.

Seethalaxmi, P. "Teaching Philosophy of Life through the Select Ghost Novels of Toni Morrison and Margaret Atwood." *Journal for Educators, Teachers and Trainers*, vol. 13, no. 4, Feb. 2022, pp. 32–36, https://doi.org/10.47750/jett.2022.13.04.005.

Senghor, Shaka. *Writing My Wrongs: Life, Death, and Redemption in an American Prison*. Convergent, 2013.

The Servant Girl. Directed by George Jonas, written by Margaret Atwood, Canadian Broadcasting Corporation, 1974.

Sethi, Anita. "Birdwatching with Margaret Atwood." *Financial Times*, 26 Oct. 2016, www.ft.com/content/9e1e1506-9b04-11e6-b8c6-568a43813464.

Shadwell, Thomas. *The Tempest; or, the Enchanted Island: A Comedy, as It Is Now Acted at His Highness the Duke of York's Theatre*. London, 1674.

Shahalimi, Nahid, editor. *We Are Still Here: Afghan Women on Courage, Freedom, and the Fight to Be Heard*. Random House, 2022.

Shakespeare, William. *The History of King Lear*. Edited by Stanley Wells, Oxford UP, 2000.

———. *Macbeth*. Edited by G. K. Hunter. *Four Tragedies:* Hamlet, Othello, King Lear, *and* Macbeth, Penguin Classics, 1995, pp. 787–955.

———. *The Tempest*. Edited by Stephen Orgel, Oxford UP, 2008.

Shakespeare, William, et al. *The Tempest; or, The Enchanted Island. A Comedy, as It Is Now Acted at Their Majesties Theatre in Dorset-Garden*. London, 1690.

Shakespeare Behind Bars. Directed by Hank Rogerson, produced by Rogerson and Jilann Spitzmiller, Philomath Films, 2005.

Sharpless, Rebecca. *Cooking in Other Women's Kitchens, 1865–1960*. U of North Carolina P, 2010.

Sheckels, Theodore F. *Margaret Atwood and Social Justice: A Writer's Evolving Ideology*. Cambridge Scholars Press, 2023.

———. *The Political in Margaret Atwood's Fiction: The Writing on the Wall of the Tent*. Ashgate, 2012.

Sheckels, Theodore F., and Kathleen Mackin Sweeney. "Scene, Symbol, Subversion: The Evolving Uses of Mapping in Margaret Atwood's Fiction." *American Review of Canadian Studies*, vol. 31, no. 3, 2001, pp. 403–21.

Sheehey, Maeve. "Census Data Shows White Population Shrinking below 60 Percent." *Politico*, 12 Aug. 2021, www.politico.com/news/2021/08/12/census-data-white-pouplation-shrinking-504253.

Showalter, Elaine. *Teaching Literature*. Blackwell, 2003.

Siddall, Gillian. "'This Is What I Told Dr. Jordan . . .': Public Constructions and Private Disruptions in Margaret Atwood's *Alias Grace*." *Essays on Canadian Writing*, vol. 81, 2004, pp. 84–102.

Skloot, Rebecca. *The Immortal Life of Henrietta Lacks*. Crown, 2011.

Smith, Karen R. "What Good Is World Literature? World Literature Pedagogy and the Rhetoric of Moral Crisis." *College English*, vol. 73, no. 7, July 2011, pp. 585–603.

Snipe, Margo. "Clinicians Dismiss Black Women's Pain. The Consequences Are Dire." *Capital B*, 6 Sept. 2022, capitalbnews.org/black-women-pain/.

Somacarrera, Pilar. "A Prince of Asturias Award for the Queen of Canadian Letters: Reading Margaret Atwood's Texts in Spain." *Made in Canada, Read in Spain: Essays on the Translation and Circulation of English-Canadian Literature*, edited by Somacarrera, Versita, 2013, pp. 108–28.

Sophocles. *Antigone*. *The Oedipus Cycle: An English Version*, translated by Dudley Fitts and Robert Fitzgerald, Harcourt, 1977, pp. 186–245.

Spivak, Gayatri Chakravorty. *Death of a Discipline*. Columbia UP, 2003.

———. Translator's preface. Derrida, pp. ix–xc.

Staels, Hilde. *Margaret Atwood's Novels: A Study of Narrative Discourse*. Francke, 1995.

———. "Margaret Atwood's *The Handmaid's Tale*: Resistance through Narrating." *English Studies*, vol. 78, no. 5, 1995, pp. 455–67.

———. "*The Penelopiad* and *Weight*: Contemporary Parodic and Burlesque Transformations of Classical Myths." *College Literature*, vol. 36, no. 4, pp. 100–18.

Star Wars. Directed by George Lucas, Twentieth Century–Fox, 1977.

St. Aubyn, Edward. *Dunbar*. Hogarth Books, 2017.

Stein, Karen. "A Left-Handed Story: *The Blind Assassin*." Wilson, *Margaret Atwood's Textual Assassinations*, pp. 135–53.

Steinem, Gloria. "I Was a Playboy Bunny." *Outrageous Acts and Everyday Rebellions*, by Steinem, Holt, Rinehart and Winston, 1983, pp. 29–69.

Stevenson, Robert Louis. *Strange Case of Dr. Jekyll and Mr. Hyde*. 1886. Edited by Katherine Linehan, W. W. Norton, 2003.

Stewart, Tracy M., et al. "Rates, Perceptions and Predictors of Depression, Anxiety and Post Traumatic Stress Disorder (PTSD)-Like Symptoms about Covid-19 in Adolescents." *PLoS One*, vol. 17, no. 4, 2022. *ProQuest*, https://doi.org/10.1371/journal.pone.0266818.

Storrie, Ashley. "Ashley Storrie: Swept into Another Realm." Interview by Phil Treagus-Evans. *The Reading Lists*, 2023, www.thereadinglists.com/ashley-storrie-reading-list/.

———. "If 'The Handmaid's Tale' Was Scottish." *YouTube*, uploaded by Ashley Storrie, 22 Sept. 2017, www.youtube.com/watch?v=gVEoQWJvLFg.

"Sudbury a Symbol of Hope: Margaret Atwood." *Sudbury.com*, 23 Nov. 2009, www.sudbury.com/lifestyle/sudbury-a-symbol-of-hope-margaret-atwood-226457.

Sullivan, Rosemary. *The Red Shoes: Margaret Atwood Starting Out*. HarperCollins Publishers, 1998.

Sutton, Madeline, et al. "Racial and Ethnic Disparities in Reproductive Health Services and Outcomes." *Obstetrics and Gynecology*, vol. 137, no. 2, Feb. 2021, pp. 225–33.

Suzuki, Mihoko. "Rewriting the *Odyssey* in the Twenty-First Century: Mary Zimmerman's *Odyssey* and Margaret Atwood's *Penelopiad*." *College Literature*, vol. 34, no. 2, 2007, pp. 263–78.

Syrewicz, C. Connor. "Centering the Activity of Writing: Designing Writing Tasks for the Introductory Creative-Writing Classroom." *Journal of Creative Writing Studies*, vol. 6, no. 2, 2021, article 6, scholarworks.rit.edu/jcws/vol6/iss2/6/.

Szalay, Edina. "Quilting Her Story: The Resisting Female Subject in Margaret Atwood's *Alias Grace*." *Hungarian Journal of English and American Studies*, vol. 3, no. 1, 2003, pp. 173–80.

Tatar, Yağmur. "'Spirits to Enforce, Art to Enchant': Metatheatricality and Art in *The Tempest* and *Hag-Seed*." *British and American Studies*, vol. 26, 2020, pp. 93–100.

Taylor, Gary. *Reinventing Shakespeare: A Cultural History from the Restoration to the Present*. Oxford UP, 1989.

Taylor, Jamila, et al. "Eliminating Racial Disparities in Maternal and Infant Mortality." *Center for American Progress*, 2 May 2019, www.americanprogress.org/article/eliminating-racial-disparities-maternal-infant-mortality/.

Taylor, Jon Marc. "Alternative Funding Options for Post-secondary Correctional Education (Part One)." *Journal of Correctional Education*, vol. 56, no. 1, 2005, pp. 6–17.

Templin, Charlotte. "Layers of Time: Margaret Atwood's Handling of Time in *The Handmaid's Tale*." *Women's Utopian and Dystopian Fiction*, edited by Sharon R. Wilson, Cambridge Scholars Press, 2013, pp. 174–85.

Tennyson, Lord Alfred. "Ulysses." *Poets.org*, poets.org/poem/ulysses. Accessed 13 Feb. 2025.

The Terminator. Directed by James Cameron, Orion Pictures, 1984.

Thomas, Riley. "Women's Rebel Spaces in Margaret Atwood's *The Handmaid's Tale*." *Margaret Atwood Studies*, vol. 17, Jan. 2024, pp. 25–41.

Thompson, Ayanna, and Laura Turchi. *Teaching Shakespeare: A Student-Centered Approach*. Bloomsbury, 2016.

300. Directed by Zack Snyder, Warner Brothers, 2007.

Thury, Eva M., and Margaret K. Devinney. *Introduction to Mythology: Contemporary Approaches to Classical and World Myths*. 4th ed., Oxford UP, 2016.

Tiffin, Helen. "Voice and Form." *Australian/Canadian Literatures in English*, edited by Russell McDougall and Gillian Whitlock, Methuen Australia, 1987, pp. 119–32.

Tolan, Fiona. *The Fiction of Margaret Atwood*. Palgrave Macmillan, 2022.

———. *Margaret Atwood: Feminism and Fiction*. Rodopi, 2007.

———. "Margaret Atwood's Revisions of Classic Texts." Howells, *Cambridge Companion*, pp. 109–23.

———. "Sucking the Blood out of Second-Wave Feminism: Postfeminist Vampirism in Margaret Atwood's *The Robber Bride*." *Gothic Studies*, vol. 9, no. 2, 2007, pp. 45–57.

———. "Twenty-First-Century Gileads: Feminist Dystopian Fiction after Atwood—*The Handmaid's Tale, The Natural Way of Things, The Water Cure,* and *The Testaments*." Ostalska and Fisiak, pp. 155–67.

Trounstine, Jean. *Shakespeare behind Bars: The Power of Drama in a Women's Prison*. St. Martin's Press, 2001.

Troy. Directed by Wolfgang Petersen, Warner Brothers, 2004.

Turner, Sasha. *Contested Bodies: Pregnancy, Childrearing, and Slavery in Jamaica*. U of Pennsylvania P, 2017.

"2022 Fast Facts." *American Association of Community Colleges*, 2022, www.aacc.nche.edu/2022/02/28/42888/.

Tyler, Anne. *Vinegar Girl:* The Taming of the Shrew *Retold*. Hogarth Books, 2016.

"Unfit." *The Handmaid's Tale*, created by Bruce Miller, season 3, episode 8, Hulu, 2019.

United States, Congress, House. Defense of Marriage Act. *Congress.gov*, www.congress.gov/bill/104th-congress/house-bill/3396. 104th Congress, House Resolution 3396, passed 12 July 1996.

United States, Congress, Senate. Healthy Marriages and Responsible Fatherhood Act of 2004. *Congress.gov*, www.congress.gov/bill/108th-congress/senate-bill/2830?s=1&r=18. 108th Congress, S. 2830.

United States, Department of Education, Office for Civil Rights. "Dear Colleague Letter." 4 Apr. 2011, www.ed.gov/sites/ed/files/about/offices/list/ocr/letters/colleague-201104.pdf.

Usher, Thomas. "Turning Shakespeare's 'The Tempest' into an Aboriginal Story." *TVO Today*, 16 Aug. 2016, www.tvo.org/article/turning-shakespeares-the-tempest-into-an-aboriginal-story.

van Dooren, Thom. *Flight Ways: Life and Loss at the Edge of Extinction*. Columbia UP, 2014.

———. *The Wake of Crows: Living and Dying in Shared Worlds*. Columbia UP, 2019.

Van Rys, John. "Narrative Truth in Canadian Historical Fiction: In between Veracity and Imagination." *Truth Matters*, edited by Lambert Zuidervaart et al., McGill-Queens UP, 2013, pp. 155–72.

VanSpanckeren, Kathryn. "The Trickster Text: Teaching Atwood's Work in Creative Writing Classes." Wilson et al., pp. 77–83.

VanSpanckeren, Kathryn, and Jan Garden Castro. *Margaret Atwood: Vision and Forms*. Southern Illinois UP, 1988.

Van Wormer, Katherine, et al. *The Maid Narratives: Black Domestics and White Families in the Jim Crow South*. Louisiana State UP, 2012.

Waltonen, Karma, editor. *Margaret Atwood's Apocalypses*. Cambridge Scholars, 2015.

Wang, Vivian, et al. "With Four Deaths in Iran and More Cases on Three Continents, Fears of Coronavirus Pandemic Rise." *The New York Times*, 21 Feb. 2020, p. A1.

Watkins, Susan. *Contemporary Women's Post-apocalyptic Fiction*. Palgrave Macmillan, 2020.

Wells-Lassagne, Shannon, and McMahon Fiona, editors. *Adapting Margaret Atwood:* The Handmaid's Tale *and Beyond*. Palgrave Macmillan, 2022.

Werner, Marta L. "Sparrow Data: Dickinson's Birds in the Skies of the Anthropocene." *The Emily Dickinson Journal*, vol. 30, no. 1, spring 2021, pp. 46–89. *Project Muse*, muse.jhu.edu/article/795762.

West, Emily. *Enslaved Women in America: From Colonial Times to Emancipation*. Rowman and Littlefield, 2015.

White, Deborah Gray, "Let My People Go." *To Make Our World Anew: A History of African Americans to 1880*, edited by Robin D. G. Kelley and Earl Lewis, Oxford UP, 2000, pp. 169–226.

Whitman, Walt. "Song of Myself." 1855. *WaltWhitman.com*, www.waltwhitman.com/song-of-myself.jsp.

Williams, William Carlos. "Landscape with the Fall of Icarus." 1962. *Poets.org*, poets.org/poem/landscape-fall-icarus.

Wilson, Sharon R. *Margaret Atwood's Fairy-Tale Sexual Politics*. U of Mississippi P, 1993.

———, editor. *Margaret Atwood's Textual Assassinations: Recent Poetry and Fiction*. Ohio State UP, 2003.

———. "Mythological Intertexts in Margaret Atwood's Works." *Margaret Atwood: Works and Impact*, edited by Reingard M. Nischik, Camden House, 2000, pp. 215–28.

———. *Myths and Fairy Tales in Contemporary Women's Fiction: From Atwood to Morrison*. Palgrave Macmillan, 2008.

———. "Quilting as Narrative Art: Metafictional Construction in *Alias Grace*." Wilson, *Margaret Atwood's Textual Assassinations*, pp. 121–34.

Wilson, Sharon R., et al., editors. *Approaches to Teaching Atwood's* The Handmaid's Tale *and Other Works*. Modern Language Association of America, 1996.

Winterson, Jeanette. *The Gap of Time:* The Winter's Tale *Retold*. Hogarth Books, 2015.

———. *The Stone Gods*. Hamish Hamilton, 2007.

Wolf, Maryanne. "Why It's Hard to Read in the Electronic Age." *To the Best of Our Knowledge*, hosted by Anne Strainchamps, NPR, 26 July 2015.

Wordsworth, William. Preface to *Lyrical Ballads*. 1800. College of St. Benedict and St. John's University, faculty.csbsju.edu/dbeach/beautytruth/Wordsworth-PrefaceLB.pdf.

"World 'Moving Back towards "Handmaid's Tale,"' Margaret Atwood Says." Interview by Linsey Davis. *YouTube*, uploaded by ABC News, 9 Mar. 2022, www.youtube.com/watch?v=-42q_VkuGPY.

Wright, Lauren. "Mayday: Rethinking Reproductive Justice Protests Utilizing Margaret Atwood's *The Handmaid's Tale*." *The Palgrave Handbook of Reproductive Justice and Literature*, edited by Beth Widmaier Capo and Laura Lazzari, Palgrave Macmillan, 2022, pp. 621–37.

Wrobel, Claire. "Gender and Surveillance in Margaret Atwood's Novels, from *Bodily Harm* (1981) to *The Testaments* (2019)." *Law, Surveillance and the Humanities*, edited by Anne Brunon-Ernst et al., Edinburgh UP, 2023, pp. 252–72.

Yeo, Jayme M. "Teaching Shakespeare Inside Out: Creating a Dialogue between Traditional and Incarcerated Students." *Teaching Social Justice through Shakespeare: Why Renaissance Literature Matters Now*, edited by Hilary Eklund and Wendy Beth Hyman, Edinburgh UP, 2019, pp. 197–205.

York, Lorraine. *Margaret Atwood and the Labour of Literary Celebrity*. U of Toronto P, 2013.

Zabus, Chantal. *Tempests after Shakespeare*. Palgrave, 2002.

Zajac, Paul Joseph. "Prisoners of Shakespeare: Trauma and Adaptation." *Studies in the Novel*, vol. 52, no. 3, fall 2020, pp. 324–43.

Zimmerman, Barbara. "Shadow Play: Zenia, the Archetypal Feminine Shadow in Margaret Atwood's *The Robber Bride*." *Pleiades*, vol. 15, no. 2, 1995, pp. 70–82.